The Crime
That Never Was

The Crime
That Never Was

Carl A. Coppolino, M.D.

Justice Press, Inc.
Florida

LIBRARY OF CONGRESS
CATALOG CARD NO.: 80-81163

      Coppolino, Carl A.
        The Crime That Never Was.

      Tampa, Fla.: Justice Press, Inc.
      450 p.
      8008   800306

ISBN 0-936802-00-6

Printed in the U.S.A.

To my wife, Mary

ACKNOWLEDGEMENTS

My thanks extend to the many people whose combined efforts freed me from Florida's dungeons.

My wife, Mary, deserves the most thanks. Without her love and support, without her determination to succeed, without her guidance, it is doubtful I would have survived those torturous twelve-and-half years.

To Representative Arnett Girardeau rests my eternal gratitude. His love and concern for his fellow man is an example all of us should note and follow.

Last but not least, my thanks go to the Free Press in these United States of America. My liberty is a direct result of a tireless, inquiring, relentless pursuit of truth and justice. What the Free Press accomplished for me should help muzzle some judges and courts who attempted in recent years to put fetters on the bulwark of our freedom: The Free Press.

CONTENTS

Foreward   *xi*

Part One   *1*

   The Beginning of a Nightmare

Part Two   129

   The Nightmare

   The Nightmare Continues

Photographs End of Part Two   202

Part Three   203

   Stirrings of Awakening

Part Four   233

   Early Morning Sunlight

FOREWORD

As a recent dental graduate and a minority citizen who was deeply involved in the civil rights movement, I was scarcely aware nor concerned with newspaper articles reporting the indictment and conviction of Dr. Carl A. Coppolino of second degree murder. However, over a decade later our paths crossed by virtue of a series of oddities.

Mary Coppolino, Carl's wife, approached me in my capacity as Chairman of the Correction, Parole, and Probation Committee of the House of Representatives for the State of Florida. Her obvious sense of hopelessness and yet strong belief in her husband's innocence convinced me that I should at least hear her problems, even though, I felt, there was nothing I could do to help because of the strong support for Carl's conviction and continued imprisonment from the Attorney General's office.

Some months later, while visiting Mary Coppolino's home community, I had an opportunity to read the last brief presented to the Parole Commission by James M. Russ, when parole had been denied again.

The written words of the brief seemed to leap from the printed page. Doctor Helpern, the New York City Medical Examiner, supported by his associate, Dr. Umberger, literally convicted Dr. Coppolino on faulty highly technical scientific testimony that any second-year medical student could repudiate. This faulty evidence not only served to convict Dr. Coppolino but was upheld by the Appellate Court and used as a precedent in other criminal cases.

After a year and a half of collecting information and scientific studies, I had the irrefutable proof that Dr. Helpern and Dr. Umberger had intentionally fabricated the facts in their perjurious testimony against Dr. Coppolino which resulted in his conviction.

Dr. Carl A. Coppolino's book, *The Crime That Never Was*, is more than a story of his conviction for a cime that never occurred, it is also a ringing indictment for the crimes committed by agents of the State of Florida in the name of justice.

Dr. Coppolino was paroled in October, 1979 after losing 12 years of his life on a conviction for a "crime that never was." His legacy, this book, expressing the day-to-day dangers threatening a person's very survival in our prison system, is written by a most capable intellectual individual, and may well urge you, the reader, to demand better management of our prisons. Your future safety depends on making improvements in the quality of prison administrators, from the cabinet position of Secretary down to and including the correctional officers.

Dated: February 23, 1980

Representative Arnett E. Girardeau, Chairman
Committee on Correction, Parole, and Probation

House of Representatives
State of Florida

"You're wrong **there**, *at any rate," said the Queen. "Were you ever punished?"*

"Only for faults," said Alice.

"And you were all the better for it, I know!" the Queen said triumphantly.

"Yes, but then I **had** *done the things I was punished for," said Alice: "that makes all the difference."*

"But if you **hadn't** *done them," the Queen said, "that would have been better still; better, and better, and better!" Her voice went higher with each "better," till it got quite to a squeak at last.*

Alice was just beginning to say "There's a mistake somewhere—," when the Queen began screaming, so loud that she had to leave the sentence unfinished.

Through the Looking Glass, *Lewis Carroll*

PART ONE

The Beginning of a Nightmare

APRIL 28, 1967
FRIDAY, 2:00 p.m.

The cell door to the felony tank of Sarasota County Jail slammed shut behind me. I was back. Nothing had changed, even though six months had passed since I'd inhabited this filthy dungeon. The stench of urine, stale air, bad food, dirty bodies, and fear filled my nostrils. I gagged.

I stood, my back leaning against the steel wall. The rough cloth of my white coveralls scraped along the sides of my body, irritating my skin and further adding to my misery.

I walked into the cell block and threw my few belongings on the unoccupied top bunk. There was no bed linen—only a filthy plastic mattress. But that didn't bother me. It was the same mattress I had previously hugged to my body for three long months.

The day room was occupied by seven men, all younger than I, and all dressed in the same white coveralls. A radio blared in a corner of the room, spitting out my name at regular intervals.

"Dr. Coppolino was convicted of killing his first wife, Carmela Coppolino, by a Naples jury this morning. At 9:30 a.m. the jury handed down a verdict of guilty of *second degree murder* climaxing a month long controversial and sensational trial. Judge Silvertooth of Sarasota sentenced the young doctor to life in prison at Raiford."

1

"Hi, Doc!"

One of the young prisoners, his face covered with angry red spots, smiled at me. He got up from the bolted metal bench and wiped his right hand across his filthy coveralls.

"My name is Pimples," he offered.

I judged him to be about 18 years old, if that. Yet his smile revealed broken and black-encrusted teeth. We shook hands.

"I bet you've had a long day," he commented.

I nodded. "Yes, a long, long day," I said, thinking how the "day" had begun . . .

APRIL 28
7:00 a.m.

I awoke with the sun shining in my eyes. Our room at the *Buccaneer Inn* in Naples was situated in the east wing. It looked like any one of the thousands of plastic motel rooms that dot the State of Florida. My wife, Mary, stirred beside me and in her sleep rolled into my arms. I brushed her dark hair away from her closed eyes. For just a moment I forgot that today my fate would be decided upon by the jury. I quickly returned to reality and again felt that gnawing sense of sadness.

The first time I had felt this sadness was on the previous night. F. Lee Bailey, still in his courtroom-blue shirt, was on the telephone at the bar of the *Buccaneer Inn* making arrangements for a victory party of cold champagne and sandwiches. I was in no mood to listen to his forced gaiety.

Disgusted, I left the cocktail lounge and went up to our room, leaving Mary, reporters, well-wishers, and Bailey's sycophants. I threw myself on our motel bed, fully-clothed, not caring about my new tan suit. Defeat! That was all I thought about. The blackness of depression closed all around me. Somehow I just knew that the jury was going to convict me.

Perhaps 10 minutes passed before the door to the room opened and Mary entered. She said that Bailey had sent her because he didn't want me to be alone.

"Come down and join the party, Carl," she pleaded.

"What do you think, Mary?" I tried to keep the worry out of my voice.

Mary sat on the bed alongside me. She smoothed out the wrinkles in her dress. Then she looked down at me, intensely. She suddenly smiled, lighting up my bleak world.

"I think we have a winner," she said. "No intelligent jury could convict you of a crime that never happened."

I looked up at her. "That's the problem," I thought, as I held her left hand and fingered her wedding band. The jury had not understood a word of the complicated medical testimony. Then there was the line of Helpern and Umberger—

I released her hand, wrapped my arms around her waist, and lowered her face toward mine. I kissed her gently at first, then harder. Our mouths opened and joined. Like the very first time we kissed, Mary set me on fire.

She gently pulled away from me and took a deep breath. The late afternoon sun had cast several shadows in the room. One touched her face. And from its mist her eyes spoke of countless desires. She said wistfully, "Let's go join the party."

Today it would all be over. My watch read 7:30 a.m. I slowly removed my arms from under Mary's warm, naked body and sat on the edge of the bed.

She stirred beside me and murmured, "What time is it?"

"Time to go."

I bent down across her breast and gently kissed her lips. Mary opened her eyes and put her arms around my neck and kissed me for a long, long time. Suddenly, she thrust me away and looked up. There was a twinkle in her eyes. "Do we have time?"

I bent toward her, not wasting precious time with words.

After a quick shower and shave I dressed in a gray raw silk suit—my winner's suit. It was the same suit I had worn when the Freehold, New Jersey jury acquitted me on what must have been the most laughable murder case in that state's judicial history.

Mary wore a white dress. The rays of early morning sun caught her brunette hair and caught its shine. She *was* beautiful!

I walked out on the balcony and took a long look across the pool. I felt miserable. Mary followed me and took my right hand in hers. She stood silently beside me drinking in the early morning scene. Suddenly, we turned together and walked out of the room.

The breakfast room of the *Buccaneer Inn* was cheerful. Polished mahogany wood gave strength and dignity to the fragile crystal vases filled with freshly-cut flowers, which sprinkled the bright room.

Mary and I joined the table of Bailey and his investigator, Andrew Tuney. Tuney's large Irish frame sagged, indicating defeat. His blue suit was wrinkled and spotted. The unshaven chin and sunken blue eyes completed the picture of dejection.

As I greeted him, I noticed that Bailey's hands, which always shook normally, now jerked spasmodically as though they had a life of their own. He had difficulty even holding his coffee cup. The gray in his rapidly disappearing hair seemed more pronounced that morning.

Breakfast was a quiet, almost mournful affair. Bailey's big concern, at the moment, was the timing of the verdict. How soon would the jury come to a decision? He was scheduled to give a lecture to the National Law Association that very afternoon in French Lick Springs, Indiana—a lecture for which he had already received a substantial sum of money. It was just one of the many, many business deals in which Bailey had been involved during the trial. At one point, Twentieth Century Fox motion picture studios had appeared in Naples in the persons of Brad Dexter, producer, and Sid Furie, director. These men and Bailey talked about a Coppolino movie and a Coppolino book-movie production, proper-ties purported to be worth millions, predicated upon an acquittal. They had come to Naples to hear the prosecutor's side of the story. When the State of Florida rested its case, lies and all, Dexter and Furie left, convinced that I would be acquitted, and that we would all participate in a profit-able movie venture.

Despite the knowledge that Helpern, New York's chief medical exam-iner, and Umberger, his head of toxicology, had obviously lied on the witness stand, Bailey had never given a single thought to the possibility of a conviction. That was how sure he was of the situation. Expenses during the trial had far surpassed the sum of money I had agreed to pay him, but Bailey wasn't concerned. He was willing to make up the difference in cost from his own pocket. Often he would joke with me about the fact that he had already spent enough money to buy the *Buccaneer Inn*, and that he was going to get it all back and a great deal more through television and motion picture deals.

No, Bailey wasn't worried. All that bothered him now was the incon-venience of waiting for the jury's verdict.

I was worried. I knew I was innocent. I knew that the medical evidence from our experts showed I was innocent. However, I had heard the lies of Helpern and Umberger and watched while the hostile eyes of the local people on the jury tried to understand the highly scientific testimony.

I was worried because several days earlier Circuit Judge Silvertooth had calmly said at a hearing in his chambers that he didn't understand what was going on. If the Judge couldn't understand my position, how could I expect the local jurors to understand?

Bailey, Mary, and I arrived at about 9:00 a.m. in front of the Collier County Court House, a modern complex of glass and steel. The court-room was completely air-conditioned and fitted with bleached wooden benches covered with upholstered pillows, similar to those found in many theaters.

Court was scheduled to convene at 9:00 a.m. With every court session, the lines of spectators grew exponentially as the curious, bored, haters, and well-wishers jockeyed for the few public seats. The Press, which included photographers and television cameramen, was well represented, both nationally and internationally.

The early morning light filtered through the courtroom and highlighted the dark circles under Judge Silvertooth's eyes. His lips were pinched, accentuating the furrowed creases that indented his cheeks.

The 12 members of the jury briskly filed into the courtroom and took their seats. No one looked at me, and no one smiled.

Bailey, seated on my right, began drumming his fingers nervously on the defense table. Russ and McEwen, my Florida attorneys, sat passively on my left.

I glanced across the aisle to the prosecutor's table. Assistant Attorney General George Georgieff, fat, in a rumpled gray suit, sat slumped in his chair. Despite the early hour and the temperature of the air-conditioned room, his skin was high-lighted with beads of sweat like dew on a melon. To his right sat Frank Schaub, State Attorney of the Twelfth Judicial Circuit. Schaub, pale and nondescript, kept picking at a mole on his face. To Schaub's right sat William Strode, Assistant State Attorney. Strode, tall and smartly dressed, was responsible for the presentation of the state's position on all medical evidence. Events which were to take place years later would bring questions from reporters on how much, if anything, Strode knew about the falsification of the state's medical evidence against me. But that would come later. Today Strode looked like a used car salesman anxious to close a deal.

Judge Silvertooth repeated the Court's instructions and admonitions to the jurors.

On the previous day, Thursday, Judge Silvertooth's charge to the jury had taken almost 30 minutes. He had instructed the 12 men in the details of the State's charge against me; he told them they could return one of five verdicts: 1. guilty of first degree murder with no recommendation of mercy; 2. guilty of first degree murder with a recommendation of mercy; 3. guilty of second degree murder; 4. guilty of manslaughter; or 5. not guilty.

The jury left the courtroom shortly before 5:30 p.m. and deliberated for an hour and ten minutes before breaking for dinner. They had returned to the jury room in the Collier County Court House at 8:30 p.m.

By 10:30 p.m., the newly-slected foreman of the jury, Harry Miller, a Naples mortgage broker, had told Judge Silvertooth that the jury hadn't reached a verdict and that, "under the present circumstances, I think it's best we go and sleep."

Now on this clear, beautiful, sunny Friday, they would continue to decide my fate. I looked at them for the thousandth time and wondered what each of these jurors was thinking:

Francis Gidley, retired;
Captain Fredrick H. Hite, Jr., retired U.S. Navy man;
Edward N. Hempel, retired;
Eugene Brisson, construction foreman;
Jack L. Stark, air conditioning serviceman;
Ray Charles Green, TV repairman;
James Homer, furniture salesman;
Harry L. Miller, the jury foreman, mortgage broker;
Henry Brantley, sanitation man;
Virgil Marcum, realtor;
Charles L. Howison, retired;
Leo Chickering, realtor.

Without knowing it, they were all destined to become pawns in the greatest miscarriage of criminal justice in Florida's legal history.

At this point Bailey jumped up. "If it please the Court . . .", Bailey began. He told Silvertooth that if the verdict did not come in before 9:30 a.m. today, he would have to leave the case to Russ and McEwen. He said he had a noon speaking engagement at French Lick Springs, Indiana.

Snickers from the press gallery and court spectators reached my ears and, I am sure, the ears of Judge Silvertooth and the members of the jury.

I looked at Mary, who sat directly behind me. From the look of disgust on her face, I knew her feelings concerning Bailey's remarks.

Judge Silvertooth ignored Bailey's outburst and the members of the jury filed into the jury room to resume their deliberations.

Andy Tunney and Mary took seats in a corner of the courtroom away from the curious onlookers and reporters. Bailey had scooted to the Clerk's office to begin his daily business calls. McEwen and Russ drifted away, lost in their own private thoughts.

Pressure was building up inside me. I searched the courtroom for Paul Holmes. Holmes, a former newspaper reporter with *The Chicago Tribune*, had been instrumental in freeing Dr. Samuel Sheppard, and he had attended not only this trial, but my New Jersey trial as well. Holmes was not only a good reporter and excellent judge of human nature, but, even more important, he was a close, personal friend.

I found Holmes sitting alone in the last row of the courtroom and sat down beside him, determined to get an objective opinion from this wise old gentleman. But nothing he said could alleviate this depression I felt.

"No question you'll be victorious, Carl," Paul began. His watery ancient eyes darted about my face, but they failed to settle anywhere. He took another puff on his ever-present cigarette, a practice which was illegal in the courtroom. He ignored the flow of cigarette ashes as they streaked his suit. Holmes' bloodshot eyes squinted up at me. "The gods hide the truth from our eyes," he continued. "But this trial was not a search for truth. This trial had you as the legal defandant, but in reality tried, if you will, F. Lee Bailey."

"That bad! Right, Paul?" I shot back.

"Nonsense! Who can dispute the unassailable scientific evidence of Dr. Foldes? Certainly not the State of Florida's witness, Dr. Umberger, not when he out of his own mouth proclaims from the witness chair that his tests were worthless!"

I sighed. Paul's argument wasn't new. Mary and Bailey had hammered that very point to me last night. They had added that Dr. Foldes was the world's foremost expert in succinylcholine, and that he had found none in Carmela's body; therefore, there was no murder, no crime. How could I be guilty of a crime that never happened?

"Paul, that jury . . .," I began. I never finished my sentence. The Bailiff called the court into session. The jury had reached a verdict. It was 9:30 a.m.

I hurried back to the defense table. Mary had already resumed her seat right behind me. All the other seats were occupied by The Press and others who were eager to hear the awaited verdict. They were to be disappointed.

In an unprecedented move, Judge Silvertooth cleared the courtroom of all spectators charging only court staff, the attorneys, Mary, and me to remain.

The jury grimly filed in. Again, no one looked at me. Today, as I write this, I can still visualize their faces. The feeling of sadness that had been dogging my footsteps now overwhelmed me.

"Gentlemen of the jury, have you reached a verdict?" Silvertooth intoned from his raised bench.

"We have, your honor." Foreman Harry Miller started toward the bench, verdict in hand.

"All the jurors will line up before the rail, please," said the judge, stopping Miller. They did.

I watched as the verdict went from foreman to clerk to judge. My eyes were riveted on Silvertooth's hands as he carefully unfolded the precious document. His eyes darted back and forth across the paper like a moth dancing his dance of death with a candle flame.

I stared at Silvertooth's face, searching for a clue. Nothing. On my right, Bailey moved restlessly in his chair. His hands spasmodically grasped at the edge of the defense table.

Silvertooth handed the verdict back to Margaret Scott, the count clerk. His face remained impassive. "Publish the verdict!" he ordered. His voice virtually boomed. A death-like stillness enveloped the courtroom. My heart sank.

In an old, raspy voice, the clerk, a determined lady, intoned: "We, the jury, find the defendant guilty of murder in the second degree, as charged. So say we all."

Bailey stiffened. He struck his right fist to his skull. The muscles of his neck quivered. The fingers of his left hand trembled so badly that the sheets of paper lying on the defense table started to vibrate.

Red McEwen rose hurriedly to demand a polling of the jurors.

I turned and looked at Mary, but I couldn't see her. It seemed as if the courtroom lights had dimmed. A black fog had settled between her and me. She was only three feet away, yet her features were blurred. I blinked rapidly, desperately trying to tear away the fog. McEwen and Russ were on their feet on my left. Bailey's shouted words lingered in my ears. Suddenly, I was able to see Mary.

Her face was a lifeless mask; it matched the color of her dress, white. She gazed at me unblinking, and then it seemed that her stare passed through me and that she was locked into another scene.

I slowly turned back and faced the jury. I listened as each juror agreed verbally that the verdict read by the clerk was his verdict.

Russ pointedly asked juror number four, Edward N. Hempel, if this was his verdict. Hempel sat slumped in his chair, tears streaming down both sides of his face and dripping on the jury rail like raindrops on a mournful day. "Yes," he whispered. "It's my verdict."

Russ immediately made a flurry of oral motions; among them were postponing sentencing and continuing bail. All were denied. Silvertooth refused to seriously consider any motion. He was anxious, almost eager, to get to the sentencing.

"Will the defendant rise and approach the bench," Silvertooth ordered.

Silvertooth's voice seemed to reach me from a distance. I stood up, squared my shoulders, and slowly approached the high bench. Bailey stood on my right, Russ on my left.

"You, Carl A. Coppolino, having been convicted by the jury of the offense of murder in the second degree, the court now judges you guilty of the ffense of which you have been convicted. Have you anything to say as to why such a sentence should not be imposed upon you?" Silvertooth asked.

I turned to my right. "Don't bother to answer the bastard," Bailey whispered. "It won't do you any good." His voice seethed with anger.

Silvertooth cleared his throat and peered down at me. Reading from a card, he continued, "It is the judgment of this court in the sentence of law for the crime of which you stand convicted, that you be taken by the sheriff of Collier County, Florida, and be delivered to the authorities of the state prison at Raiford, *there to remain for the remainder of your natural life.*"

Silvertooth banged his gavel, got up, tugged at his black robes, gave me a hot look, and walked out of the courtroom.

Sheriff Hendry, who was standing behind me during the sentencing procedure, took me by my right arm and led me out of the courtroom through a door that led to a small conference room that is part of the Collier County Jail. I didn't look back.

The conference room was dim and contained a long mahogany table surrounded by several chairs. I slumped into one of the wooden chairs. Dazed, I wiped my forehead with my breastpocket handkerchief and loosened my tie. Life in prison! The thought kept going around in my head like a broken record.

I have no idea how long I sat staring at the room's dingy beige wall. Vaguely I sensed I wasn't alone. There was a detective standing quietly by the door.

"I want to see my wife and my attorney," I said.

The detective shuffled his feet and crossed his arms. "They know where you are," he retorted.

I felt the dull ache starting in the middle of my chest again, *angina pectoris*—a cardinal sign that my heart muscle wasn't receiving sufficient blood. But I no longer had the strength to care.

Suddenly the door to the conference room opened and Bailey, with Russ in tow, walked toward me.

"Well, that's the system!" Bailey joked, slapping me on the back.

I looked up at him dumbfounded.

"Now keep cool and calm," Bailey continued. "We are going to beat this conviction. It's ridiculous!"

Russ took the chair next to me and began shuffling papers. He remained silent. He never once looked directly at me.

"What went wrong?" I asked, not recognizing the sound of my own voice.

Bailey slapped Russ on the shoulder. "At least we don't have to worry about running around for stays of execution," he said gleefully.

"For Christ's sake," I screamed. "What am I doing with a life sentence?"

Bailey remained silent.

"They know you are innocent, Carl," Russ mumbled beside me.

"A lot of good that does me," I snapped.

"I must leave you now," Bailey exclaimed. He was pacing back and forth watching me. "I'm due in French Lick Springs, Indiana, at 1:00 p.m."

Bailey turned to Russ and said, "You tell Carl the procedure from now on." He turned on his heels and walked out of the room, slamming the door behind him.

Russ looked at the closed door. "Those reporters will tear him apart," he said, softly.

I couldn't have cared less. Before I could comment, the door swung open again. I looked up expecting to see Mary. However, it was a physician to check on my cardiac status. After all the fuss the State Attorney's office made trying to convince the world that I didn't have a heart condition, despite graphic evidence to the contrary, and after doing to me what they set out to do—now, just to be sure I didn't cheat the state out of their satisfaction by dropping dead of a coronary— now, they sent me a physician, concerned about my welfare.

As soon as the physician was satisfied I was going to live to serve the life sentence and left, I turned to Russ and asked, "Where's Mary?"

"She is checking out of the motel and going back to Sarasota to your children. There is nothing she can do here."

Russ outlined for me the procedure that would be followed. He would file a motion for a new trial and a motion for continuation of bond. Meanwhile, I was to be moved to the Sarasota County Jail.

"I will stay right on top of this," he added, gathering his papers together.

We walked across the room to the door, and Russ left me in the hands of the detective.

I was taken further into the jail, where I was fingerprinted and my picture taken (mugged, as it is called).

One half-hour later, my wrists handcuffed in front of me, I was escorted down a long corridor by two deputies and the physician. We were leaving for Sarasota.

I passed an open door. It was the changing room. Judge Silvertooth was in the midst of taking off his judicial robes. I stopped and looked at him. He turned to me and smiled.

I extended my cuffed hands toward him in a gesture of supplication. Words tumbled in my head as I looked at Silvertooth's smiling face.

"I'll see you soon," I whispered.

He looked at me and said, "Sure."

I walked out of the Collier County Jail. For a second I was blinded by the bright sunlight. However, through the glare I could make out milling groups of bodies. The noise and activity increased as I was noticed. Newspaper reporters, TV cameramen and photographers surrounded me. The deputies started to push their way through the crowds, dragging me along with them.

Some of the reporters shouted; "Don't give up, Doc!" Others screamed, "Turn this way!" as they scrambled to take their exclusive photos.

I recognized John D. MacDonald, the noted mystery writer. He stood transfixed as though watching a funeral procession pass by.

The deputies led me to a state car. I was pushed into the back seat. A deputy sheriff sat on either side of me, while the physician rode up front with the driver.

The car traveled north on U.S. 41, passing through town after town. No one said a word.

My mind was numb. I saw the highway, stores, pedestrians, and other cars, but I didn't really see anything. The driver started some small talk, but let it die when he was ignored. It seemed as if everyone had withdrawn into his own private hell.

It was a three-hour trip by car from Naples to Sarasota. Two hours into the trip, the driver pulled over into a side road and cut the engine.

We waited. Nobody breathed a word. My wrists ached from the tightly-applied handcuffs. The heat began to rise in the car. The physician squirmed in his seat and lowered his window. A puff of air caressed my sweaty face. I leaned forward and tapped the physician on the shoulder with my manacled hands.

"Can you loosen these cuffs?" I asked. "My hands are swelling." The physician continued to look out of the window, not moving, not talking, I leaned back.

Still no one spoke. We waited.

After about 30 minutes, I could see another car approaching. It stopped alongside. Sheriff Ross Boyer of Sarasota County got out of the car and walked over.

Quickly, I was transferred to Boyer's car. Inside sat Boyer's chief deputy, Jack Royal, and his administrative aide, Tony Montagnesi.

Despite my mental exhaustion, I recognized the car switching procedure for what it meant: high security precaution. It foreshadowed the atmosphere that would permeate my entire period of imprisonment.

Boyer, a tall and stately southern man, quiet, yet firm in his official duties, took the handcuffs off me as we continued the drive to Sarasota. Ross tried to engage me in conversation.

"I'm sorry this happened, Carl," Boyer began.

I didn't answer, but kept staring out of the car window watching the trees flash by.

"The verdict really surprised me," Boyer persisted. "It doesn't make sense," he added.

I turned and smiled at Ross. "You don't have to tell me how stupid the verdict is. I know! But I still have a life sentence! What do you say about that, Sheriff?"

"Well, I'm a law man," Boyer said, moving uncomfortably in his seat next to me, "and I have to abide by the court's decision, but I don't mind telling you that there was something fishy about the State's medical evidence."

I whipped my head around and stared at him. Boyer sat impassive, looking at the back of the driver's head.

Not another word was spoken during the ride to the Sarasota County Jail.

I could see a crowd of newspaper reporters and photographers in front of the jail. The car stopped. I got out, escorted by Sheriff Boyer.

"What's Bailey going to do now, Doc?" one of the news reporters shouted. Another screamed, "Is your wife going to leave you?"

I ignored them.

The chief jailer, Jerry Grady, fingerprinted me and took a mug shot. The pockets of my suit were emptied and their contents placed in a brown personal property envelope for safekeeping.

Boyer escorted me into the elevator and up to the second floor. I walked down a dirty hall to an open clothes closet where I took off my "lucky" suit, and stepped into a pair of tight, heavy white coveralls.

Again and again I ran it through my head. Not a single new detail, and it no longer shocked or even surprised me that the only sense I could make of my conviction was that it made no sense at all.

And the root of it. My crime that never was. I considered that too, and that misguided woman who came to me back in 1963, who came to my home to be cured of smoking by means of hypnosis, and who then decided to make me a wife killer in her mind and in the eyes of the world.

Why? Because she had "fallen in love with me." I know, as a doctor, that it can happen. I will admit that I didn't handle this aspect of my life very well. But had I known that both her husband and my wife Carmela would be dead of natural causes within a few years . . . and that this woman, operating out of some delusion, would tell the authorities that I had hypnotized her into becoming a murderer . . . well, what would I have done?

I still couldn't answer that. I still can't. What do you do when a seemingly rational person turns into a deluded avenging angel before your eyes?

Her charges became a case and went to trial. I was tried in New Jersey for the murder of her husband. I was acquitted because they were satisfied that all the evidence pointed to one and only one conclusion. No crime had been committed!

Then I was tried in Florida for the murder of my wife. I was convicted on evidence that any novice medical assistant would laugh at. The verdict was based on conclusions drawn from a body exhumed long after death—but on tests of the body that are not valid even 48 hours after death. The evidence was drawn from tests that proved nothing.

Now, suppose you were innocent and events jumbled into place in a way that made you look superficially guilty—Remember, we're talking about you now, not me—Suppose you were found guilty and sent to jail. You'd believe that you were going to be set free in no time, and you'd be raging with resentment for each minute they took out of your life. Each minute. You'd never resign yourself to being a convict. You'd numb yourself, maybe, but when you thought about it—each and every time you thought about it—you'd be up in arms with righteous indignation. And now, every minute of your time would be wasted . . . your work or business would be falling apart . . . your family would be growing up without you . . . and you'd be just as innocent as the day they charged you with the crime you had never committed.

I was 34 when all of this began. I had suffered five heart attacks. My first wife had recently died, and Mary and I were putting together our family of four children. And today I was beginning a life sentence . . .

"Hi, Doc," another of the prisoners called out. "I heard the news. Tough break!"

"Yeah," a red-headed prisoner added, "but you've got the world's best mouthpiece. He'll spring you!"

"Want some coffee?" one bald-headed man with watery gray eyes asked.

Without waiting for my reply, he handed me a grease-covered, cut-down milk container half-filled with a hot, black liquid.

"A Ross Boyer special coffee blend," the redhead giggled.

I murmured, "Thanks," and sat on the metal bench. I was exhausted. The coffee tasted good as I leaned against the bars which ran from ceiling to floor.

I must have dozed off, because Grady's bald head appeared suddenly at the bars. "You've got a visitor, Doc," he shouted.

The cell door swung open, and I shuffled down the corridor toward the elevator. Grady held me by my left arm.

I straightened my coveralls and ran my fingers through my hair while the elevator crept down to the first floor. I could see Grady's watch. It read 4:00 p.m.

"Who is it?" I asked.

"Your wife."

Grady shoved me out of the elevator, opened the door to a detective's office, and closed it behind me.

I blinked my eyes.

"Hi." Mary's voice came from the center of the room. Her hair was brushed back from her face, highlighting the bright smile on her lips. I adored her.

We clung to each other, tightly. I shuddered as a cry escaped from my mouth. Minutes passed as we held each other, not saying a word.

Slowly I loosened my grip and brushed her lips with mine. I stepped back and held her by the shoulders. Mary cocked her head to the right. Her eyes began to fill with tears. "I love you, Carl."

I sighed.

"I want only you," Mary sobbed. "And I mean to have you. We'll keep on fighting."

"Why, Mary? Why?" I asked hoarsely.

She shook her head, and I squeezed her shoulders for support.

"Why do you want to go on? Why should you continue to believe me?" I cried.

"Because I know all there is to know, Carl. Remember I was present throughout the complete investigation. I talked with a scientist like Foldes and his assistant, Smith."

She brushed a strand of hair from her tear-streaked face.

"I know you didn't kill Carmela because there was no crime committed. Besides, I love you," she softly added, her voice breaking.

I dropped my arms, turned away, and started pacing the floor.

"I don't know, Mary."

I started to list all the reasons why it was best for her to leave me and make a new life for herself—the bad publicity; social ostracism; the emotionally and financially exhausting fight ahead of us which we might or might not win; the time involved with possibly years wasted; and my own health, which was poor. Any moment I could be hit with a fatal coronary; I wanted her to understand that then she would have nothing.

"No, Carl, you're wrong," she countered. "Even if the worst happens, I will have had you and your love, no matter what the conditions. And for me, that's enough. That's my life."

"Give me six months," Mary urged. "I'll have something going for sure within that time." She held out her hand and grabbed my arm to stop my pacing.

I looked at her. "What about bond?" I asked.

"Lee will be here this week and we'll see. But I'm not hopeful."

"What do you mean?" I began to shout.

Mary fell quiet. "Look, I have to go. Ross Boyer was good enough to give me a few minutes alone with you. He knows how much we need each other."

"How are the children?" I asked.

"Fine. Look out the window at nine tonight and you will see Monica and Lisa. They will be in the Ford convertible. I'll visit you at the regular time on Sunday."

Mary crossed the room and opened the door.Grady was standing there. She turned, blew me a kiss, and left. The jailer took me back to the felony tank.

APRIL 28, 1967
9:00 p.m.

I climbed the cell bars like a monkey, straining my neck to see acrossthe street. The light from *Mrs. O'Leary's Saloon* bathed the dark street with a golden hue. I spotted the Ford parked at the corner under the streetlamp. Mary and the children, Lisa, 4, and Monica, 8, were walking up the street, then down the street, never once looking up in my direction. But Lisa held one hand behind her back and kept it waving.

That's how I visited with my children the first night after my conviction.

APRIL 30, 1967
SUNDAY

What a restless night! The heat and filth of the felony tank were almost unbearable. My mattress reeked with the tears, fears, and sweat of past bodies. I was another victim.

I had eaten neither Friday, nor Saturday. The meals were shoveled into cake pans. Every meal looked like some sort of goulash. And the beans were always wormy.

My body stank. The odor was so bad I thought everyone was looking at me. Of course, that wasn't true as I was smelling them, as well!

I was determined to take a sponge bath, shave with cold water, and try to make myself presentable. Mary would be here at 2:00 p.m.

Visiting at the Sarasota County Felony Tank was unique. The steel cell door to the tank had imbedded in its center a six-inch rectangular plate glass. Through this opening, a prisoner saw his visitor and shouted messages, with only a few minutes allotted to each man.

Eight men! Perhaps some would not have a visitor, I thought selfishly.

I needn't have worried. "Murphy's Law" was operating at full capacity. All eight men had visitors that Sunday!

Heidi, my 19-year-old stepdaughter, was the first to stand in front of the glass. She cried and I comforted her. I had to forget myself enough to make sure that lovely Heidi would not have guilt feelings, and that her life would not be marred by the twisted stories and lies told about me.

Mary was next at the window. Dressed in a pink dress, she looked supremely regal, utterly beautiful. From her I learned that a motion for a new trial, indigency plea, and motion for bond had been filed by Jim Russ. Judge Silvertooth had set a hearing date for the motions for Thursday, May 3rd.

"Thursday!" I shouted.

Mary nodded with a smile on her beaming face.

"Then I'll be free!!" I shouted in joy.

"I don't know. We will see," Mary quickly countered.

For an instant I wanted to rant and rave at her: "You don't know? What do you mean, you don't know?" But I bit my tongue, and swallowed my frustration. After all, how *could* she know?

"How rough is the publicity?" I asked her, changing the subject. I felt I knew the answer since my cell was filled with newspapers from across the country carrying similar screaming headlines as the ones in Florida.

A tired smile crossed Mary's face. "We'll manage."

"What do you mean?" I persisted.

"The newspapers are full of the story, daily," she answered bitterly. "The phone keeps ringing. And now the tourists drive slowly past the house pointing and whispering."

"I feel as if we're freaks," Heidi interrupted.

"What about the younger children?"

"They are playing with their friends, Carl. They may have a problem tomorrow when they go back to school," Mary added ominously.

I bowed my head against the cold cell door. Those poor children! A mother dead, a new stepmother, and now their father convicted of murder—in prison for life! And what could I do? Absolutely nothing!

Sensing my mood, Mary tapped on the door. I lifted my head and looked through the glass plate at her face, lined with fatigue.

"I love you," she mouthed, and added, loudly, "Don't worry about anything. Just take care of yourself and stay well and all for us!"

Visiting time had run out. I waved goodbye through the glass plate. Heidi shouted, "Look out of the window at nine tonight."

APRIL 30
9:00 p.m.

I was back on the bars, like the proverbial monkey, watching Heidi walk up and down the street with Coco, the brown family poodle, in tow. Now and then she stopped, bend down and whispered to Coco. I imagined that he turned his head and looked up in my direction, tail waving.

"Hello Coco!" I called, insanely, again and again. Finally, I slid down the steel bars, exhausted.

MAY 1, 1967
MONDAY

I received a letter from Bailey. It had been written at 5:30 a.m. Saturday, April 29th'

Dear Carl:
I arose this morning at 5:00 a.m., unable to sleep because of the many

racing thoughts swirling through my mind as to what can be done most swiftly and efficiently to reverse your current situation. Let me say, at the outset, that after some serious reflection I am satisfied that yesterday's verdict amounts to a legal acquittal.

I am sorry that I had to rush off at such an inopportune time and leave you with only peripheral reassurance. Had I anticipated the possibility of conviction, I, of course, would have cancelled my appearance earlier in the week. However, under the circumstances, I had given my word and made a commitment to several hundred lawyers, and could not break it any more than I could break my word to you. Although departure at the moment may have seemed callous, I am sure that you would rather depend on one who takes his promises seriously.

Since it appears that the jury was prejudiced against you rather severely for sufficient reasons to convict you on preposterous evidence, we may be most thankful that their verdict was abortive. You will never be tried again on murder in the first degree. Although I think the degree of the conviction will dispose of the case on appeal, you have two other very strong points, either of which would bar further prosecution upon reversal: the denial of a speedy trial would certainly prejudice you demonstrably inasmuch as the State's principal evidence was not obtained until after that trial date went by; and the insufficiency of the evidence, because of its speculative and experimental nature. My principal concern at the moment is that of getting you freed on bail while the machinery of appeal is warmed up to operating speed. Again, it is fortunate that the conviction was non-capital, for bail is much simpler to get under such circumstances . . . I know that of great concern to you is the matter of finances for such appellate and further work as may be necessary. It is apparent that the cost of a transcript alone is going to be substantial, and that you are, in every sense of the word, indigent. I have not even begun to count the costs of this trial, but as you may suspect I am personally on the hook for many thousands of dollars, in addition to the leftover bills from New Jersey . . .

There is not much more to say at the present time, except that you may continue to count on me to give you every inch of representation I can muster without regard to your ability to pay, as I have in the past. You are now in the shoes of Sam Sheppard in a sense, for until you are out and free you are necessary and unfinished business. I remain completely convinced of your innocence and further convinced that there was no murder. Although we have not finished yet, we have come a long way since the day you and I embarked on what was to have been the most hopeless case in U.S. history. I am grateful that Paul Holmes has been present to record the story, for now it very badly needs to be told. Ironically people will probably be more prone to read it under the circumstances than if you had been acquitted.
I was most upset to learn that someone had the termerity to question Mary about money yesterday. It was a callous and thoughtless act and may result in some shift of personnel. If anyone at any time comes to you with money questions in connection with this case, refer them to me at

once. I told Mary long ago that I did not intend to ask her for any of her own funds, and I meant it then as I do now.

Keep your chin up. You have survived this long only because you have been able to take a pounding. The world holds success for those who can take it as well as dish it out, and the strongest people are those who fight hardest when the storm is at its peak. We'll lick 'em, somehow. All of the staff, who are your friends, are very much behind you.

Lee

Bailey was soon to change his story.

MAY 2, 1967
WEDNESDAY

It was early afternoon when Grady came for me. Mary and Bailey were waiting in the detective's office.

Fortunately I was able to find a clean pair of coveralls. They were too small for me, so my bare lower limbs looked like misplaced piano legs. While they did nothing for my appearance, who can measure a psychological lift? At least I was clean.

As I approached the detective's office, I could hear angry, muffled voices behind closed doors. I opened the door and walked in.

Bailey's face was a deep red and Mary's mouth was small and tight. Her hands were down at her sides closed into fists. *Now what?* I thought.

"Ah, Sweetie," she said. Her face relaxed as she stepped into my arms for a long kiss. Her body felt really good, and her perfume, Shalimar, literally made my head swim.

I shook hands with Bailey and asked what the shouting was all about.

Bailey jammed his hands deeply into the pockets of his blue suit and began pacing up and down. "I need money," he said.

"You've been paid," Mary snapped.

I held up my hand and said to Mary, "Let him speak, please."

"Look," Bailey said, and stopped his pacing, "I have run up bills in your defense that are out of sight. I have to pay them off!"

"He wants more money," Mary interrupted, ignoring my previous request to let Bailey speak.

"Look, Lee," I said. "You agreed that the $40,000 I had to fight both the State of Florida and the State of New Jersey and the appeals, if God forbid I should lose, was more than enough."

"He wants to take the $16,000 mortgage that we hold on your old house on Longboat Key and sell it for $10,000 quick cash!" Mary shouted. "We'll lose $6,000 for nothing!"

Lee exploded. "Now, look!" He turned toward Mary.

"I'm not going to discuss it any further," Mary snapped and walked out of the room, slamming the door behind her.

"What the hell's the matter with you, Lee!" I shouted, feeling completely out of control. "I get a life sentence and all you have on your mind is money! Look," I added desperately, "I'll try to see if I can raise more money."

Lee shook his head. "It's not good enough. I want an assignment on all the book and movie rights to your story—on all the royalties until your bill is paid. And if you don't sign, I'm not going to represent you any further."

I sat down stunned. It took all the control I possessed not to push the panic button.

"Lee," I pleaded softly, "I don't own any rights. You know that. They are all in Mary's name. I can't sign anything over to you because I don't own anything!"

"Get her to sign!" Bailey demanded.

"I can't do that," I answered patiently. "She is an independent individual. We love each other completely and support one another. You know that. But we are also self-sufficient. One doesn't own the other!"

"Balls!" Bailey snapped. "She is nothing but a millstone around your neck. You ought to get rid of her!"

Appalled, I didn't answer. Bailey's outbursts were so infantile I treated him like a child. I ignored him.

"What about the hearing?" I asked, trying to change the subject.

Bailey went on in great detail to explain how the media was on my side, and that the State of Florida was being looked upon unfavorably and even being ridiculed because of the absurd verdict. He planned to appear on several T.V. talk shows, like those of Johnny Carson and Joe Pyne, and would tell the nation what this country already knew: Namely, that I was convicted by a jury made up of hicks and fishermen who were unqualified to judge the scientific evidence in the case. Bailey went on to say that Judge Silvertooth was incompetent and never should have allowed the State's medical evidence. Bailey had already heard from sources that Helpern hated him so much that he, Helpern, had falsified the evidence

—that there never really were tests performed by Helpern and Umberger.

"We are not licked, Carl," Bailey continued. We are going to show the world what the State of Florida really is, a cesspool."

Bailey continued his pacing. "I don't know about the bond hearing. The law is in your favor, but I don't think Silvertooth has enough balls to apply it. Right now the good judge figures he is a community hero and to hell with jeopardizing that for you. Understand?"

I nodded. I understood all right, but I was speechless.

"Forget the motion for a new trial and the indigency plea. We're going to lose them, but I need them for the record," Bailey said. "Take care of yourself and smile," he added. "I can't stand sad clients."

Bailey shok my hand, opened the door and turned.

"I'll find Mary and send her back to you. I hope she's cooled off. She fights harder for you when you're in a jam," Bailey observed with a twinkle in his eye.

My mind was in a whirl. Money! Mary! Bailey! Maybe no bond! Then what? What will happen next? The thoughts of going to Florida State Prison! No, I couldn't think about that. Never that horror!

The door opened and Mary was back. It was really the first time I had had a chance to look at her. She was wearing her blue silk wedding dress—it now seemed so long ago since we had been married—and a strand of cultured pearls. We sat and held hands quietly, looking at each other, enjoying this moment of togetherness.

I remember every detail of what Mary wore, this time and every other time she would visit me in all those years in prison. The styles and colors are indeliby etched on my memory, not because I care about clothes but because I care that Mary cared to take such special pains to please me.

"Don't look for any relief, Carl," Mary said. She plucked at a piece of thread from her blue dress.

"Why?" I squeezed her hands tightly.

"I spoke with Bill Herford. You know he does all of Judge Silvertooth's law research. He told me the judge is totally against any relief for you."

"But why?" I cried. "I was out on bond before and during the trial, a ridiculous bond of $15,000. Silvertooth knows we have roots in the community—that the children attend school. Nothing is going to happen."

Mary shook her head. "You don't understand, Carl. There is a lot of clamor in the newspapers. Florida is delighted they beat the great F. Lee Bailey. Schaub, as much as he is usually despised by people in Sarasota, has become their hero. There's too much community pressure and Silvertooth is not going to fight it. Why should he?" Mary asked rhetorically.

"He's a judge! A professional man!" I yelled. "It simply isn't right and he knows it!"

Mary looked at me as if I were Lisa, who was four years old.

"For all your intelligence, almost brillance, all your knowledge of people as a physician, you still don't know anything about reality do you?"

I exploded. "I don't want a nickel-and-dime analysis. I don't want lectures. I want results!"

"I love you completely, my darling," Mary answered. "But you have a lot to learn."

As it turned out, she was right. Very right.

MAY 3, 1967
THURSDAY

The Big Day. My first crack at freedom! What a beautiful day!

Dressed only in my boxer shorts, I hung onto the bars of my cage. I could see the sunlight bouncing off the shiny hoods of the cars parked across from the jail.

Mrs. O'Leary's, the corner saloon, was doing an active business at 10:00 a.m. Now and then, I caught sight of and recognized newspaper reporters walking up and down the sidewalk, even though my hearing wasn't until 5:00 p.m., and was to be held at the Court House in Bradenton rather than Sarasota.

I decided to get dressed on the theory of unexpected visitors. Jailer Grady brought me the gray suit Mary had dropped off and he told me to put all my personal property in a brown paper bag which he handed me, since I wasn't coming back!

My heart leaped!!

Persistent questioning of Grady yielded nothing. All he would tell me was that sheriff Ross Boyer wanted me ready with all my belongings. It would take an hour to drive to the Bradenton Court House, and the Sheriff wanted to arrive in plenty of time. "Security, you know," Grady added, rubbing his bald head.

There was that word again: *Security!* I felt uneasy about the turn of events. But I was obviously in no position to find out anything, and could not guess the reasons behind Boyer's orders. Logically, I could reason that since I wasn't coming back, it could mean only one of two things—

freedom, on bond to go home to Mary and the children (please God!), or a transfer to Raiford. I shuddered and stopped speculating.

My portable radio gave the news every half hour that I would be in court that day for a hearing on a motion for a new trial, an insolvency plea, and a motion for bond.

I couldn't understand Bailey's strategy concerning the insolvency plea, other than the fact that it would be a touch of irony to have the taxpayers foot the bill to overturn a railroaded conviction. However, I felt that the motion would only serve to further alienate Silvertooth. And despite what Mary had said about the outcome of the bond hearing, I thought, given the chance, Silvertooth would follow the law and release me on an appeal bond.

MAY 3, 1967
3:00 p.m.

Grady came for me and I hurriedly went down the elevator to meet Sheriff Boyer.

We walked out of the jail into the driveway, bathed in the afternoon sun. There were only two photographers furiously snapping pictures. The rest, I imagined, were at the Bradenton Court House.

Boyer and I sat in the back. He hadn't handcuffed me, and for this I was grateful. The front of the car was occupied by the driver and chief jailer, Jack Royal.

During the ride to Bradenton, I tried to question Boyer on what would happen, but he wouldn't comment. Ross refused to answer my question concerning the reason for his order that I take along my personal property.

"Try to sit back and relax, Carl. Take in the scenery," Boyer advised, breaking off all conversation.

I took Boyer's advice, leaned back in my seat, and watched the outside world go by—the free world. I hoped I would rejoin this world after today's successful bond hearing.

The car pulled up to the curb across from the steps of the courthouse. One look told me I was in trouble. The steps were covered with hundreds of people— reporters, photographers, T.V. cameramen, and the ever-present spectators. I wondered how many were responsible for the hate mail directed toward Mary that had been arriving at my home.

Boyer took out a pair of handcuffs. "Sorry about this, Carl, but I have to put them on for appearance sake."

I stuck out my wrists. There was no point in arguing. Boyer had his job to do.

With flashbulbs popping in our faces, Boyer and Royal threaded me through the crowd. We quickly went up the steps and into an anteroom off the courtroom. After the door was shut behind us, Boyer took off the cuffs. A black detective handed me a hot cup of coffee, and I sat down in a rickety wooden chair to wait.

After 30 nervous minutes had passed, Bailey arrived. There was little small talk. Boyer left, Bailey opened his briefcase and whipped out a legal paper, and placed it on the table. "Sign," he commanded.

I slowly read each clear, crisp typewritten word. It was an assignment to Bailey of all letters, literary rights, and royalties to my story.

"What's the point of my signing this?" I asked Bailey. "You know I don't have anything to assign to you. Mary has all the rights. I told you that last week."

"Never mind that," Bailey insisted. "Sign it or I don't go with you into that courtroom. Besides, I want to use it as an exhibit in our indigency plea."

I didn't bother to fight him any longer. I signed.

MAY 3, 1967
5:00 p.m.

The attorneys for both sides had entered the courtroom and taken their places. Russ, McEwen, and Bailey for me; Schaub, Georgieff, and Strode for the State.

Now it was my turn. The deputy sheriffs of Bradenton, one on each side and one in front marched me into the courtroom. A glance told me that every seat was taken. I sat next to Bailey at the defense table and twisted my head around to find Mary. She was nowhere insight.

"Where's Mary?" I asked Bailey.

"I don't give a shit," he snapped, not looking at me.

I grabbed his right arm. "What the hell does that mean?"

Bailey turned to me. "I am through with that wife of yours. I'm finished. I'm fed up. She can shift for herself and can start right now by trying to get into this courtroom."

I sat stunned and speechless at Bailey's conduct.

Again I twisted my head looking for Mary. After multiple eyeball-to-eyeball confrontations with the curious, I found Mary sitting in the back next to Bud Montgomery, owner of Montgomery-Roberts Department Stores in Sarasota—a man committed to helping me and my wife, in any way he could. I failed to catch her eye; then it was too late.

The baliff rapped on the door "Hear ye! hear ye! The courst is now in session. Judge Silvertooth presiding. All stand!"

We stood. Silvertooth strode into the room and briskly walked to the bench. His black robes pulled at his trousers revealing a pair of green socks. After he sat, we sat, and the ritual began.

The first argument was presented by Red McEwen. He said that the jury's verdict should be rejected by Judge Silvertooth and I should be freed because of 17 major points all of which had been listed in a lengthy motion filed in Naples on Tuesday.

They included complaints about the testifying of some of Schaub's prosecution witness, the actions of Schaub himself before the jury, and allegations that Schaub failed to prove many of the things he promised to prove to the jury.

Bailey was next to argue. He felt a new trial was not even warranted because I had been, in effect, acquitted of first degree murder in Naples and should not be tried again.

He hammered at the contentions held by us that the second degree murder verdict was inconsistent with a charge of poisoning.

"There is no case in the United States of second degree murder from poisoning that has been sustained. If the jury had returned a verdict of manslaughter, as you told them they could have," Bailey said to Judge Silvertooth, "we would find ourselves in an even more laughable situation."

"The jury tasted the sweet blood of Carl Coppolino in returning a verdict satisfactory to the public," Bailey continued, "but the eyebrows of lawyers across the country are raised at Florida's new concept of second degree murder."

Bailey concluded, "The law of Florida, however inadvertently, has acquitted Coppolino of everything."

Schaub argued that under Florida law, if the evidence supports first degree murder, juries are permitted to agree on any of five lesser degrees of guilt. He accused Bailey of invading the province of the jury.

Schaub and Strode refuted each of our 17 points in support of a new trial and reminded Silvertooth he had been privy to all the testimony and facts during my four-week trail.

Silvertooth, at this point, smiled and said, "I am fully familiar with the facts, gentlemen," and Strode sat down.

Silvertooth then denied the following motions: *a.* motion to set aside the jury verdict and enter a directed verdict for acquittal for the defendant; and *b.* a motion for a new trial for the defendant.

The hearing for the plea of insolvency was embarrassing for me. Bailey insisted I take the stand. He asked me very simple questions concerning my finances.

Frank Schaub handled the cross examination and asked me many questions concerning bank accounts I had throughout the country. It was difficult to explain to the Court how I moved the same several thousands of dollars from one bank to another to take advantage of favorable interest rates at different banks in different parts of the year, and not have it appear that it was a huge sum of money. Schaub made it appear to the Court that each bank account was a differnt account rather than the same account moved several times from place to place.

Then Bailey called Mary to the stand. The court leaned forward eagerly as she walked with dignity to take the oath and the witness stand.

Bailey asked only one question concerning my stock account. And Mary responded that I had sold it to her to raise the cash for his fee. The irony was in the fact that with this same transaction I had included the transfer to Mary of any story of literary rights. Yet Bailey refused to accept it!

Strode cross-examined Mary on the stock account. She pointedly showed him that it was her money, not mine.

Silvertooth quickly denied the insolvency plea. The bond motion was scheduled to be heard next.

My body began to respond to the mental anxiety. As I sat forward in my seat eagerly awaiting Silvertooth to begin, my hands dripped cold sweat. I could feel the tight steel-like bands of pain across my chest. I prayed: "Dear God! No coronary attack! Not now!

"We are running late," Silvertooth intoned piously. "I will entertain other motions at a later date." Now came the gavel.

Pandemonium broke out in the courtroom. Reporters raced for the door searching for a telephone. Murmurs of disbelief spread throughout the spectators. The crowd was disappointed. Silvertooth had cheated them.

I turned to Bailey. "What the hell does that mean?"

"I'll see what goes with His Honor," Russ answered.

"I'll follow you," Bailey added.

Out of the corner of my eye I watched Mary and Heidi approach. I was surrounded by deputies, but they allowed my family to come and sit with me.

Mary held my head in her hands and kissed me on the lips. Heidi held me tight as if I'd disappear if she didn't. She kept saying, "It'll be all right! It'll be all right!" I felt very loved. The three of us talked and speculated on the reasons why the bond hearing was postponed. I informed Mary and Heidi that I was forced to take my personal property from the Sarasota County Jail and asked her what was going on, or if she had heard anything?

She shrugged her shoulders and said, "Lord, who knows? I fear we have no control over the situation."

Bailey flopped into an empty chair beside us. His ever-trembling fingers tapped incessantly on the table. He shook his head.

"You are going to Raiford," he said looking me straight in the eye.

"Right now?" I asked increduously.

"Right now," he emphasized, ignoring Mary.

Mary grabbed my hand. "You'll be better off there, Carl. The food and sleeping conditions are much better than Boyer's jail. We can come visit you."

"I've never been to a prison," Heidi coyly added, teasing me.

Boyer approached and grabbed my left arm. "Let's go!"

Hurriedly I kissed Mary and started out of the courtroom. I could hear Mary's voice behind me. Keep your hopes up, Carl!"

Boyer put on the handcuffs just before we walked outside into the now setting sun. The steps were jammed with newspaper reporters and T.V. cameramen. Boyer and Royal hurried me down the steps to a waiting state car. The driver gunned the motor and we were off. My wristwatch registered 7:30 p.m.

It's approximately 250 miles from Bradenton to the town of Raiford, site of the Florida State Prison. In fact, the prison is known as Raiford rather than FSP.

Night had fallen and the headlights of the car picked out the cheap tourist motels along the highway.

I tried not to think, but it was difficult. Prison was an unknown quantity. My only frame of reference was those old James Cagney/Humphrey Bogart prison movies. All I could visualize were those cell doors clanging, the beatings, tortures, and prison murders. (It would turn out to be *just* like that! Mercifully, I didn't know it at the time.)

My pathetic handful of personal belongings rested at my feet in a large paper sack. The top of the bag contained letters—opened, read, and censored by the jail officials—from Mary, which I read first with the help of the flickering lights along the highway.

One was an upbeat letter filled with positive thoughts about how we would be successful in our fight, and another was a plea to give her six months before I made a decision about us. (My thinking still led me to the conclusion that Mary and the children would be better off with a new name, and a new life.) Another was a love letter. Tears welled in my eyes as I looked out the window, seeing nothing but the face of my wife.

There were other letters—all hate mail—some from so-called Christians saying I should repent! Repent for what? If anybody should repent, I thought, it should have been Helpern and Umberger! Other letters were plain nasty, a disgrace to the human race and an insult to anyone's humanity.

Not a word had been spoken since we left Bradenton. Boyer, Royal, and the driver had, no doubt, other things on their mind, and I was too wrapped up in my own pain.

It was about 10:00 p.m. when we stopped at a restaurant along the highway. Boyer had removed the handcuffs a long time ago. Inside the restaurant the driver, Royal, Boyer, and I occupied a quiet table in the rear.

Funny thoughts ran through my mind as I sat there and looked around at a "free" citizens eating their suppers. It occurred to me that I should bellow, 'I am being held against my will!" Or yell, "Who would believe that the infamous Dr. Coppolino sentenced to life in prison and under maximum security precautions, dressed in a business suit, is leisurely having dinner tonight at a highway restaurant?"

We all ordered the same meal—steak, salad, coffee, and dessert. Boyer opened the conversation: "We will be arriving at Raiford in about two hours."

I nodded. "Then what?"

Boyer sippied his coffee, then answered, "I'll turn you over to the prison officials. You'll leave either by parole or by overturning your conviction in the appeal courts."

"Ross, what do you think my chances are in the appeals court?"

"Like I told you before, it's a rotten conviction. Either you poisoned your wife or you didn't; it's premeditated first degree murder or nothing."

Boyer chewed at his salad. "I never felt we had any hard evidence," he added, softly.

Royal and the driver were engaged in small talk, ignoring us.

"Remember Ross, you said something to me about the State's medical evidence being questionable? What did you mean?"

Boyer leaned back in his chair and slowly looked around at the scurrying waitresses. He caught the attention of one of them and signaled for more coffee. I didn't push, didn't move, but held my breath. Naturally, I knew the State's medical evidence was phony; we all knew it, but so what? Knowing and proving, especially after conviction, would be very, very difficult. So I waited, patiently.

Sheriff Boyer turned and looked at me. "There was something fishy going on at *The Cove Inn*," he said dropping his voice. *The Cove Inn* was the place where the prosecution held their strategy sessions.

Boyer sipped at his fresh cup of coffee. "I kept hearing reports," he continued, "that Helpern and Umberger were constantly changing their testimony to match the day's courtroom activity. And that Schaub was afraid they were doing too good a job and that it would blow up in his face."

"You are going to have a tough way to go," continued Boyer. "Now that Florida beat Bailey, they are not going to give up easily, to anything! Schaub and Georgieff will see to that."

"Mostly because of Schaub?" I prompted.

"That bastard!" Boyer exploded. "He's sick! I never agreed to that business of repeated subpoenas of your young daughters."

I felt hate for Schaub rushing within me. He was the person who tried to destroy my marriage by trying to turn Mary and me against each other; the person who tried to destroy my young daughters psychologically; and the person who tried to turn my older stepchildren against me. The fact that he failed in these efforts didn't lessen the hatred I felt for him.

"Do you know what the son-of-a-bitch had the nerve to do, Carl?" Sheriff Boyer asked. Without waiting for an answer, he went on. "Schaub was scared about this case dealing with Helpern and Umberger and, by the way, he was surprised, maybe more surprised than you when the jury came back with that ridiculous conviction. Yeah, Schaub was scared considering the time bomb he was playing with. So he gave an interview to a local Naples radio station. He went on the air saying that if he, Frank Schaub, lost the case, it was the fault of the Sarasota Sheriff's Department and that Sheriff Ross Boyer was incompetent; that we never investigaged the case properly; and that we didn't supply his office with concrete evidence. "How could we, Carl?" Boyer asked excitedly. "There wasn't any evidence!"

Boyer paused to catch his breath. The waitress brought us our steaks. We ate, silently.

"You know, I have the tape of that interview," Boyer mumbled, his mouth full of food. "I have it in a tape recorder sitting on my desk in the office. Sometimes I play it and hate Schaub's guts a little more each day."

MAY 5, 1967
ABOUT MIDNIGHT

It was slightly after midnight when the state car pulled up in front of the well-lit monstrosity of barbed-wire topped fences, guard towers, and concrete that was the fortress called Floria State Prison. Boyer had called ahead by car radio, so the officers at the steel-locked gates were waiting for me. He gave the turnkey my commitment papers and shook my right hand. I held in my left hand the brown paper sack that contained my worldly possessions.

"Good luck to you, Carl. Do you have any money?" Boyer asked.

Numbly I shook my head. My eyes darted around, trying to take in everything at once.

"Here." Boyer said, thrusting a 10 dollar bill into my right hand.

"Thanks," I whispered. "And when you see Mary . . ." my voice broke.

"I know what to tell her," Boyer finished for me.

The fat turnkey butted in. "Hey, Sheriff," he blabbered, the wad of chewing tobacco getting in the way of his tongue. "If you ain't in a powerful rush, this here prisoner can give you his fancy duds to take back." He scratched his food-stained brown shirt that covered an enormous belly. "He ain't going to need them no more here."

Boyer looked at the turnkey with disgust in his eyes and nodded. Two prison guards dressed in wrinkled, ill-fitting brown suits led me down a poorly-lit dingy corridor to a room with a steel door. Inside, one guard ordered me to strip off all my clothes. The other gave me a pair of shower slides, white boxer shorts, and gray coveralls. In addition, he handed me a bedroll which consisted of a muslin sheet, a pillow case, and a blanket. In turn, I jammed my raw silk suit into a brown paper sack and handed it to one of the guards.

The other guard took me to the communication center of the prison, the control room. Inside the control room there were seven guards dressed in their brown uniforms. I stood in the center of the room and waited, holding in my hand Mary's letters and my shaving gear. I looked around the nondescript room. An old Longine clock on the fly-spattered green wall registered 1:00 a.m.

The gate guard handed the control room officer my commitment papers and the 10 dollars Boyer had given me.

"You got anything else, Coppolino?" the control room guard asked from behind his badly scarred wooden desk.

I shook my head.

"Hey! You answer me, boy!" the guard commanded. "And in this place you answer and put "Sir" on the end! You understand that now, boy?"

"Yes, Sir!" I answered.

The guard nodded his head, pleased.

"What's his number?" he asked one of the other guards.

"018591."

"Okay," he grunted. Squinting up at me from his desk, he yelled, "You hear that? That's who you are, 018591. Somebody calls that number out, you answer. 'Cause you ain't no fancy doctor in this place. You're only a dirty old inmate," he laughed, "number 018591. You understand?"

I nodded.

"Boy," the guard shouted with much agitation, "are you bitten with the dumb ass? I told you to answer and put 'Sir' on the end of it!" He wagged his finger in my face. "Now I'm going to remind you no more, boy! You understand?"

"Yes, Sir!" I answered softly.

"Take him to 'F' floor."

Two guards led me down the same dingy corridor and up two flights of filthy metal stairs. They unlocked and locked two floor-to-ceiling steel doors behind us. I found myself walking down a concrete catwalk, screened in on my left side; on my right side, I passed cells closed in by steel bars.

The catwalk was dimly lit by a bare lightbulb, hanging from the middle of a black ceiling. I could hear the clanging of plumbing and the moans of tortured souls, trying to sleep.

A guard approached us from the opposite direction. "You got an empty?" my keeper asked him.

"Naw! Got a single in this one," he said, gesturing to a dark cell. "Got crazy Tony in there."

"Get him out!" ordered my keeper.

A partially-bald man came flying out of the now unlocked cell.

"What the hell are you motherfuckers trying to do to me?" he screamed. He stood with bare feet in the middle of the dank corridor, his white, now gray, boxer shorts held by a single metal snap. "I'm sound asleep! Can't you cocksuckers wait until morning?"

"Now, Gentile," cooed the "F" floor guard, "we've got to make room for our special guest."

Tony Gentile turned and gaped at me. His fat face broke into a broad grin. "You must be the Doc! I heard about it on the radio. Geez, I'm sorry," he said sticking out his hand. "It's real tough."

Gentile turned back to the guard and yelled, "Why didn't you tell me it was for the Doc? You no good bastard!" He turned and walked down the corridor with the guard.

"Okay, Coppolino! In here!" ordered my keeper, pointing to the now vacant cell.

I walked into the pitch black cell. The steel door slammed behind me and the lock snapped shut. I was alone. I inspected my cage by the dim rays of the light coming from the catwalk. It was a room about 6x9 with a double bunk and a scarred metal stand sitting in one dark corner. In the opposite corner was a chipped porcelain sink. Brownish water dripped from a green-coated single tap.

I put my belongings on the top bunk and covered the gray slick mattress of the lower bunk with a muslin sheet. There wasn't a pillow; I made my own. I folded the blanket and stuck the pillow case on top of it.

Next I sat down on the bunk and re-read Mary's letters by the same dim light. One of the letters contained stories about the children and Coco, our poodle, as if nothing horrible had happened. It was just a normal letter sent from a loving wife to her husband who was on, perhaps, a business trip. It was the beginning of Mary's attempts to make our life together "normal," or as normal as possible, so that we could pick up the pieces of our lives someday and go on living. Exhausted, I was finally overcome by sleep.

MAY 5, 1967
5:30 a.m.

The banging and rattling of the steel bars woke me.

"Hey, buddy!'

I looked up and saw a thin, blond convict holding a bucket of steaming coffee.

"Got a cup?" he asked.

"No, I don't."

"Never mind, I'll be back."

The convict shuffled off, his slides slapping against the concrete floor of the catwalk.

I rolled out of the bunk, washed my face, shaved, brushed my teeth, and combed my hair purely by feel because there wasn't a mirror in the cell. Finally, I urinated in the sink because there wasn't a commode, either.

The bars to my cell door rattled.

"Here!" The convict handed me a red plastic cup filled with hot black coffee.

"Thanks."

Sitting on the edge of my bunk, I sipped the coffee.

The convict didn't move. "You must be the Doc? Ain't you?" His blond hair kept falling into his eyes. He kept rubbing his sniffling nose with the back of his hand.

I nodded.

"Yeah! I heard the hacks talking about you. They've been talking all day about getting their hands on you," he grinned. "They figure to make things tough for you—like tear you a new asshole. That's the talk. Like sort of putting you in your place." He blew his nose with his bare fingers and wiped it on his gray pants.

"Now don't let them get to you, Doc! They're a bunch of illiterate bastards, and they can't stand nobody with smarts. But they've got the key and don't you forget it!" he observed. "But don't sweat it! They ain't going to fuck with you too much. They're scared shitless of your publicity and lawyers and all the stuff you've got outside," the convict added.

He smiled at me. "Really, these cocksuckers got no balls! So keep your mouth shut, and your eyes open. You'll do okay." He split his mouth into a toothless grin and waved.

"Thanks," I mumbled, trying to make sense of what he had just said. I felt lost, like some captive on another planet; it certainly couldn't be Earth, where I knew the customs, responses, and language. I didn't have time to dissect it all, because suddenly a voice boomed at me.

"Okay! Coppolino!"

I looked up and saw a short, gray-haired prison guard standing outside my locked cell door. A "hack," I thought, since I had already started to think of them in that term.

"Get your shit together," he ordered. "We're going for a walk." He unlocked the cell door.

I grabbed my shaving gear and letters and threw them into the brown paper sack. I stepped out onto the catwalk. It was 9:00 a.m.

The sun was high in the cloudless sky and I could feel the heat through my thick coveralls.

"My name is Officer Harris," the guard offered.

I nodded, forgetting the instructions on answering that I had received the previous night from the guard in the control room.

"I'm going to take you to the West Unit, our receiving center. There's no reason for you to be here in lock-up."

Harris led me along the concrete walk and down a flight of concrete and metal steps. This was the front way out. I was in a section of the prison called *The Rock*, Harris told me.

We passed what seemed to be hundreds of convicts, some wearing blue uniforms, others dressed in white. Some passed by and called out, "Hello, Mr. Harris!" and the guard would answer playfully.

I could hear voices swirling about me. "There's the Doc!" "That's Coppolino!" "Well, they got the poor bastard!" "I knew he'd never beat it in Florida!"

We went out of the main prison through a huge gate called the West Gate. I took a good look at the surrounding buildings that made up the prison and learned more from Officer Harris.

In 1967, Raiford had actually been three prisons, situated on an 18,000-acre reservation midway between the towns of Starke and Lake Butler, a long way from anywhere. The indigenous pine forest of north Florida had been cleared for more than a mile around the prison buildings to provide farmland and to make escape more difficult.

One prison was the ancient, decaying main prison called *The Rock* or Raiford— and now in 1980 called the Union Correctional Institution. It was built in 1927 and first housed 1700 to 1800 men.

As we walked through the West Gate, Harris pointed out the landmarks. To the right was the visiting park with tables, benches, and small patches of lawn edged with flowers. It was in there that visitors would come with food and spend six hours with their loved ones each Sunday. To the left was a red brick building, the Chapel. Then came the hospital, laundry, and finally the West Unit.

I heard Harris' running commentary, but really wasn't paying attention. I kept saying to myself over and over, "When are they going to let me out of this horrible place?"

The West Unit was the receiving center for Florida State Prison in 1967. It consisted of multiple dormitories containing double bunks stacked two feet apart, a fly-spattered mess hall, several offices that housed classifications, records, a psychologist, and a small Chapel and dispensary. There was a tiny canteen run by a convict. Here I was able to purchase toilet articles and the daily newspaper.

Around the West Unit was a yard that contained a softball field, weights, and a shed with metal tables and chairs holding dominoes, checkers and chess sets.

Harris took me to Records. This section was staffed by convicts who did all the menial work, but, on this occasion Mr. Carmichael, the supervisor, personally fingerprinted me and took my picture for the file—called my *jacket*.

Next we went to the West Unit control room staffed by Lieutenant Chambers, a dour-faced man who wore thick-lensed eye glasses, and his associate, Sergeant Chessar, a small, rotund, easy-going guard who found a home eating out of the public trough. The man who did all the work was their clerk, a convict named Santos, a tall, husky, black-haired Mexican-American.

"Ah, *Amigo!*" greeted Santos, shaking my hand as if we had known each other for years instead of less than a minute.

"So you're *the* Doctor Coppolino!" he beamed. "I am Santos, a political prisoner serving life for murder."

"Cut the crap now, Santos!" laughed Harris. "Log him and assign him a bunk."

"*Bueno!* Senor Harris!"

Santos picked up the log book. "You have a heart trouble, no?"

"Yes, I do. How did you know?"

"It's been in the paper, *el medico. Bueno!* Here! For you, I have a bottom bunk in the back away from the T.V. where it's nice and quiet."

I thanked Santos and Officer Harris and I left to find my quarters.

The huge dormitory was only partially occupied by convicts. Some were reading, others playing chess, and a few were curled up sound asleep on their bunks.

When I entered the dormitory, all movement stopped. The convicts watched, but said nothing. Harris pointed out my bunk and instructed me as I put on sheet, blanket, and pillow case. Then he left.

Santos came into the dormitory just as I finished storing my shaving gear in a metal drawer attached to the underside of the bunk. He had a sad look on his face.

"*Pardone me*, Dr. Coppolino," Santos said, "but you must move." His eyes filled with tears.

I looked up from the bunk at Santos. "This is the bunk you assigned me?"

"*Si*. But me *jefe*, Lieutenant Chambers, he said; No! You get a top bunk and up front right under the T.V. No favors for you," he confessed.

Santos looked so crushed that I laughed, relieving the tension. "Forget it, *Amigo*. The air smells better the higher you go," I observed. "Now I can watch T.V. with no obstacles," I added.

Santos joined in my laughter and shook my hand. Later he would save my life, but that is getting ahead of my story. At this point, we had already become good friends.

I unmade my bunk and moved to my new location, a double bunk up front, under the T.V., close to the showers. The lower bunk was occupied by a weasel-faced convict named Morris. Morris was from New York, a junkie, serving five years for possession of heroin.

"Got any pills, Doc?" Morris asked eagerly.

"No."

Morris clued me in on the routine: lights out at 9:30 p.m., lights on at 5:30 a.m., breakfast at 6:30 a.m., bunk made up for inspection before 9:00 a.m., showers at 5:00 p.m., count at 6:00 p.m.

"You stand by your bunk, Doc," Morris instructed. "The hacks call your name and you answer by your number."

Then came mail call.

Morris was a wealth of information, a good teacher in survival. He was full of tidbits like "Don't leave anything around, not even a toothbrush, because somebody will swipe it. Stay away from the queers—don't even talk to them—their old man may get the wrong idea. Don't get into any gambling games. Keep your mouth shut."

Morris made it plain that he was flat broke and wanted "tailor-mades" —prison slang for commercial cigarettes, like Camels, Lucky Strikes, etc.—as compared to the roll-your-own variety called *Rip*. Morris and I made an agreement—for so much money a week Morris would make up my bunk, keep an eye on my personal property, and in general look out for me while I learned the language and reflexes of my new world.

It was the best contract I ever made. My mind was so fogged that invariably I'd leave my watch, my wallet, or anything else I had, on my bed as if I were at home. Morris would pick it up behind me and admonish me by saying, "Hey, Doc! You ain't home now. Somebody's going to steal your shit if you ain't more careful!"

"That's why I have you, Morris," I'd reply. And Morris' face would beam with pride and importance.

MAY 6, Saturday
5:30 a.m.

"Everybody up!" shouted the guard.

I opened my eyes, but the bare lightbulb's glare forced them shut again.

Morris was up already, sitting at the edge of the bunk below me. He had a plastic cup full of coffee in his right hand and a "tailor-made" in his left.

"There's yours," Morris pointed. He had made me a cup of coffee.

I grinned down at him. "I think I'd better get some groceries today at the canteen, if we want to eat." We both agreed that breakfast would be horrible at the mess hall.

But that was easier said than done. The 10 dollars I had turned in could not be drawn on for another week. I was broke. However, I need not have worried. Suddenly I found that my fame had preceded me.

All that morning the men of the dormitory trickled over to my bunk and introduced themselves with names like "Lefty," "Indian Joe," and "Fat Hughie." Many asked if I needed anything. They were willing to share what meager goods they had. Morris handled all the formalities and quickly said "yes" to all the offers.

Soon our metal drawers were filled with Maxwell House instant coffee, both state and tailor-made cigarettes, soap, cookies, candy, shaving equipment, etc.

Morris carefully made a list of who gave what, so I could replace the goods. But I could not replace the spirit of generosity these men spontaneously gave me. It was the one bright spot in my prison day.

Morris continued with my education after we finished breakfast which for him consisted of cookies, coffee, and a cigarette. He began pointing out all the convicts he knew and gave me some background material on each of them.

"This guy, Doc, for instance, he's a creep!" Morris gestured toward a pudgy, baby-faced convict who didn't look older than 18. "He's a baby raper. Somebody is going to kill him. So stay away!"

Another description: "This guy is a moocher. He'll bleed you to death." The convict Morris pointed out looked like any wino on any town's skid row.

Another: "This guy is a stone queer. I know you don't play that shit, Doc. But you get too friendly with this kind and his old man thinks you're making a play for his queen and then one night you wake up with a shiv in your guts."

I shuddered, imagining a knife blade going into my belly.

"Who needs it?" Morris continued. "Just stay cool until the cons get to know you."

The morning went fast. I watched the work squads leave, those who would mow the lawns, cut grass with yoyo swing blades, pick up paper, and clean the latrines.

Morris pulled a house man job that morning, sweeping and mopping the floor.

Strange, but my name was passed over that first morning.

"You better get yourself a permanent slot, a steady work assignment," advised Morris. "With a steady work assignment the hacks can't fuck you over. Because, believe me, some sorry hack is going to assign you to latrine detail. They'd love to stand there and watch the famous Doctor Coppolino scrubbing out shit bowls for life."

There was wisdom in Morris' words. The signs were plain to see. I was in for a rough time in the Florida State Prison system. Nobody was going to be able to help me and I had better start doing things for myself right now.

"You know of any openings, Morris?"

"Yeah! I hear the preacher is looking for a clerk. You could do worse, you know."

"Which way?"

Morris pointed out the way to the Chapel.

I was on my way.

Chaplain Kaiser, a Baptist minister, was a seedy-looking, small man dressed in a plain gray suit. Kaiser wore the same suit everyday I knew him. It stuck to him as though he had slept in it.

I introduced myself to Chaplain Kaiser and was immediately assigned as his clerk. I would work from 8:00 a.m. to 5:00 p.m. every day except Saturday. On Sunday I would help him with church services.

"By the way, Doctor," Kaiser asked, "did you know that your family can visit you tomorrow, since it is Sunday?"

My heart leaped. "No I didn't know!" I answered eagerly. Then my heart fell. There was no way Mary could be aware of this.

My face must have reflected my thoughts because Kaiser asked me what the problem was. I told him.

"Oh? Well, we'll take care of that!" Kaiser reached over and picked up his telephone.

"What's your home phone number?" he asked.

I told him. And within a minute he had Mary on the telephone and was telling her about being able to visit Sunday.

"Yes," Kaiser said, answering one of Mary's questions, "he's fine and sitting beside me in my office. No. I'm sorry, Mrs. Coppolino, you cannot speak to him. It is against regulations. However, he is fine. I'm looking right at him. I'll be glad to ask him."

Kaiser turned to me. The pale green walls of his tiny office seemed to make him look smaller and paler.

"Your wife wants to know how you feel and if you have your nitroglycerin tablets with you."

"Tell her I'm fine, Chaplain, and that I'll get my tablets as soon as possible."

He conveyed my response to Mary and then broke the connection. "She'll be here tomorrow."

MAY 7, 1967
SUNDAY

I awoke and was out of my bunk before lights came on at 5:30 a.m. It was my plan to take a shower while the water was hot.

The heat in the dormitory was almost unbearable. I wore the same pair of coveralls given to me when I first arrived at the prison. To my mind, I smelled awful. I did the best I could, sprinkling after-shave lotion over the coveralls to kill most of the odor.

At 9:30 a.m. Santos called me and handed me my pass to the visiting park. Mary had arrived.

I hurried up the broken concrete walk out of the West Unit past the closed laundry, oblivious to guards and convicts. As soon as I entered the visiting park, I spotted Mary.

She stood still in the morning sun. Her blue wedding dress and string of pearls stood out—she was a goddess among rabble. Her brunette hair was cut short and had two spit curls, one in front of each ear. She was absolutely breathtaking and for a moment I couldn't see through my tears.

I opened my arms and we held each other, very tightly. After a long moment I realized we weren't alone. Claire and Heidi stood behind Mary, misty-eyed.

We sat at an empty table away from the mingling crowd and the girls started to unload all the food they had prepared for me.

I wasn't hungry but made a determined effort to eat at least a little portion of each serving. After all, they had finished cooking this meal at 3:00 a.m. and left the house at 4:00 a.m. driving straight through. It was a routine Mary would repeat weekly for over five years.

Everyone tried to talk at once. What I did learn, finally, was far from encouraging. I needed a transcript of the trial before Bailey could appeal the case. Mary told me it would cost one dollar per page and run about 4000 pages, but worse than that, it would take between four and six months before the transcript could be ready for Bailey and the other lawyers. Mary promised to try and rush Bell, the court reporter. She was already talking with him every day by phone, on the theory that he would speed up the transcript just to get rid of her.

"By the way," Mary said "the bond hearing is now set for the end of the month."

"Thank God," I sighed. "You have no idea what this place is like! Let me . . ."

"Carl," Mary interrupted, "don't torture yourself. Remember I told you I didn't think you had a chance with Silvertooth for bond. You had better put it out of your mind, and try to adjust."

Claire and Heidi began teasing me about how lucky I was not having to stay home and put up with all the publicity. They told me about the daily newspaper stories, about the telephone calls from reporters, and about the curious sightseers driving past the house and talking to them if they could.

"Did Sheriff Boyer tell you about leaving me ten dollars?" I asked Mary.

"Yes. And I paid him back. We may have a bad problem according to Boyer," she said, looking at me intently.

"A very bad one?"

"Maybe," Mary continued. "Your ex-father-in-law, Dr. Musetto, went charging into Sheriff Boyer's office last week. He was ranting, according to Boyer, that he was going to take Monica and Lisa away from us because neither one of us was a fit parent. He was in a real rage."

I looked at Mary, then Claire, then Heidi. They started back waiting for my reaction. I knew Musetto was a sick man and capable of anything. In fact, there was talk during the trial that he tried to put out a contract on my life, a fact that made Sheriff Hendry of Naples, Judge Silvertooth, and F. Lee Bailey very nervous. There was no great danger in Musetto's threats, since Mary had legally adopted Monica and Lisa in 1966. Musetto had no legitimate complaint, but it could turn out to be a messy situation which could give Mary and the children still more grief and strife if he persisted in this insane manner.

"What did Boyer say?" I finally asked.

Mary smiled. "Ross told Musetto that he was an old fool, and that he had no standing at all. And further, that if he persisted in bothering us, he'd lock him up."

Claire who was 15 added, "Monica and Lisa are our sisters, and he can't take our sisters away from us. So don't you worry, Carl."

"No way, Poppa Carl!" Heidi chimed in, holding my arm. "Don't worry. Stay well, and come home to us. We need you."

"Now, tell us all about your strange life here," Mary said. I told her and the girls about Morris and Santos, the count procedure, the guards, especially the one called Bradley, whom the convicts called "Track Down" because he was illiterate and had to use pebbles to keep track of the number of convicts on his work squad. Then there was the guard named Hansel who sported a moustache and wore a tri-pointed brown hat like those stylish during World War I. He was the spitting image of Deputy Dog, the cartoon character, and this fact provided his nickname for the convicts.

Then there was the local sadist, a guard by the name of Ross, a braggart who rode the men mercilessly, but was deathly afraid of making his rounds alone like the other guards. Ross needed the protection of a fellow guard, and rightly so.

"How do you feel?" Mary asked. "How is your chest?"

I shrugged my shoulders. "I still don't have any cardiac medication, but I'll try to get some this week."

The end of visitation hours, 3:00 p.m., came very quickly. It was time for Mary and the children to leave and start the 250-mile trip back to Sarasota.

We hugged and kissed and brushed away a few tears. Then they were gone.

WEEK OF MAY 6

On Monday I took an I.Q. and psychological test and had an interview with the psychologist, Mr. Winkie. Mr. Winkie was a fat, slovenly individual who sat behind his desk, constantly picking his nose. During our interview he told me that I had scored one of the highest, if not the highest, I.Q. in the history of Florida State Prison—I discovered my I.Q. was somewhere between 147 and 157. Then he proceeded to tell me that I had an aggressive, individualistic personality with a strong character, not given to taking orders. This was a negative finding according to the prison psychologist!

I countered by asking this fat slob, whom I loathed even looking at, if physicians, since they dealt daily with decisions involving life and death, had to be highly motivated and strong individuals?

"Yes, that's true for physicians. But you ain't a doctor anymore," Winkie added, rubbing his nose with the back of his left hand. "You're an inmate!"

I laughed. "For a psychologist, you're quite ignorant. There isn't a power on this earth that can take away my medical degree and knowledge."

Winkie flushed a deep red. I had made an enemy, but I didn't realize how much of an enemy until years later. In his confidential report for my file, Winkie classified me as a very agressive inmate with a very high escape risk factor. This report, plus a push from the Attorney General's office, ensured that I would be transferred to Florida's hell hole, the maximum security prison called the East Unit.

Later, that same day, I learned I had received help from an unexpected source.

Court of Record Judge Robert J. O'Toole stated to The Press that my conviction for second degree murder was ridiculous and that the legislature needed to repeal the law.

O'Toole was president of the Criminal and Civil Court of Record Judges Association of Broward County. In a letter to Representative James Eddy of Broward County, O'Toole said, "The State cannot try him (Coppolino) again for first degree murder and obviously he is not guilty of second degree murder."

Eddy, who was a representative from Pompano Beach, held a news conference and said; "How can there be no premedidation in a poisoning? If there was premeditation, he should have been found guilty; if not, he should have been acquitted."

Meanwhile, Judge O'Toole continued his attack against my conviction. In Fort Lauderdale he told newsmen, "The State never asserted that Coppolino committed the crime of second degree murder and never contended he was guilty of that charge. It's absurd."

On May 9 Mary sent a letter to Judge O'Toole. It read in part:

I have no idea where your sympathies lie, but your coming forward and having the inner fortitude to stand for justice, knowing the public is well pleased to have my husband in jail regardless of how he was put there, is indeed a ray of light in the dark world of despair in which I find myself.

However, there was no further action by Judge O'Toole. His voice was silent.

MAY 8
TUESDAY

I had an interview with my first classification officer, a man by the name of Adams. Adams would be the first of many, many classification specialists—some good, most ill-trained—whom I would come to know and hate through the years.

Adams was a rotund, whiskey-voiced individual whose main fascination with me was my alleged crime. That's all he wanted to talk about. He kept telling me that I was a murderer, and that I could look forward to spending at least 10 years in prison. He wanted me to describe to him the method I used to murder Carmela!

I ignored most of his questions and answered the others with monosyllables. By this time I realized what ignorant, bigoted, hate-filled fools had total control over my life.

Foolishly, I did ask Adams to classify me to Avon Park Correctional Institution (APCI), which was a minimum security facility for "honor" convicts and for those who had firm family ties and no previous record—a category I certainly fit into.

Most importantly, A.P.C.I. was about 80 miles from Sarasota as opposed to the 250 miles Sarasota was from the West Unit and Raiford. This would make it much easier for Mary and the children to visit with me.

Adams sneered. "No way! Forget it! That's a nice, soft location. Not for the likes of you!" So ended our interview.

The rest of the week progressed normally; I arose at 5:30 a.m., showered, shaved, dressed, and was out of the dormitory by 6:30 a.m. I lined up for breakfast and fought the flies and cockroaches for my share of grits, gravy, and molasses. Then it was off to the Chaplain's office at 8:00 a.m.

Lunch was at 12:00 noon. It usually consisted of black-eyed peas, corn bread and bologna. We went back to work at 1:00 p.m. and returned to the dormitory at 5:00 p.m.

By this time I was out of coveralls and wearing a blue cotton shirt and blue cotton slacks. My number, 018591, was stenciled in black on my shirt pocket and the side of my slacks.

Looking back on that week, that first prison experience, I thought it was like dying. Just to exist in that jungle called for a severe psychological readjustment; a Death of what and who I was and a rebirth to being whose number one thought was survival.

Morris kept combing the West Unit for me to find any kind of reading materials, no matter what the topic. And I retreated into my books to find some peace and sanity.

I started a routine of reading and writing that I continued throughout my imprisonment. By the time I left in October of 1979, I had accumulated literally hundreds of poems, essays, short stories, and three fully- or partially-completed books. I devoured anything to kill the clock between visits.

It wasn't long before I witnessed an act of violence. There was a convict in the dormitory who was previously a deputy sheriff. His name was

Pruitt. He didn't last a week. The convicts first stole his wristwatch and anything else of value he possessed and taunted him to retaliate—report it, try to take it back, whatever. Next, they severely beat him during the night, resulting in his sustaining two black eyes and a broken nose. On the third night, they set fire to his bunk. Finally the guards took him away and locked him up in a single cell for his own protection.

The following weeks brought visits from Mary, who brought with her piles of bad news.

First: The court reporter, Bell, still hadn't transcribed the trial records so I was halted from any efforts to appeal my conviction. In addition, Mary had to send the money for the transcript in advance!

Second: Bailey was still threatening not to follow up on the appeals unless he received more money.

Third: The earliest I could expect the bond hearing was June 1st.

Fourth and most important: The newspapers were filled with the statements of Bailey and Umberger over Umberger's testimony in my trial.

Bailey charged that Umberger had told him privately that the verdict of second degree murder was wrong if it was based on his (Umberger's) testimony. Bailey went on to say that Umberger didn't know why Carmela died.

To compound the situation, three chemists, March, Calise, and Coumbis, out of Umberger's laboratory were fired by Dr. Milton Helpern for approaching Bailey at my trial in Naples and offering to cooperate with the defense.

According to the newspapers, Helpern said the suspended chemists "went to Mr. Bailey and told him the investigation by Umberger was no good."

My heart leaped. What did March, Coumbis, and Calise know? Did they have the proof of what Bailey and I suspected and Boyer hinted at—namely, that Helpern and Umberger falsified the evidence and then perjured themselves?

Why didn't Lee Bailey put them on the stand? These men took a great risk in coming to Naples. They stuck their necks out and were suspended for their troubles. No doubt they were serious and had documentation of their position. So, why didn't Lee put them on the stand? It would take me 12 more years to find out part of that answer.

The Press, meanwhile, began pressing Dr. Umberger. Finally, in exasperation, he told the reporters, "With my testimony alone you couldn't convict anyone of stealing a chicken."

Unfortunately, the Second District Court of Appeals would think differently.

MAY 17
THURSDAY

It was time for my medical examination. Doctor Karl Heinz Zaffke was a man in his 60s—Prussian in appearance, with white hair slicked back, and rimless eye glasses. He graduated from the University of Heidelberg, Germany, in 1936. In 1939 he was inducted into the German army as an army physician, and remained one until Germany's collapse in 1945. From 1945 until 1956 he practiced medicine in South America. He joined the Florida prison system in 1959.

Doctor Zaffke took my medical history, concentrating on my cardiac problem. I signed medical releases so that Doctors Kelly of New Jersey and Page of Sarasota could send him my medical records. I wanted to give Dr. Zaffke as much of the past medical history as I could, so he would be in a better position to help me with my cardiac difficulties and preserve my life, so I could leave the prison and be reunited with Mary and the children.

I need not have bothered.

Dr. Zaffke gave me a most perfunctory physical examination and refused to allow me to carry nitroglycerin, a life-saving medication for patients who have had a heart attack and later suffer with angina pectoris. He did prescribe peritrate, a questionable cardiac medication. Essentially Dr. Zaffke concluded that there wasn't anything radically wrong with me.

Years later when I became so seriously ill that death was imminent, Dr. Zaffke admitted to me that he was under orders from the then acting hospital administrator, who had told him the Attorney General's office felt I was a malingerer despite evidence to the contrary, and that I should be treated with some suspicion.

MAY 30

Lieutenant Chambers called me into the control room and told me to gather up my personal property so that he might inspect it. I was then to leave with the two deputy sheriffs from Sarasota that were waiting for me at the main gate of the prison.

By this time I had written a number of poems dedicated to Mary and our children, essays and other scraps of writing—all on plain white paper. These papers plus my shaving gear were the extent of my personal property and it all fit, loosely, into a shoe box; however, I wasn't going to get away that easily.

Chambers grabbed my writing and began to rant and rave that I was using state property, and that I had no business writing anything. He asked me who I thought I was, and said that I seemed to forget I was nothing at all but a number, and finally, that he was going to take my writings and destroy them.

I exploded. "Unless you give me back these papers right now, you ignorant redneck," I screamed, "I'll have your name splashed all over the newspaper. I'll open the public's eyes to what goes on in this West Unit, the unit you run!" I snatched the papers out of his hand, scooped my shoe box off his desk, and walked out.

I never heard a word about that incident. Later, Santos told me that Chambers looked at my retreating back with shock all over his face. No doubt this was the first time he had been rebuffed by a convict. The episode did show me that I had some powerful tools at my disposal if used correctly, namely publicity, or the threat of publicity. It would be a lesson driven home many times in the future.

I was sent to the laundry where I shed my blue uniform and put on a pair of tight brown slacks and a spotted white shirt. All I could think of was that the bond hearing was set, and I was going home!

The trip down to Sarasota took five hours and I was handcuffed all the way, sitting in the back seat of the state car. The two deputies, Wade Coker and Max Frimberger, rode up front, armed with 357 Magnums in their holsters.

On the approach to Sarasota down U.S. 41, it seemed that the streets had already changed. Yet it had been less than a month since I'd seen the same stores, and the same motels.

I arrived at the County jail at 6:10 p.m. Grady, the jailer, took my shirt and slacks and gave me the same pair of white coveralls. Before I went up to the second floor and the felony tank, I telephone Mary, and informed her that I was at the jail. She promised to see me before the bond hearing scheduled for the morning.

JUNE 1

The sights, sounds, and smells of Sarasota's County Jail felony tank had not changed in the last 26 days. Ditto for the food.

During my previous visit I asked Sheriff Boyer and the jailer, Jack Royal, why they didn't try to humanize their jail. After all, most of its inhabitants were innocent of any crime until a jury said otherwise. *No way!* That was their answer. The county gave them a pittance, and they had to feed and care for their prisoners with this insufficient amount of money.

The radio, which belonged to one of my cellmates, kept repeating on the half-hour the earth shattering news that: "Convicted murderer, Doctor Carl A. Coppolino, will petition Judge Silvertooth for an appeal bond today. Flamboyant Criminal Attorney F. Lee Bailey will not be present, but Coppolino will be represented by Orlando Attorney James Russ, and Tampa Attorney Red McEwen."

The knowledge that Bailey would not be there both relieved and bothered me. It relieved me because Bailey was obnoxious about the question of money. In addition, he was excoriating the State of Florida on television talk shows, in The Press and in his paid speeches, none of which would help me and all of which would make my life miserable in the prison system. It bothered me because I knew that as hungry as Bailey was for publicity, he would not miss an opportunity for wide press coverage if it looked like I would be released on bond. Actually, it didn't look good at all.

One half-hour before court time, Grady brought me my gray suit and underwear that Mary had dropped off at the jail. Within five minutes, I was ready.

The Sarasota County Jail and Court House were combined. Grady escorted me down the elevator and through two locked steel doors.

I entered Judge Silvertooth's brightly-lit courtroom to find every seat occupied by Sarasota spectators. Mary and Claire were seated in the front row, waiting for me.

Red McEwen was seated at the defense table gazing out into the distance at an unseen object.

Mary hugged me around the waist and kissed me hard on the lips. She broke away and whispered, "It doesn't look good. So control yourself and remember we love you."

"You mean Silvertooth is going to deny . . ."

Mary interrupted me with a kiss, ignoring all the spectators. "Sh!" she said. "I told you before not to expect anything from Silvertooth. I checked again with Bill Hereford and the Judge is not going to put you out on the street in his county!"

During this conversation, McEwen stood quietly by my side. His rimless glasses tilted on his forehead, and his hands thrust into a muted plaid suit gave the appearance that my attorney was already defeated, rather than beginning a fight to have me freed.

"I really don't know what to do," he mumbled. "Russ prepared the motion and he is supposed to argue it. But he isn't here yet." He fiddled with the papers in his briefcase. "I really don't know what to do," he observed for the second time. "Bailey keeps me completely in the dark."

Despite my anxiety, I was concerned about McEwen. As past State Attorney for Hillsborough County and a long successful career as a Seminole attorney, Red McEwen had the "smarts" that most men could never hope to attain in two lifetimes. Yet he was ignored by Bailey and, therefore, in a weakened position to help me.

"If Russ doesn't show up and Silvertooth starts this hearing, I may have to put you on the stand," McEwen said.

I didn't like what was happening. Mary said that it didn't look good. McEwen had been cut out of the defense strategy by Bailey; Russ, who was acting for Bailey, had written and filed a motion for bond, but wasn't present. And Schaub sat at the prosecutor's table, all smiles. It was obvious what was going to happen, what Silvertooth would rule, but I refused to see it.

The bailiff announced Judge Silvertooth. Heidi, Claire, and Mary, again wearing her blue wedding dress and black stockings, took their seats in the first row. Court was in session.

McEwen turned left, then right, as I took my seat at the defense table. I didn't know what was going to occur.

Just then the back door to the courtroom flew open, and Russ rushed down the aisle to the defense table. A wave of relief washed over me as Russ and McEwen conferred briefly. They decided to put Mary and Claire on the stand.

The thrust of my family's testimony was their love and devotion to me, the fact that I had a home and roots in the community, and that I was accepted by my neighbors.

Mary elaborated on how much I was needed at home: "He gives Heidi a sense of security and well-being. He has made efforts to help her develop self-confidence."

Mary had emphasized to Judge Silvertooth how I provided Monica with the last link to the child's past life. She explained that Lisa operated on Daddy-power and "she is the least able to understand why her Daddy isn't home."

Claire followed Mary on the stand. She said, "He is my Father as far as I am concerned. I have problems with boys and little love things, you know, and he helps me with these. He's very understanding and he is very good at revealing reality to me."

"Have you missed him?" McEwen asked Claire.

"Oh, yes," Claire answered so sweetly and sighed, "very much."

With their testimony and the law on our side, surely I thought I had to be released on an appeal bond! After all, there were many other convicted felons, felons who were convicted, not on circumstantial evidence like me, but convicted on solid eye-witness evidence, and who had previous criminal record, yet received appeal bonds.

Silvertooth denied bond with a few terse sentences and quickly adjourned the court.

Even though Mary had warned me repeatedly that this would be the outcome, I sat immobilized. Heidi broke into deep sobs. Claire kept shaking her head, "No! No!" Mary sat still, stone-faced.

Mary, Russ, McEwen, Heidi, Claire, and I walked into an anteroom next to the courtroom to discuss the next step. Here, Russ paced up and down fuming and fussing about "Silvertooth's stupidity, Silvertooth's law."

Russ said, "We'll appeal this denial," his fists clenched by his sides. "It's contrary to the law, Carl. It can't stand. Don't worry about it."

I sighed. "How long will it take?" I had my arms around Heidi, her sobs starting to subside.

"Oh. About two months," Russ answered. "We'll need a transcript of this so-called bond hearing. I'll file a notice of appeal right now." He turned to McEwen who had been standing next to Mary, his hand patting her shoulder in comfort. "Let's go, Red, and file this motion." They left the room.

Sheriff Boyer said I could have a few minutes alone with my family.

"Well, Mary, now what?" I asked.

"You heard Russ. We appeal."

I shook my head. Something began to bother me. All these negatives: being turned down in court, the attitude of the prison officials.

"Mary, I think I am going to be the Sam Sheppard of the 1960's."

Boyer stuck his head in the door. "Time to go."

"Sweetie, I won't see you tomorrow," Mary said. "There will be photographers waiting to snap your picture as they drive you back to Raiford. And I am tired of seeing us in the newspaper. All right?"

"That's fine with me," I agreed. I kissed her and the children.

"I'll see you Sunday with Lisa," Mary promised.

PART TWO

The Nightmare

JUNE 2, 1967

When I arrived at Raiford, I turned in my suit at the laundry and put on a pair of coveralls. The control room asigned me to *The Rock*—"G" floor.

My cell on "G" floor held 10 men on double bunks, yet was built to accommodate four. There was a commode and sink on one wall. A card table and four chairs sat in the middle of the cell floor.

I was exhausted. I said "hello" and introduced myself to the other nine men, most of whom had heard or read about me. Then I made up my bunk and fell into a deep sleep.

JUNE 3
SUNDAY

Mary visited me with Lisa. While Lisa walked around and examined the flowers along the pathway in the visiting park, Mary and I enjoyed the day and refused, by mutual agreement, to talk about any unpleasantness.

I came closest to losing control when Lisa, sitting on my lap in her new white dress, kept asking me to come home with her and Mommy; she said that Coco, the poodle, missed me and that she wanted me to read her a story when she went to bed, the way I used to do.

JUNE 4
MONDAY

That morning's *Miami Herald* contained an article by Gene Miller accompanied by a picture of Mary and Lisa and Coco. In this article Miller related that Mary and Lisa had visited me in a park setting and that Mary had cooked and brought food so we could have a picnic.

Later that morning, I was called to the control room at *The Rock* and told to pack my "shit" because I was being transferred to the East Unit, the maximum security prison. No matter how I persisted in my questioning, I could not find out why I was being transferred. It was not until much later that I learned the Attorney General's office had seen Gene Miller's article in the *Miami Herald* and was outraged that my family and I might be enjoying ourselves! How sick can people get? I wondered.

There wasn't anything I could do but follow orders. I had heard from the other convicts about the East Unit. It was hideous. The men were psychotic and dangerous, the guards brutal, the food repellent, and the visiting conditions primitive compared to the visiting park at Raiford.

"Don't ask questions!" snarled the control room guard. "Just pack your shit."

"I guess they're worried about their prize prisoner, 'eh Lieutenant?" observed another guard.

A third guard sneered at me: "No more picnics, Coppolino!"

Within the half-hour I was walking up the ramp into the back entrance of the East Unit, my personal belongings clenched between my manacled wrists.

The ultimate prison—the East Unit—housed 1200 prisoners in 13 wings, plus Death Row.

As I walked up the ramp, I could see approximately 20 vicious German

Shepherd dogs patrolling between chain-linked, barbed-wire fences. I passed through two remote control gates and four more sliding steel gates to reach the inside where the men were housed.

The handcuffs were removed and my personal property was locked up in an octagonal-shaped, steel control room fitted with bullet proof glass. I was ordered to walk down a long, wide concrete and steel corridor to "W" wing. My work assignment? Kitchen help.

The entrance to "W" wing was actually the second floor of the three-tiered wing, with approximately 32 one-man cells on each tier. There was a clothing room and communal shower on each tier. The second tier, in addition, contained a day room with one television set. That was where I stood, lost.

"Hi! My name is Lucky Holzapfel."

I turned and clasped the extended right hand. Floyd (Lucky) Holzapfel was a short, heavy-set man with thinning brown hair.

Holzapfel and Joseph J. Peel, former municipal judge of Palm Beach County, had life sentences for the murders of Judge Chillingsworth and Mrs. Chillings-worth. Their names and story had been and were still prominent in the Florida newspapers since 1959.

"You must be Dr. Coppolino!" Holzapfel added, laughing.

"Yes. And it seems I read something about you and Joe Peel."

"You think you have publicity, Doc? Ours was fantastic! At least your case is screwy and hard to believe—plus you don't have solid blocks of opposition like Joe and I have."

Holzapfel thrust his hands in his blue slacks and began pacing the floor in the day room. "We have everybody against us—the lawyers, judges, newspapers, sheriffs' associations, other law enforcement agencies, plus all the members of the Chillingsworth family. Everybody!"

Suddenly he stopped pacing and grinned. "Enough of my problems, Doc. Where's your personal property?"

"At the control room."

"Wow! It'll be there for some time. Come with me," Holzapfel beckoned. "You'll need a cup, coffee, comb, shaving gear, and a toothbrush."

"I'm going to move across to 'J' wing," Holzapfel said over his shoulder as I followed him down the catwalk to his cell. "But I have extras and you can replace them when you draw from the canteen."

I walked into Holzapfel's cell intending to help him, when all of a sudden Holzapfel barked, "Get out!"

Hurriedly I backed away onto the catwalk.

"I didn't mean to scare you, Doc!" Holzapfel said apologetically, "but they have a rule here—nobody else in the cell but the one assigned to it. And the way the hacks are on me and you, too, we'll both get D.R.'s and have to go to their kangaroo courts."

"What's the idea, Floyd?"

"It's supposed to cut down on homosexuality. But the way the prison officials encourage homosexual activities, the rule is a big joke!"

Holzapfel made me a cup of instant coffee using the hot water from the tap of the porcelain wash basin. The rest of the cell consisted of a steel cot bolted to one wall, a metal locker, and a seatless porcelain commode. There was a radio and speaker built into the concrete green walls above the cots which was controlled up front. It was turned on at 7:00 a.m. and turned off at 10:00 p.m. There was a switch on the wall which gave a choice of two radio stations. One played primarily rock music and the other played Country and Western music.

"Let me tell you something about your new home," Holzapfel said, handing me the hot cup of coffee. He stepped out on the catwalk and propped his foot on the lower rung of the steel guard rail.

"There are about 40 hacks for each eight-hour shift. That means 40 hacks to watch 1200 men. And they are real nervous—ready to jump on you for any minor infraction of the rules. The rules change daily; there isn't one firm standard set of rules. Therefore, the hacks have you coming and going."

"There are three chow halls," Holzapfel continued, pausing momentarily to sip at his coffee. "The doors to the chow halls are locked so if anything comes off, it will be contained. The squads line up for meals and are randomly distributed among the three chow halls; this cuts down on any prearranged planning by the men. We eat with spoons only. No knives or forks. The hacks are scared of anything that could be made into a weapon."

"Yet they sell double-edged razor blades in the canteen, Floyd?"

"You figure it out, Doc. I've given up long ago."

"Did you see the electric gate at the end of the corridor?" he asked me.

"Yes." I tried not to react to what Floyd was telling me, but icy fingers of fear prodded my belly. Where was I? What was this place? I felt as though I were buried in a concrete mausoleum and no one outside knew about it.

"In back of that electric gate, Doc, are five maximum security closed wings, including Death Row. I sat for five years on Death Row. It's called 'R' wing."

"Then there is 'P' wing or *soup row*," he grinned. "That's where Captain Combs and his goon squad send you if they think you've been a naughty boy."

"Is that the result of the D.R. court you mentioned before?" I tried to hold down the sense of panic that was threatening to engulf me.

"Right! And don't think you've got a chance in that discipline court.

Godwin, who is the superintendent here and a fair man, will go along with his correction officers nine times out of 10 to boost morale."

"I've got to go now," Holzapfel said, shaking my hand. "Where did they assign you?"

"The kitchen."

"That figures. You're a physician. So they put you on the slop line! Real intelligent!" He ran his fingers through his thinning brown hair. "I'm working in the medical clinic. If you need anything, come down on sick call. It's at 5:30 a.m."

JUNE 5, 1967
TUESDAY

"Okay, Coppolino! Get your ass out of bed! Time to go to work!"

The guard's voice jolted me out of a deep sleep. I looked at my wristwatch: 5:00 a.m. I rolled out of the bunk. I could hear the voice of my keeper as he thumped down the catwalk, screaming at the other convicts. I made myself a cup of instant coffee, washed, shaved and combed my hair. Next I slipped into my uniform, a white shirt and white pants with a blue stripe from top to bottom on the side of each leg. I couldn't change my shorts nor socks for another three days, but I planned to rinse them out when I returned from work.

I gulped my coffee and walked out of my 9' × 6' cell, slamming the steel door shut behind me. I was ready.

There were 20 men assigned to the kitchen detail. We marched double file out of "W" wing down the brightly-lit concrete and steel corridor. Fat, sloppy Sergeant Thompson waddled beside us, glaring at each man in turn.

We marched through two electrically-controlled gates, operated by the control room. At each gate a remote television camera scanned each face. Finally, we approached a large metal machine that looked like the outside rim of a large steel doorway. It was a metal detector.

I watched as each convict took off his wristwatch, ring, and belt and placed them on a wooden table resting alongside the metal detector. The convict walked through the detector, picked up his belongings from the table, and went on his way.

The metal detector gave off a screeching sound as a thin black convict passed through.

"Okay, boy!" snarled Thompson. "Get that Goddamn metal off your fucking body! It's too early in the morning for clowning!"

The black convict sullenly removed a metal chain with a large cross from around his neck. Reverently, he placed it upon the wooden table.

"Hurry your black Nigger ass!" Thompson screamed.

The convict gave Thompson such a naked look of hatred that I involuntarily shrunk back.

The convict moved (shuffled would be a better description) through the machine again, which mercifully remained silent. He picked up his chain and cross from the table and moved away. The black man never uttered a word or looked back. I relaxed.

It was my turn. Dutifully I took off my Timex wristwatch and black belt, placed them on the wooden table, and walked silently through the detector. Breathing a sign of relief, I grabbed my personal property and began to move away to join the other men.

"Hold it!" snapped fat Thompson.

"You!" he pointed at me. "Button that shirt!"

The second button from the top of my shirt was unbuttoned.

"Oh! Ah! Thanks. I guess I was too much in a hurry this morning," I commented pleasantly.

"You!" Thompson shouted. "Are you a wise ass?" he screamed. "You think you're slick, Coppolino, eh! Well, let me tell you something." Thompson's voice got louder and louder. His face turned a deep purple. Spittle formed at his blubbering lips. "There are rules, and you smartass college inmates are going to follow them!" Thompson took a deep breath, his hands clenched into granite fists. "You understand me, big shot?" he roared.

I stood still, rooted in shock to the spot. My eyes were open in amazement at the amount of raw venom and palpable violence directed toward me by someone I never knew and didn't want to know.

"Yes, I understand," I replied in a strong, quiet voice.

"And say, 'Sir' to me. Say it nice and loudly," Thompson bellowed, glaring at me.

There was complete silence. My fellow convict workers stopped moving and were intently watching this drama being played before them.

This was it. The test. I took a deep breath.

"You keep riding me, and I'll see you in Godwin's office," I snapped at Thompson, and walked away from him without a backward glance.

From that day on, Sergeant Thompson never uttered a word to me, but I knew that he was waiting—waiting for me to slip up so he could bury me back in the closed maximum security wings.

The large metal double doors to the kitchen opened up, and 20 men marched through. The kitchen in the East Unit was divided into a bakery unit with machinery, a vegetable room with huge colanders sitting on their swivel bases, large grills, long steam serving tables, and a dishwashing section.

I could see approximately 50 convicts milling around. Others were sitting on the tile floor, their backs propped up along the dirty fly-specked wall, sipping coffee or rolling state cigarettes.

A short, squat black-haired convict was heading my way singing, *Arriverderci Roma.*

"Ah! The Doctor Coppolino! *Paisano!* I am Pete, the best jewel thief in Miami," he said, wagging his index finger in my face. "There are none better! Welcome to the East Unit and the kitchen squad," Pete said, pumping my right hand. "Listen, Doc! I got a pain in my lower back, in my left . . ."

And Pete was off and running with his complaints. It was a ritual we would follow every morning. He became my number one patient and my number one "cheerer-upper." If ever there was a man who helped make my time easier in the East Unit, it was Pete.

"Listen, Doc?" Pete whispered, slipping into his Italian accent. "I work in the vegetable room. And we have green peppers. You like fried peppers? In oil with salt and pepper and a little bread crumbs?"

I nodded. My mouth began to water. "You bet."

"I'll call you when they're ready," Pete wheezed. "It'll be about 6:30."

"6:30 this morning?" I said increduously.

"Fried peppers 6:30 in the morning? Why not? Your stomach doesn't know what time it is."

Pete took me through the kitchen, introducing me to some "jam-up convicts," as he put it. Others he ignored, pointing out the informers, rats, squealers. "Don't talk to them!" he warned.

One of the men I met was Curtis "Bo" Adams. Adams was a thin, soft-spoken man of about 40. He had one outstanding characteristic; his fingers trembled. Adams was assigned to the bakery and I wondered how he managed not to hurt himself working around the machinery.

Adams and I hadn't talked more than five minutes before he invited me to join him in a game of chess. He pulled out a black-and-red chessboard made of paper and some black-and-white plastic chess pieces. Sitting over a flour barrel, Adams began to teach me the game. He was very good.

We played chess every morning. During our games, Adams would tell me about his involvement in the Pitts-Lee affair. At this time, Pitts and Lee were on Death Row facing execution for the murder of two St. Joe gasoline station operators. Adams had already told the authorities that

Pitts and Lee were innocent and that he was the one who had robbed and killed these men. However, the Attorney General's office did everything in its power through pressure tactics not to have these men freed. It was apparent to many, including the *Miami Herald*, the legal profession throughout the country, and Florida residents who had read and heard details from Adams, that the only reason Pitts and Lee had not been freed was the racial prejudice that permeated that section of Florida at the time. In 1975, after spending 12 years on Death Row for a crime they never committed, Pitts and Lee were finally pardoned by Governor Askew. As of this writing, they have been denied any monetary compensation for the years stolen from their lives.

Mr. Huntley, the kitchen supervisor, assigned me work on the steam table. My job consisted of ladling out the so-called food onto the trays of the convicts as they marched past the steam table. After each man had been served and marched out of the chow hall, it was my job to wash down the tables and chairs and mop the dining room floor clean.

At first brush, one would think that the prison officials were ignorant of my heart condition by having me do such medically dangerous tasks. This would be an erroneous assumption. No. They knew what they were doing. Events later on tended to firm up the feeling that was growing in me—namely, that the prison officials, under orders, were determined to break me physically and psycho-logically.

My cardiac condition demanded that I have better medication, work, and living conditions. My angina pectoris was worsened by the strenuous work I had to perform, by the stressful living conditions I found myself under and by the little or no medical care.

Unfortunately for them, but fortunately for me, I had not been brought up with a silver spoon in my mouth. I had fought for everything I ever received. I was a survivor. This background plus the love of Mary and my children proved more than a match for what would be thrown at me.

My routine never varied: Serving on the steam table; cleaning the tables and chairs; and mopping the floor after each meal. It was hard and involved long hours (I didn't get back to my cell unit until 7:00 p.m. where I would collapse with exhaustion), but I refused to complain.

Matters came to a head later that week.

On this particular day Huntley assigned me to the detail of unloading the vegetable truck that would come to the back door of the kitchen. Some members of the kitchen squad would be made to unload the heavy crates of vegetables and 100-pound sacks of potatoes.

I flatly refused. My episodes of angina were increasing in frequency and duration and I had not been allowed to carry nitroglycerin tablets. The medication ordered by Zaffke was inadequate for my condition. It did little or nothing to relieve the constant episodes of oppression in my chest.

Since I was, as far as I was concerned, the only qualified physician, I gave myself the best treatment and best care possible within the confines of this prison. I wasn't going to jeopardize my health, my life, and my family's happiness and future by complying with Huntley's demand— just for the sadistic glee of my keepers.

Huntly called the guards immediately. There were two on duty in the kitchen at all times. He told them I refused to work. I tried to explain to the brown-shirted, tobacco-chewing, mindless rednecks what my medical problems were and why I wasn't going to unload the truck, but they wouldn't listen to any of it. Within five minutes, I found myself in the office of the superintendent, J.B. Godwin.

Godwin was a huge, hairy individual who looked as if he could play professional football any Sunday of the year. His wrists were so huge that the watch he was wearing seemed buried in the thick, hairy flesh. Yet for all his girth he had a soft, modulated voice.

I didn't know what to expect from him. Rumors and fact about him permeated the prison population. His father had been superintendent of Raiford in the early 1950's at the same time that the now-director of the Division of Corrections, Louie L. Wainwright, was captain of the guards. One day George Larue, a convict in *The Rock*, had a pistol smuggled into him by his girlfriend and tried to escape. This escape attempt ended up with J.B. Godwin's father being shot to death by Larue, and with Wainwright's being wounded in the buttocks. I knew this episode had to have affected Godwin, whether consciously or subconsciously, since he was a child living on the prison grounds when the tragedy happened.

The conversation between us started innocuously.

"Sit down, Carl," Godwin said, as the guards led me into a small but comfortable office.

"Outside!" he ordered the guards. He waited until the door was firmly shut behind the retreating hacks before turning to me.

"Tell me all about it," he encouraged, leaning back in his leather-covered executive chair.

So I did. I let it all hang out—my feelings over my treatment, my thoughts, my suspicions, and ended by reaffirming my refusal to unload the truck.

After I finished, Godwin leaned forward, elbows on the desk, fingertips poised together in a cathedral shape. "This is a terrible place, Carl," he began. "There is no denying that point. I have been here a long time and I don't think I could spend any time in the East Unit as a convict without going through some radical changes. Anybody who spends any length of time living or rather existing under these conditions becomes mentally ill. The logical processes of the mind become destroyed. A man's thoughts become completely disorganized. The noise, the screaming during the night from the throats of some of our insane inmates—and we do have violent ones walking around in here—the frustrations, the steel traps, the hollow sounds from the concrete walls, the smells, the unwashed bodies, the filthy language and thoughts, and, of course, the rotten food—all these things will eventually ruin a man."

"He knows!" I thought. "He knows how it really is!"

"That's if you let it, Carl!" Godwin continued, his voice getting rougher. "You are an intelligent man, a doctor. You know human nature. You know what makes people tick. You know also what slowly destroys human beings. Now, Carl, everything you told me is true. I agree with it all. The policies for this prison and its treatment of its inmates are formulated by the director of the Division of Corrections, Louie L. Wainwright.

"In your paticular case, because of the publicity surrounding you and the crime, because of the type of criminal lawyer you have, the Attorney General Faircloth and Mr. Wainwright are deeply involved with your welfare. You have been assigned to the East Unit by their orders. I agree it isn't the place for you, but nevertheless, you are here and my immediate responsibility. My advice to you is get busy finding something to occupy your time. Stop worrying. Stop reacting to your environment. Men are not brutalized by their environment, only by their response to it."

Godwin placed his hands on his desk and got up. His huge frame and height seemed to overpower me in my chair.

"I'll speak to Mr. Huntley and have you taken off any heavy duty work, but I am not going to move you out of the kitchen. That is what Captain Combs wants you for now. So that is where you'll stay."

Godwin walked around the desk. "If you have any trouble at all, any difficulty, drop me a note in an envelope. I will call you to my office. And I mean *any* trouble, whether it be with the inmates or my staff."

He opened the door and called to the guard. "Okay. Take Coppolino back to the kitchen."

JUNE 10
SUNDAY

On Monday, June 4, I had dropped Mary a hurried note informing her of my transfer to the East Unit. However, since the mail was censored, I had no idea if my note ever left the prison. By this time, I was convinced I was the subject for special treatment; therefore, I was certain my mail was closely scrutinized.

I had received letters from Mary during the week, but they had been originally addressed to *The Rock* and then forwarded to the East Unit. I was completely delighted when the guard on "W" wing told me at 9:30 a.m. that I had a visitor. Hurriedly I dressed, putting on the cleanest white uniform I had in my cell.

I left the wing and walked down the long corridor, under the remote television cameras, in front of the officers of other wings, through two electrically-controlled gates, and paused at the control room. I had been under constant observation from the time I left "W" wing until I reached the control room. Yet when I approached the control room speaker, it blared: "Give me your name, number, and what you want!"

"Coppolino. 018591. I have a visit."

A motor hummed and the steel gate on my left slowly slid open. "Go ahead!" ordered the metallic voice from the speaker.

I went through the gate and walked down a short concrete and steel corridor. At its end I could see a closed steel gate and beyond that a metal detector machine. There were correctional officers and visitors milling around.

As I approached the gate, Whitehead, one of the more sadistic guards, motioned to me from inside a small room which was located to the left of the closed steel gate.

"Take off your clothes," Whitehead ordered.

I looked around the small room. Empty metal bins lined one wall while in front of the other wall sat a long tale. Piled upon the table were bundles of white T-shirts, white slacks, and multiple pairs of black and brown shower slides.

I took off my shirt and slacks, folding them neatly into a bundle and stopped.

"I said, take off your clothes!" Whitehead barked. "I mean *all* your clothes!"

Off came my shoes, socks and shorts. I stood before him naked and suspicious.

"Okay! Open our mouth," Whitehead screamed. "Stick out your tongue. Lift your tongue. Lift your arms out from your sides. Spread your fingers. Spread your legs."

The orders were spit out like bullets. "Okay! Now lift your nut sack. Turn around! Bend over! Spread the cheeks of your ass! The left one! Now the right one! Now your feet—one a a time!"

After each command my jaws became tighter and tighter. I felt like a slave on the auction block being examined for purchase.

"Okay, now get dressed!"

Whitehead threw me a T-shirt, pair of slacks and slides. "When you get through with your visit, you get to do it all over again," he said. A stupid malicious grin was plastered all over his face. A few weeks later, Whitehead was killed in an automobile accident. He was not mourned.

Nothing could disturb me. No matter how rough, how degrading the enemy tried to make it, I was on my way to see my Mary.

I carried nothing with me as I stepped out of the room, not my wristwatch, not even a handkerchief, and my slacks were pocketless.

The visiting room in the East Unit was about 140 feet long by 20 feet wide. It contained two bathrooms on each end—one side for the women, the other for the men. A guard sat at an elevated desk watching everybody, both convicts and visitors. There were metal chairs along the wall and some metal-upholstered couches in the middle.

Mary stood by a small counter that served as the canteen; on one end was a coffee urn. She picked up two cups of steaming brew. She turned, saw me, and smiled.

I can't explain how much I loved this woman, and what an impact she had on me then and now, 15 years after our marriage. During those early dark days of my confinement, we hung upon each other for solace and survival. It was rapidly apparent to both of us that we had *no one* but each other, having been abandoned by family and friends. The only help we could generate was the help we could pay for. As the years rolled on, this became more and more apparent, and, as a result, we turned more and more to each other. Finally nothing and nobody outside of us and the children had any importance.

Mary quickly explained what was happening in Sarasota. There was still plenty of publicity in the media, the children were fine, although some of the neighbor's children were trying to give Monica and Lisa a bad time, but Claire and Heidi were helping them and the four of them banded together.

While I sipped my coffee, she told me how Bailey and Russ were preparing the appeal on denial of bond and how she was still pushing Bell, the court reporter, to get out the transcript.

"The appeal goes to the Second District Court of Appeals in Lakeland," Mary informed me. "What do Russ and Bailey say about the bond appeal?" I asked eagerly.

She shrugged her shoulders and looked far away. Long ago I recognized that this maneuver preceded some unpleasantness.

"They think you'll get relief there," she paused.

"What do you think, Sweetie?"

"I don't know." She evaded my look.

"Come on, Sweetie," I urged. "Tell me!"

"I don't think you are going to get a thing—not bond and not a reversal. Lakeland is too close to Sarasota and the judges on the Second District Court of Appeals are 'kissing-cousins' to Lynn Silvertooth. They are not going to go against him—not in a hot case like ours—and not for you and Bailey."

"Jesus Christ!"

Mary placed her right hand on my lips. Some of the coffee spilled out of the cup in her left hand and splattered her dress, like raindrops on sand. "You asked me what I thought. That is strictly my opinion. Take it for what it's worth. I also thought you'd be free in Naples and look where that got us!"

"So you don't think the Appellate Court will go against Silvertooth on the denial of bond?"

Mary shook her head. "Especially the way Bailey is tearing up Florida in the newspapers and on television. These judges are not going to do him any favors in Lakeland. Would you like more coffee?"

I slowly nodded and slouched back in my seat. I wondered if there was ever going to be an end to all this.

Mary returned with fresh cups of coffee. "Now," she said, sitting down beside me, "tell me all about your new home."

I told her about the living conditions and being assigned to the kitchen. That brought a big laugh from her, and as badly as I felt, I joined her.

"Sweetie, they had better transfer you before it is too late! Remember how you used to help me in the kitchen with the dishes?" Mary continued without waiting for my answer. "If they keep you in the kitchen any longer, they'll wind up with no dishes at all."

I told her about my meeting with Godwin, but only touched briefly on my problems. She had enough to worry about.

Visiting hours were over. Mary was reluctant to leave, even though she felt she was visiting me in a mental hospital. That's the feeling one gets from looking at the East Unit.

"Take care of yourself for me," she said. "Remember, all we have is each other."

JUNE 12
TUESDAY

My daily routine was brought to a halt on this day. I wasn't at all happy with the cardiac medication I was receiving. I'd been having too many episodes of chest pain, the kind that goes along with the diagnosis of angina pectoris. Some pains were so severe and lasted for such a long duration that I would lie down on the cold tile floor of the empty chow hall trying to bring my mind and body to a complete rest, praying that the pain would cease. These attacks were episodes of acute coronary insufficiency—one short step to a full blown heart attack.

On this particular morning I lost consciousness and collapsed on the tile floor of the kitchen. My next recollection was of a sense of weight on my chest—as if I were being crushed in a vise. Pete held my head off the floor and tried to pour hot coffee between my unfeeling lips. Later on, I learned that as I was walking toward Pete, I fell to the floor, unconscious.

Pete told me that he couldn't find a pulse and smashed me in the chest. He took one of the peritrate tablets which I carried in my shirt pocket and jammed it into my mouth. Then he poured hot coffee in my mouth and down my throat in an attempt to get me to swallow the tablet. That's when I regained consciousness.

I lay on the tile floor, weak. Sweat dripped from very pore of my body. And the chest pain persisted—although it now seemed to be receding.

Pete had yelled for help, and the guard had called the medical clinic to bring a stretcher.

About one hour later I was hoisted on a stretcher by several husky black convicts. I didn't know them, but they surely knew me.

"That's okay, Doc!" one kept saying, as they pushed me down the corridor. "We're going to the clinic! Hold tight!"

I must have passed out again because the next thing I knew I was lying on an examining table in a small office. Floyd Holzapfel was standing over me, taking my blood pressure and pulse. He then strapped an oxygen mask over my face.

"You look terrible," Holzapfel observed. Worry deepened the creases in his lined face.

"How are my vital signs?" I asked from under the mask.

"Blood pressure 100/80, pulse 80. How's the pain?"

"Easing."

"Are you holding anything?"

"What do you mean?" I mumbled, gulping in the oxygen.

"Do you have any contraband on you?"

I shook my head. I didn't know what contraband was, exactly. But since all I had in my pockets was a handkerchief and my peritrate, I felt I must be safe.

"The medical technician called Dr. Zaffke," Holzapfel said. "You rest quietly and breathe the oxygen."

I felt a little better, but the chest pain still lurked, not as severe, but still with me. I felt very weak.

I must have had another coronary, I thought. From my own training I knew that 40 percent of the people who have heart attacks die before they can receive proper medical care. I was frightened.

About one hour later Holzapfel returned and informed me that I was going to be admitted into the clinic. That was about 9:00 a.m.

He wheeled my stretcher into an eight-bed clinic. There were two convicts occupying hospital beds. And Holzapfel moved my stretcher to the empty bed next to one of the convicts.

"Suffering Sassafras, what the hell!" the convict's voice boomed from the occupied bed.

Holzapfel made the introductions. "This is Dr. Coppolino, Dinger. And he has a little problem with his ticker."

"Carl, this black-haired monster next to you is the Dinger, also known as Jerry."

I waved unsteadily. Talking was an effort for me.

Holzapfel took away my clothes and brought me a pair of pajamas.

I lay there trying to rest, but the Dinger made it impossible. He was cursing a blue streak—cursing his rear end since he was recovering from a hemorrhoidec-tomy, cursing the heat, cursing his bedclothes, cursing his life in general. In fact, his vocabulary never improved during the 12½ years we were close friends.

At noon Holzapfel again took my blood pressure and pulse. My pressure had fallen a bit, 90/70, and my pulse had raised slightly to 84 beats per minute. This was the extent of my medical care, so far.

I was worried, really worried. The idea of dying in such a Godforsaken place terrified me. I started to think about Lisa, Monica, Claire, Heidi, the family poodle, Coco, and of course my beloved Mary. Despite my firm control, tears dropped silently from my shut eyelids, soaking my pillow.

"Hey, you!" barked the Dinger, calling me. "You're a *paisano*, right? A *Dago*, right?" He was sitting gingerly on the side of his bed, peering down on me. "Don't give these cocksuckers the satisfaction," he continued. "Fight these no good bastards!! You let your guard down and they'll bury you!"

I wiped my eyes and smiled. Later Jerry told me that I was as pale as my white sheet, and he was afraid I was going to die.

At 3:00 p.m., which was about eight hours after my attack, Dr. Zaffke arrived. He took my blood pressure and pulse and ran an electrocardiograph. Then he ordered me discharged! That's right, discharged! No serial EKG's, no period of observation, no blood chemistries, nothing except that I was to pick up three nitroglycerin tablets each morning at sick call which was at 5:30 a.m. I couldn't have any more tablets, nor any less.

Out of my pajamas and back into my white uniform, I carried my personal property which had been sent down earlier to the clinic by the officer in charge of "W" wing, through the multiple doors and electric gates, down the long corridor, back to "W" wing.

I was so drained that my legs felt like rubber. Periodically, I would stop and lean against the cold concrete wall trying to ease the dull ache that still was present in the center of my chest. There was a bedroll waiting for me at the clothing room. Somehow I made it back to my old cell. There, I collapsed on the bare mattress.

Three hours later, it was count time. I struggled out of the bunk and stood, no, swayed, on my feet in front of the window of my locked cell door so that the guard could count me as he walked by. My pulse was irregular—extra beats, which is a common complication of myocardial infarction and one which can lead to ventricular fibrillation, where the heart beats so erratically it looks like a bag of worms. The blood goes nowhere and death occurs.

What to do! I needed medication, desperately. No point in calling for help or trying to get to the clinic. I knew what kind of non-treatment to expect!

I needed something to stop the irregular heartbeats. But what? And how? I was locked in a 9' × 6' cell!

Dimly I recalled reading a medical article about a medication taken by epileptics, called Dilantin. Dilantin was useful in controlling irregular heartbeats! How much to take? Or how did it work? I couldn't remember!

I knew that one of the men on this wing had epilepsy. He might be in the day room after the count clears. Perhaps he will have some extra Dilantin, and would sell me a few capsules.

I had to find out, and now! The count cleared. I opened my steel cell door, slammed it shut behind me, and went slowly down the catwalk to the day room.

It was jammed with both black and white convicts. The air was thick with cigarette smoke, and the television was blaring a hard rock song.

The guard locked the door behind me. After 30 minutes, he would open it again for those who wished to return to their cells.

I didn't know the men on the wing very well. I walked around the day room and passed a few words to this one, then that one, and waved to another. I was looking for Georgia Boy.

Georgia Boy was a tall, heavily-muscular black man whose home was obviously Georgia. He loaded and unloaded the trucks out of the kitchen and was as strong as an ox. I spotted him in the corner of the room, playing dominoes.

I all but stumbled over and caught him by the right shoulder. "Georgia Boy!" I rasped.

He jumped out of his chair, turned on the balls of his feet, and faced me, balanced with his right hand thrust deep into his pants pockets. Later I found out he had been holding a knife.

He blinked at me and slowly his body relaxed. "Christ! You shouldn't scare me that way, Doc. You wanna talk to somebody? You go and approach them from the front, man. So they can see you coming. You know what I mean?" He grinned, showing me a perfect set of gleaming white teeth.

"Sorry, Georgia Boy, I'm not too bright about how to get along in here."

His grin got wider and wider. "You got a problem?"

Nobody was paying any attention to us. Still I motioned him over to the sidewall where we couldn't be overheard.

"You took terrible, man!" Georgia Boy said.

"That's what I need to talk to you about. I need some Dilantin. You got any to spare?"

Georgia Boy gave me a hard look. "You ain't no user. Why do you want the pills. You gonna be a junkie?"

I shook my head. "I need them for my heart. I don't feel good now, but I'll explain later."

I must have sagged because Georgia Boy eased me gently into a chair and pressed a packet of Dilantin into my hands.

"Stash them," he ordered. "And we will talk tomorrow." Then he was gone, back to the dominoes.

The guard opened the door. The allotted 30 minutes had passed.

Back in my cell, I immediately swallowed two capsules of Dilantin. At midnight, six hours later, I swallowed another. And I swallowed four more capsules during the next day. My heart rate became fairly regular, although I still felt weak.

I didn't have to report to the kitchen until the following day, and so I spent the day in my bunk. I was too debilitated to get up, walk down the corridor, and eat the daily slop served in the mess hall. I lived on instant coffee and packets of hot chocolate.

JUNE 22
FRIDAY

I went to sick call at 5:30 a.m. to pick up my three nitroglycerin pills and stopped at the mess hall for breakfast.

Even though the grits, gravy and bread wasn't the best cuisine in the world, I ate every morsel because I needed strength. "Eat while you can." Mary once said to me, "Eat every little bit—it plugs up the holes."

The rest of the day I spent resting on my bunk, and swallowing what remained of the Dilantin. I left my cell only for meals.

Georgia Boy came in from his work squad at 7:00 p.m. I caught him at the laundry room before he went down the stairs to the first tier.

"Thanks for the Dilantin. What do I owe you?" I asked.

"For you man, nothing! Not a thing! But for your information, they go for two capsules for a pack of tailor-made cigarettes." He punched me in the shoulder, "You look better today."

"What did you mean the other night when you said I wasn't a junkie. Do the men in here actually shoot Dilantin?"

"Man! Come on to the day room. Your *joint education* is about to begin."

We went into the day room and Georgia Boy explained to me how the men took Dilantin, Darvon, Librium, and practically any and all medication. They crushed it, put it into a barrel of a syringe, added tap water, shook it until the material dissolved, and then shot the mixture into their veins.

"Are you crazy?" I asked. "These drugs are to be taken by mouth. They'll burn out all your veins!"

"Oh! You is right! They sure make a mess of the veins! But Doc, the boys like to feel the buzz and that means they got to get into the veins."

I shook my head. I visualized sclerotic veins, open ulcers, and gangrene. Soon I'd see them in real life.

"Thanks for the education, Georgia Boy."

He waved at me and went on to his cell.

JUNE 24
SUNDAY

Mary took one look at me in the visiting park and ran into my arms.

"What's the matter, Darling? You look horrible."

I guess I did. I was pale with deep black rings under my sunken eyes. And much thinner than the last time she'd seen me.

When I finished telling her the story of what happened and the amount and quality of medical care I received a horrified look stole across her face.

"You could have died, Carl! You need your rest. You need medication. You need . . ."

Her voice cracked and she sobbed. I put my arms around her and held her close, stroking her forehead with the tips of my fingers. We stayed that way for a long, long time.

Perhaps there was something in our attitude that radiated the amount of pain we each felt. Whatever it was, the guard did not come over to us and tell us to unclench, as he was often delighted to do.

Finally, Mary straightened up, wiped her eyes with a tissue, smearing her eyeshadow, and blew her nose.

"Now, let me tell you my problem," she said as the small smile which started over her lips got wider and wider. "They almost wouldn't let me in today. No, I take that back! I almost visited you in a most peculiar outfit."

I studied what she was wearing, a pink dress with a white collar and a pearl necklace with pearl earrings. Nothing peculiar about that. "You look good enough to eat," I protested.

"Well, let me tell you what happened. You know each visitor has to clear the metal detector? So I am very careful not to have any metal on me, not even bobby pins in my hair. Even my bra has plastic attachments, not metal." She stopped and took a sip of the hot coffee I had gotten for her earlier. "Sergeant Dorko is in charge of the machine today," Mary continued. "I noticed that he had been in charge of the machine last Sunday, so I thought nothing of it.

"When I walked through the metal detector, it rang. I was confused. I could not understand what triggered the machine."

Mary squirmed in her chair. "Dorko said, 'Take off your shoes, lady.' I don't like being ordered, first of all, and, second of all, I don't like being addrssed as 'lady,' especially since he knows my name. And he knows that I know he knows my name. Well, I let it pass. I was anxious to see you and I didn't want to waste time in conversation. I took off my shoes and walked through the metal detector once again. And once again it rang.

"Dorko now said, 'I guess you'll have to take off your underwear, lady, if you want to get through the machine.' And that's when I exploded.

"I said, 'Listen, Sergeant Dorko—it is Dorko, isn't it? If I have to strip naked, I'll do so if that's what it takes to enter this dungeon and see my husband! Now, are you going to stop playing games or are we going to spend all morning at this?'

"Oh Carl I was mad! My mouth was trembling. I wanted to take hold of that fat slob and shake him until his false teeth flew out of his mouth!"

"What did he say?" I asked, clipping my words. I was furious.

"Dorko threw out his hands and told me to walk through the machine again before I took off any more clothing. I walked through and there wasn't a peep out of that Goddamned metal monstrosity."

"So he had it rigged. Right?"

"You bet. He can control that machine to ring whenever he wants it to. He thought he was going to give me a fit, put me under some pressure. Well, let's see if I ever say a word to him again."

I stayed two more years in the East Unit, and despite Dorko's efforts to engage her in conversation, Mary never again acknowledged his existence.

"I'm concerned about your medical condition, Carl. The State of Florida would love to have you die here and let them off the hook. Needless to say, I love you and need you and so do the children. I am going to stay overnight and see Mr. Godwin in the morning."

Later that week I was transferred from the kitchen to the school to work as a teacher's aide in science.

JULY 1967

The days at the East Unit school slipped into weeks. There was no doubt that being at the school and back to my world of books and science helped me cope with my anxieties.

My days fell into a pattern of preparing my teaching lessons, teaching class, playing chess, writing essays, short stories, poems, songs, and letters to Mary and the children and looking forward to Sunday, visiting day.

It is difficult to describe life inside the East Unit without running the risk of morbidity and self pity. Fear was the primary emotion that swept the prison. Next came anger. I wasn't detached from either emotion and could still panic or explode.

One day while playing chess with Pete in the day room, I heard a commotion at the next table. A chessboard and chess pieces hit the floor, and I heard this banshee wail. Turning, I saw a convict's eye, his whole eye, hanging out of its socket by the optic nerve. The other convict was crooning softly with a hurting sound in his voice, "I told you not to push me. I told you not to tease me. I told you not to bother me. Now look what you made me do!" I lunged to help the stricken man, when Pete shot out his arm and said "Cool it! Let it be! That other guy is a bug, a complete nut. You stick your nose in it and you are going to have to sleep with your eyes open or dangling on those strings. That crazy bastard is likely to kill you, Carl!"

And so it went, day in, day out. Frightening. Petrifying. Violence or its oppressive, lurking aura permeated all of the East Unit. Even the guards were in constant fear.

The day arrived for Bailey to argue at Lakeland my denial of bond by Silvertooth in front of the Second District Court of Appeals. When Court started, it was obvious what the decision would be even before the oral arguments.

The three Appellate Judges loomed over Bailey from their high benches and if looks could kill, Bailey would have died on the spot. This could all be traced to Lee's attack against Florida in the media. What he said and had been saying on radio, television, in speeches and interviews, infuriated these justices, according to court workers.

Later that day, Bailey and his assistant, Tanya (Terri) Plaut, arrived at the East Unit to see me. It would be the last time I was to see Bailey while I was in prison.

I opened the door to the conference room. "Hi Kid!" Bailey greeted me, a big smile on his cherubic face. His right hand was outstretched.

"What's the killer doing?" asked Terri. She was dressed in a short, tight blue outfit that accentuated her 38-C bust. "That's what Lee always called Sam Shep-pard, killer. He'd call Sam in the middle of the night saying 'Hey, Killer. If I can't sleep, you can't sleep, especially if I'm working on your case.'"

Lee laughed. "Now I've got the Sheppard of the 1960's. Sam was the Sheppard of the 1950's. It seems that the system produces a royal screwing every 10 years. Well, let's get down to business," Bailey said. He looked at his wristwatch. Terri ran her fingers through the ever-present briefcase, pulling out papers.

"How did you get here?" I asked, trying to create an atmosphere of amiability. I vividly remembered our acrimonious meeting in Bradenton.

"I flew into Jacksonville in the Lear Jet," Lee explained. "Then I rented a Cessna and landed right here in the East Unit."

"Here?"

"Yep! They have an airfield which is registered with the FAA. And I am charging you with the plane rental fee. Now, let's get down to business."

Lee thrust his hands in his pockets and began pacing up and down the dreary conference rom. "I argued your bond motion in front of the Second District Court and got nowhere."

Terri tried to clarify. "We needed the trial transcript and the assignment of errors before we could be heard by this court."

"But Christ, Lee!" I yelled, getting up and pacing with him. "The convicts in here have lawyers arguing bond motions in front of this very court without those papers!"

"I know!" Lee answered. "It's strictly a procedural technicality which the court chose to invoke in your case. And there is really nothing I can do about it."

"So they denied bond."

"I didn't say that," Lee answered. "Judge Pierce pointed out that I hadn't placed a transcript and assignment of errors in front of the court. And, of course, Georgieff, arguing for the State, pressed the issue. I explained that it might take months before we would have the transcript. However, it didn't seem to make any difference to the court."

"Nope! They were going to deny us. But this leaves the door open," observed Terri.

I sank into my chair. "I thought I'd be home, for sure," I said in a small voice. "You don't know what I'm going through. You can't know. I'm in jail, Lee, living in a jail for something I never did!"

"Mary was at the hearing and told me about your heart problems," Lee added. "She asked me to come to see you. Are you feeling any better?"

"Not much. I still go to the sick call at 5:30 in the morning and collect my three nitroglycerin tablets, which I invariably use because of the pain. The last time I saw a doctor was when I had my attack. And I'm sure Mary told you that he did nothing."

Terri kept shaking her head. "I know you're telling the truth, and I have heard similar tales from other clients of Lee's. But it is still hard to believe you've suffered such treatment in this(day and age."

"It's true, all right," Lee grunted. "That's why they call these places cans." He gestured out the window which gave a view of a guard tower and the double barbed-wire fences. "Like the 'man is in the can,' because they are the outhouses of the world. And the people who work in them, especially here in Florida, are nothing but scum."

"What happens if I die in here, Lee?"

"We'll bury you! And I'll go to the funeral," he snapped, jabbing his finger at me, "and then Florida will have won! Right?"

Slowly I nodded my head. Changing the subject, I asked, "What about this Umberger business?" I asked. "What did he mean when he said I shouldn't have been covicted on only his testimony?"

Lee smiled. "I almost had him! Andy Tuney and I had him tanked up on booze, and he kept moaning that he shouldn't have testified the way he did, that he didn't know why Carmela died, that . . ."

"Then, why the hell didn't he tell The Press?" I yelled. "For Christ's sake, you were with him!"

"Yes, but so was his boss, Helpern. That's the man who gave Umberger his orders on your case, and the man holds Umberger's job in the palm of his hands."

"Speaking about job," I began, "what did those chemists have to tell you in Naples? It had to be important for Helpern to blow up and suspend them."

"It was nothing I could use." Then with a fast switch Lee came out with, "You and Paul Holmes entered into an agreement to collaborate on a future book. Right?"

"Yes. You know that. You were the one that brought us together, when I was waiting to go to trial in New Jersey."

"Right! And Paul is almost through with the manuscript. In fact, he'll be here some time next month to show it to you." Lee sat down beside me. "I told you, Carl, in Bradenton, that I spent a hell of a lot of money in your defense."

Christ, I thought, he's still on this money kick!

"The original 40 thousand dollars we agreed on isn't enough," Bailey continued. "I've gone way over. Why, the money I owe Dr. Foldes and Montefiore Hospital is almost 20 thousand alone!"

"Now, wait a minute, Lee! Before you say another word, let me remind you that you knew what I had, and you said it was more than enough. Then you went wild and spent money like there was no end in sight!"

"It was for you I spent the money, Goddamn it!" Bailey shouted. "It was to set you free from two ridiculous charges!"

"Yeah. But, Lee, where did you think the money was going to come from? I told you what I had."

"I know! But I also knew I had two winners. Foldes proved beyond any shadow of a doubt that there wasn't any succinylcholine in Carmela's body. And I was in the envious position any defense attorney would love—*I not only believe you were innocent, I had proof you were innocent.* I didn't have to rely strictly on a belief, since I had the best scientific brains in the United States telling me the same thing—that you were innocent, because there was no crime! *Carmela had not been murdered!*"

"Tell that to the Naples jury!" I cut in bitterly.

"Those farmers! Those Florida redneck fishermen! They were lucky they could sign their names!"

"Maybe so," I goaded, "but those so-called fishermen convicted me.

And I'm sitting here with a life sentence!"

"Who would ever dream you would be convicted, in a no-evidence case!" Bailey yelled. He got up and resumed his pacing. "I spent the money because I knew we would get it back by selling the book and the movie rights."

He lit his fifth cigarette and began puffing furiously. Terri was sitting quietly, watching us.

"Remember Brad Dexter and Sid Furie?" Lee asked.

"Yes. Brad Dexter is a movie producer for Paramount Pictures and Sid Furie is a director."

"They had spent a week with us or was it a weekend in Naples? I remember them. I liked them. Remember they stayed until the State rested its case?"

I nodded.

"They wanted to be sure you were innocent before they'd make me an offer. They heard the State's case and saw for themselves that there wasn't a shred of evidence. They were going to make me a firm offer for your story, after the acquittal."

"So?"

"Of course, that's all changed now! Anyhow, that's why I spent the money. I knew that when I walked you out of that courtroom, a free man, I would get it back and then some. Now then, back to Paul Holmes." Lee crushed out his cigarette, and continued pacing. "You both got an advance on the book, right?"

"Wrong! Mary got the advance. She holds all the rights. I told you that in Sarasota. I told you that in Bradenton, but you didn't want to listen."

Lee stopped his pacing and stood in front of me. His face was expressionless except for a tightened jaw. "I want that money," he growled.

"You're talking to the wrong person," I answered softly. "Mary is the one you have to talk with."

"I can't talk to her!" Bailey shouted. "It's like talking to the wall! I can't get through to her."

I kept a straight face, but I knew my eyes were sparkling with delight. I had translated Bailey's outbursts; it meant, "I can't have my own way when I deal with Mary!"

"Now Lee," I said in a soothing tone. "I'm locked up in this maximum security prison. I can't do anything with Mary. She's her own person. I don't own her. You'll have to talk to her."

Lee sighed. "Come on," he gestured to Terri. "Let's go. I'm late."

"What about the appeal?" I asked.

"As soon as I get the transcript, I'll file an assignment of errors, and then a brief. The court should overturn this conviction 90 days after I file.

So you're looking at maybe six more months in prison."

Bailey nodded his head good-bye and walked out of the conference room. We didn't shake hands.

Terri lingered behind. "Try to get your wife to send us the money," she urged sweetly, taking a deep breath and pushing her breast out at me.

I smiled. "You are as pretty and as conniving as ever, Terri."

She left the room and hurried down the corridor after Bailey.

On the following Sunday Mary told me that Bailey tried to get her to sign over the book rights to him. She told him tha she wasn't his client, that I was and that she had bought the rights.

"What did he say to that?"

"Oh, pretty much what he told you. I asked him if handing over the book rights to him would mean that he would come to the East Unit, pick you up, and bring you home to me?"

I laughed.

"You laugh," Mary said, "but Lee didn't laugh. He threw up his hands in disgust and walked away from me. I guess I'm not his favorite sweetie. What do you think, Carl?"

"Naw!" And now I roared with laughter.

The Second District Court of Appeals didn't take long to act. On Wednesday, July 19, at 3:00 p.m., Judges Woodie A. Liles, William P. Allen, and William C. Pierce jointly issued the following statement:

> "The appellant has filed a motion for a review of the order of the Circuit Court of Collier County, Florida, denying his application for bail and moves this court for an order admitting him to bail pending disposition of the appeal in this cause, and upon said consideration it is ordered that the said motion be, and same is, hereby denied."

AUGUST, 1967

Mary, bless her, besieged, begged, and pleaded with Bell, the court reporter, to such an extent that finally after four months of waiting, the trial transcript was finished.

Bailey had until September to file the assignment of errors that were made by Silvertooth and/or the prosecutor. There were many, according to Lee. Meanwhile, all I could do was wait, wait, and wait.

Because of the vile food and my constant state of anxiety, I began to lose weight rapidly. I was getting that gaunt, sick look. I could see worry reflected in Mary's eyes on visiting day. I used every bit of my medical knowledge to keep my cardiovascular system from falling apart. Constant dull chest pain and exhaustion dogged my steps. I wasn't the only convict neglected by the medical department. Every day I would hear stories about convicts poorly treated, not treated, misdiagnosed, and dying. It was a chamber of horrors. Any minute could have been my last.

The director of the East Unit school, Mr. Richard Warren, would call me each day, sometimes two and three times a day to ask my professional medical opinion on the illnesses of some of the convict students. He would ask me what could be done to treat them. Many men suffered from influenza and developed high fevers. This was due to their undernourishment and lack of resistance.

Simple substances such as vitamin supplements were prohibited by prison rules. It wasn't a question of the State's buying the vitamins, because many of the convicts had money and would have been glad to purchase their own vitamins. The answer from both the medical staff and Captain Combs was always the same: No!

Gradually I found myself answering hundreds of medical questions in any one week period. The men were starving for help, help in the forms of answers, help in the form of somebody to talk with, somebody who would care—somebody, who, perhaps, could get them treatment.

The beginnings of an idea bubbled in my head. Why not practice medicine? Certainly there was a need; that was obvious. And most important, the convicts trusted me. They knew I was concerned only about their welfare, and whatever I learned or was told by them would remain in confidence.

I couldn't dispense medication, because I didn't have access to any. The little I could get my hands on had to be hidden, and not in my cell.

My cell was a "hot spot" because of the frequent shakedowns. The guards would come into my cell, throw my bedding on the dirty concrete floor, root through my personal papers, including mail from Mary and the children, and scatter everything all over the cell. When I would come back to my cell after school, it would be in shambles. This happened at least twice a week, and, of course, created inside me a wealth of hatred for these guards.

If I practiced medicine, I could advise the men what to do and tell them what medication to get; they could take their chances dealing with the convicts who worked in the medical clinic by stealing or by finagling the proper medications.

I started my underground medical clinic. I was available at all times, in all places of the prison. I tried to get the men living on my wing of the prison to see me on Saturday or Sunday. During the rest of the week I would see the other convicts in the gymnasium or out on the yard.

One night after school I felt trapped, so I decided to go to the gymnasium. The gymnasium in the East Unit was a large, airless auditorium similar to one in a high school. It had a stage, where band jam fests were held, two basketball courts, and a section loaded with weightlifting equipment. In the back of the gym was a set of offices. This was the meeting place for the East Unit, where all messages were passed on and all business transacted. Homosexual love affairs began and termi-nated here. There were two guards assigned to the gym to prevent fights and bloodshed. Sometimes they were not successful.

On this particular night, which was my first night in the gym, there were two basketball games in progress, a weightlifting contest in one corner of the room, and some sort of skit or play being practiced on the stage.

I sat on one of the folding chairs with my back against the wall. I was watching and listening. Occasionally I waved at some of the men and shook hands with others. I didn't know any of them except by sight.

Out of the corner of my eye I spotted a medium-sized, sandy-haired, middle-aged convict approaching me. He was dressed in whites, strode with assurance, and had a professional air about him.

"Hello, Carl!" he said, a big grin lighting up his face. "I'm Joe Peel."

"Hello!" I answered, grasping his outstretched hand. "Sit down here with me."

"No. Too many rats. Come with me to my office. I'm the clerk for the coach. Besides, I have something I want to show you."

He led me past the weight lifters, across the gym floor, through a steel door into a spacious, airy office.

"Grab a chair," Peel said as he plugged in the coffee pot.

The room was dominated by a large table that held oil paintings, some finished, others in progress.

"Yours?" I asked.

"Yes. You like them?"

I did. The paintings of the animals were life-like and the landscapes were excellent. "I'm no expert, Joe, but I like these."

"How do you take your coffee, Carl?"

"Black and hot."

Peel sat down beside me and I took a closer look at him. By now he had been locked up for some six or seven years, and while time had taken its toll in a receding hair line and slightly pasty skin, he still had a strong, positive attitude.

"What do you think of your new home?" Peel asked.

"Need you ask? How the hell have you maintained your sanity?"

Joe shrugged. "Oh! I've kept myself busy. I have an active law practice, you know. The poor devils in here don't know a thing about appeals or their rights, and the prison officials are not going to help them, especially the blacks. They get the biggest screwing." He sipped his coffee and fell silent.

"I noticed they are the one who usually have the most medical questions and who need the most help," I said.

"That's it! These Goddamn rednecks hate a black man and give him a rough way to go all the way around!"

I filled Joe in on my ideas for an underground medical clinic. I explained how I felt I could be most effective under the primitive conditions we found ourselves. Peel agreed to help me by vouching for me to convicts who didn't know me and by sending me men who were sick and had no treatment.

Finally we reached the topic of F. Lee Bailey, and Peel handed me a newspaper clipping.

"This is what I have for you. I think it can work into something."

I took the clipping and noticed it was from the *New York Daily News*. The headlines read:

THREE AIDES SUE HELPERN FOR ONE AND ONE HALF MILLION
by William Federici

The body of the article started:

Three city chemists, charging Chief Medical Examiner Milton Helpern for violating their civil rights, are suing him for one and a half million for his action against them during the Dr. Carl Coppolino murder trial in Florida.

The chemists, James March, Richard Coumbis, and Joseph Calise, stated in papers filed in Federal Court that they have been dismissed because they had disclosed vital information to defense counsel F. Lee Bailey.

Dr. Helpern, served with the papers late yesterday by a federal marshall, told *The News* he was turning them over to the corporation council office to handle. He insisted that two of them had actually only been suspended. The third, Coumbis, was only a provisional employee and has been dropped, a Halpern spokesman said.

Helpern's own testimony was considered the State's most importance evidence in winning the conviction of Coppolino. The doctor was accused of killing his wife, Carmela, by using a mysterious muscle-relaxing drug, hitherto considered untraceable. The chief medical examiner's office was called in by Florida to conduct tests in tracing the drug, succinylcholine.

Bailey had the three chemists flown to Naples, Florida, questioned them at length, but never put them on the stand.

Helpern, a world-renowned pathologist, is being sued by the chemists for $500,000 each on grounds that he liabled them with "false and malicious statements" to the press and television.

"What is this vital information that the chemists gave Bailey?" Joe asked.

"I haven't any idea. Of course, we knew the testimony by Umberger and Helpern were lies when it happened. But I don't know anything about these scientists," I answered, pointing to the clipping.

Peel listened intently as I repeated the hints that Sheriff Ross Boyer dropped about the quality of the State's medical evidence and Boyer's suspicions that Frank Schaub and William Strode, the prosecutors, may have known the testimony was suspect. Then there was the business about Umberger's news conference.

"The way I see it, Carl, the two points you have are the quality of the medical evidence, and the allowing of the jury to come back with a second degree murder conviction in a case where the State postulated premeditated murder by poison," Peel said. "Florida is sitting around with egg on its legal face. Your case, which is so much in the public eye, will be discussed for years to come by lawyers throughout the country. It will find its way into seminars and textbooks. And if there was hanky-panky with the State's medical expert witnesses, Helpern in particular, as that newspaper article hints, then watch out because the shit will hit the fan for sure!"

"So you think I have a winner?"

"Are you kidding? Not in a Florida court! They'll die before they'll admit they were wrong and you and Bailey were right! No, your chances rest in the federal court system."

At that point, the whistle blew and we had to leave the gym. It was back to the cages.

I made any number of unsuccessful attempts to find out from Bailey's office the nature of this vital information given him in Naples. It had to be something important, and in my favor. Otherwise, why would Helpern take such a drastic step and fire them?

Maybe, I thought, this would help move Sheriff Boyer to reveal more than simply a hint. I had no doubt in my mind that Boyer knew more than he was saying.

It took 12 more years before I found out what these chemists told F. Lee Bailey.

Paul Holmes arrived at the East Unit that August. He brought the completed mauscript of our joint efforts called, *The Trials of Doctor Coppolino*. Despite our collaboration, Holmes was listed as the single author, since it was felt my name on the book would make the work self-serving. I disagreed and felt my name would help promote sales above the initial printing. The publisher and Holmes dis-agreed and resisted any changes. The book was released with Paul Holmes as the sole author.

Holmes told me he had sent a copy to Bailey so that Lee could use any part of it in preparation of the brief in my appeal.

"Paul," I asked, "what do you think my chances are? I always valued your judgment."

He chuckled, and in his distinctive whiskey voice said, "My boy, if there ever is a list drawn up enumerating the travesties of justice, your case would be number one. Now, I know Doctor Sam Sheppard, and I lived with that case, for many years. I like to think it was my book that made Sam a free man. He too, was innocent, but the injustice meted out to him does not approach yours."

"Marilyn Sheppard, Sam's wife, was murdered, brutally murdered. There is no question about that. However, your former wife, Carmela, died a natural death. And there is no scientific question *about that*. Yet here you sit, a condemned man, condemned to spending the rest of your life in this honeycomb of concrete and steel. Lord, I'm thirsty," Holmes added, smacking his lips.

"Water?" I laughed, knowing Paul's propensity for huge quantities of bourbon.

He pinned me with those piercing watery eyes. "Don't try to ruin my day."

"You haven't answered my question, Paul. Will I get legal relief? Where? and in what areas?"

"You'll not receive it in Florida, sorry to say. But you no doubt have worked that out for yourself. I look for Lee to overturn your conviction in either the United States Supreme Court or one of the federal courts."

Holmes lit another cigarette, his fourth in 45 minutes. "As far as what point will finally overturn the conviction, it could be one of several." He began ticking them off on his fingers: (1) the medical evidence, tainted as it was, should have been throw out by Judge Silvertooth; (2) the lesser offense of second degree murder, "which is proposterous"; and (3) possibly this matter of the chemists.

"I met with these people, Carl," Holmes said. "I talked with March, Coumbis, and Calise, and I remember how excited they were, especially Dr. March, over the fact that Helpern and Umberger were not telling the truth on the stand about the so-called tests on Carmela's tissues."

"What happened?" I eagerly asked.

"I don't know because they were close-mouthed under Bailey's orders and spoke only in generalities."

I told Holmes the hints dropped by Sheriff Ross Boyer.

"You can forget any help from Boyer," Paul said. "I hear he is running for head of the Florida Sheriffs' Association based upon the publicity generated by your arrest and conviction. Now here is the manuscript. Read it."

"Before I do that, Paul, I'd better tell you about Bailey's visit."

I proceeded to tell Holmes about the assignment of book rights and royalties that belonged to Mary and about Lee's pressures on me in Sarasota and Bradenton and now here at the East Unit. As I recited the facts, Paul became more and more agitated. Finally he exploded. "Bailey doesn't need the money! Mary does! And Lee knew you didn't own the rights. He knew that Mary bought them from you. I don't understand Lee. I think his head has grown excessively large in a very short time. Read the manuscript."

I did and enjoyed it. The book turned out to be the best, most complete and eloquent rendition of facts concerning my two trials. I watched Paul leave. I was never to see him again.

SEPTEMBER-OCTOBER, 1967

The trial transcript and the assignment of errors were filed. The number of errors listed by Bailey totaled 101. According to the rules, Bailey had 30 days to file his brief.

Speculation in the press about what was happening to me or my family had not slackened. The Orlando daily newspaper, the *Sentinel-Star*, ran an article under the byline *Peggy Poor*, anxiously informing their readers that as soon as Mary Coppolino filed for divorce, the readers would be among the first to know!

No doubt no one expected us to last, since divorce was so prevalent and

and closeness grew with each day of our ordeal. The visits continued and despite the unpleasant surroundings, Mary and I found our own happiness. Mary often said to me, "I'd rather be married to you who loves and accepts me as I am than be alone. Or worse, be with somebody else, physically, where there is no love."

Yet I persisted in my belief that she would be better off away from me. "Mary, suppose you left me," I began one visiting day, "and found somebody who loves you as I do, and whom you love? Wouldn't that be a better life for you and the children?"

But she wouldn't buy it. "I'm not a little teenaged girl! I've seen and tasted life before I ever knew you existed, and I am experienced enough to know that there could never be anyone else but you!"

"Mary! It's more than that. It's my heart. I'm not exactly the picture of health." I stopped talking because she sealed my lips with a warm kiss.

"Oh, don't worry. If something happens to you, I'll do something," she teased. "Then I'll find somebody!" she added, her eyes twinkling.

I roared with laughter. "You're too much! Come on, I'm sorry," I urged anxiously.

"Oh! Don't you go Italian on me!"

"Seriously, Mary, what will you do if I don't leave here . . . if I die here . . . ?"

She looked out past the barred windows to the barbed wire fences. Mary was silent. I didn't dare intrude. I watched her eyes. They were on those wretched German Shepherd dogs trying to find a scrap of shade to shield them from the merciless September noonday sun. Minutes went by.

"Mary!" I called out, exasperated.

"Oh, Carl I was looking at those poor animals."

"Never mind the animals. They get better care than I do."

"Yes, but they have nobody. You have me, and you will always have me. No matter how long it takes, or what effort it takes, someday we will have a life together!"

NOVEMBER, 1967

It was inevitable. This was jail, not Boys' Town, and not every inmate was a pal. Not every crazy could be avoided. It wasn't long before I found became more so as time went by. But we did stay together, and our love myself a victim of violence. I got punched in the nose. There I was minding my own business, standing in the doorway of my cell, having a minor disagreement—anyway, I thought it was a minor disagreement—with a big bruiser of a convict named Jimmy, who was six-feet, three-inches tall and weighed 250 pounds. Me? I stood five-feet, eleven-inches and weighed 145 pounds.

The last time I threw a punch was back in 1946 in high school. That fight was over a girl, who on the very next day left me for the school's football hero. From that day on, I had sworn off fighting.

Anyway, there we were, Jimmy and I, discussing our differences of opinion over a test grade I had given his friend, Randy. A year later Randy would die in a hail of police bullets during a liquor store hold-up. And Jimmy would be shot to death during a similar robbery several years later. But right now *I* was on the receiving end.

Crack! I never saw Jimmy throw his right, but a tremendous burst of force against the vicinity of my nose rocked me back on my heels. I staggered, wove, and slumped to the floor of my cell. Jimmy turned and ran down the catwalk. I don't know who was more shocked, he or I.

Slowly I struggled to my feet and staggered to the wash basin bolted to one wall of my cell. Blood poured dwon my mouth and chin, splattering my white shirt, and into the white porcelain sink. Some of the blood splashed onto the concrete floor of the cell.

I peered into the mirror over the sink and groaned. Terrific! My nasal cartilage was protruding through the skin. Not only did I have a broken nose, but a compound fracture to boot. To top off the whole affair, it was 12:30 p.m., which meant the whistle would blow at 1:00 p.m. for the school squad to line up and march down the corridor to the school.

I couldn't report the incident; that was out of the question. With my name, there would be an investigation that could go as high as Tallahassee. Since I couldn't report it, obviously I couldn't go to the medical clinic for help. I had to become my own patient and reduce the compound fracture myself.

Quickly I filled the sink with cold water, took off my blood-splattered white shirt, and washed my face free of blood. Using the state soap which is caustic, almost a pure lye, I made a thick paste and applied it to the wound and nasal cartilage like a poultice. I kept it in place for 10 full minutes. Next, I flooded my face with cold water, washing away the poultice. Blood was running freely out of the fresh wound and from both of my nostrils. I washed my hands with the caustic soap, still allowing the blood to flow freely from the wound.

Then I grasped the end of my nose with my right hand. I stabilized the upper part of my nose with my left. Pull! Twist! And push! And I had reduced my nasal fracture, and set the cartilage and broken turburnates.

Next I packed each nostril with moistened toilet tissue. Finally I palpated, molded, and manipulated my nose so that its outline in the mirror looked fairly straight. Mary commented on the following visit that my nose looked better than before the blow.

I was left now with an open laceration that was shaped similar to a puncture wound. This I covered with an old band-aid I found among my shaving gear.

Next, using my only hand towel, I washed the blood off the floor and the sink. I'd be in deep trouble if the guards decided that afternoon to shake down my cell and found dried blood stains.

By this time, the whole wing, 95 convicts plus the guard, knew what happened. But nobody said a word. They were waiting to see what I was going to do. Would I report it? Would I scream to Godwin? What would I do?

Even though I had been in prison for several months, I wasn't trusted. After all, as one convict told me later, "You ain't a criminal, Doc. You ain't one of us, really!"

It was 12:50 p.m. I had ten minutes left before the whistle would blow. I persuaded the house man to open up the laundry and give me an extra white shirt.

The whistle blew. It was time to go.

I lined up with my partner so I would be next to the wall, away from the peering eyes of the guards in the corridor. Little did I know that they already knew and were speculating on the method I would use to handle the situation.

Next I put on my sun glasses. Many of the men wore sun glasses, day and night; therefore, this in itself wasn't unusual.

The eight minute march to the school seemed never to end. After I reached my office, I asked Mr. Warren if he would send somebody up to the medical clinic for ice cubes. He took one look at my face and nodded.

When the ice cubes came, I fashioned a rough ice pack out of my handkerchief and set it on my nose and both eyes and prayed. I prayed that there would be no swelling or discoloration; I prayed that the administration wouldn't find out, officially. Only one of my two prayers was answered. What a pair of black eyes I had!

That night, Jimmy came to my cell to apologize. He was a frightened man. The convicts didn't like the idea of what he had done to me, when all "the doc does is help people!" Jimmy had heard rumors that he might wake up with his throat cut from ear to ear.

I spent the rest of the day defusing the incident. I certainly didn't want Jimmy killed. The final result was that the incident was soon forgotten and I had been accepted by my fellow convicts. This pleased me since it—and my handiwork on my own injury—allowed my underground medical clinic to flourish.

Mary became concerned over my attack. She was afraid that I would be hurt or killed because I was surrounded by mentally unstable convicts. Without my knowledge, she approached Godwin with her fears. Godwin did nothing to alleviate her anxiety when he flatly refused to have me transferred out of the East Unit to *The Rock*. She asked him what he would do if my compound fracture became infected and I developed a bone infection (osteomyelitis). Godwin re-sponded by saying, "Nothing. Carl chose not to report the incident and as far as I am concerned, it never happened. He'll have to take care of it the best he can."

THANKSGIVING-CHRISTMAS, 1967

Holiday time in prison is at best dreary and at worst shot through with depression. Mary and the children spent the holidays with me. We had a lot for which to be grateful. Our family remained intact.

Lisa was five years old, curious and starved for my attention. She spent much of her time when visiting, not only with me, but also with the canteen workers in the visiting park. These two men named Charlie and Bob, lifers, made it a point to be extra nice to Lisa. So Lisa received triple doses of attention during each visit. Even the hard-hearted Sergeant Dorko was touched by Lisa's childish innocence.

One visiting day I stood by the electric gate, waving goodbye to Lisa and Mary, as was my custom. This particular Sunday, Sergeant Dorko pressed the release button and allowed the gate to slide open so that a correctional officer could make his way out of the visiting park to the corridor.

"Run, Daddy!" Lisa cried, when she saw the gate open. "Run, Daddy!" she called again, standing next to Sergeant Dorko, with her hands out-stretched toward me. The dying afternoon sun caught some of the colored sequins on her white dress. "Run, Daddy! We'll take you home!"

It broke my heart.

The Sunday following her fifth birthday, Lisa and Mary came to visit.

Naturally I was eager to hear the details of her celebration.

"I got this pretty dress," Lisa announced, showing me a white-and-blue outfit that offset her blond hair and mediterranean skin.

"And what did you do on your birthday?" I asked.

"Well, Daddy," she sighed. "I had a party and Terri Sue and the other children came. Everybody asked me where you were, Daddy. And I told them that you were far away and that you were working. And that you knew it was my birthday and had sent me presents and that I was going to go and see you!"

It took all I could do not to cry. This simple, delightful child with all the joy of the world shining in her eyes was sitting in a maximum security prison, but was happy because she was talking with her Daddy!

My first bad episode of abject depression occurred around this time. It was the Christmas season and what it symbolized. That triggered it, but the underlying cause was my physical condition. It was deteriorating badly and fast.

My ankles were swollen by the end of each day. Heart failure? Protein deficiency? I didn't know and obviously didn't have access to reliable medical testing facilities in order to find out. It was cold that winter of 1967-1968, bitter cold. I was living in a tomb of concrete and steel, sleeping under a thin army blanket. The thermometer stood around the low twenties. I was cold very, very cold.

At 5:30 in the morning, the cold air down the drafty corridor chilled me to the bone as I trudged to sick call to pick up my three nitroglycerin tablets. All my efforts to get another blanket were useless. Nobody else could keep a second blanket either.

Mary spoke to Godwin about getting me an extra blanket. Nothing. Finally I solved the problem by stuffing sheets of newspaper between my muslin sheet and the army blanket. This created a heat thermal layer and helped me keep warm.

When I walked around my cell, I draped the blanket around my shoulders, Indian style.

Bailey's long appellate brief was finally filed in December. Bailey had used the senior law class of Harvard University in a unique way. Part of the project for the class was writing and arguing the appeal in my case to a "mock appellate court."

The Harvard law school's research effort ended up in the brief. Their class argument before this mock appellate court prevailed: a three to zero decision to reverse my conviction based on two points: 1) the medical evidence presented by the State violated even the most rudimentary conditions of reaching the level of reasonable medical certitude and, therefore, Judge Silvertooth never should have allowed it entered into evidence. 2) The second degree murder conviction was ludicrous in the face of the State of Florida's charge of premediated poisoning.

This finding of fact, of course, meant nothing in the "real world" of the criminal justice system of the State of Florida, but it did make me feel better that logic, reason, and law prevailed elsewhere.

Late in December, I had my progress report. This came up every six months and gave the convict a chance to talk with his classification officer about his future plans, mailing and visiting lists, changing of quarters or jobs and transfers.

My classification officer that year was Jim Reddish. Reddish was a rotund, moon-faced redneck from Starke. His father was sheriff of a nearby county. The East Unit convicts were well aware of the type of help and consideration Reddish gave them, especially the black convicts. It was spelled out in one word: *none.*

I was called in to the Administration Building to see Reddish.

"Come in, Coppolino!"

Reddish sat back behind his desk, chomping on a cigar. His eyes, what I could see of them since they were buried in his pudgy face, were cold.

"Why did you kill your wife?" First question.

"I didn't." First answer.

"You're convicted, ain't you?"

"Certainly I am."

"Well?"

"Well, what?"

"A Florida jury found you guilty. And you had a high priced-lawyer like Bailey. Now you're telling me you ain't guilty?"

I remained silent.

Reddish glared at me. Then he jotted some notes in my record. "What parole plan do you have in mind?"

"I'm not interested in parole, Mr. Reddish."

He dropped my record. "Oh! You're not interested in parole?" He picked up my record again. "I see here you have a wife and four children. Do you plan to spend the rest of your life in here?"

"No," I answered softly. "I have complete certainty that this ridiculous conviction of mine will be overturned."

"I know! I know!" Reddish sputtered. He took the cigar out from between his fat, wet lips. "You're appealing the case and expect to win. But suppose you don't?"

He jabbed the cigar in my direction. "What happens next when you fail in court? That *is* what is going to happen, boy! Then what?"

I took a deep breath, and forced myself to relax. "I haven't given it any thought," I answered in a tight voice.

"Well, you better think about it! Anything on your mind?"

"Yes. I want to transfer to *The Rock*."

"Forget it."

"Why? What am I doing in this place?"

"Time." Reddish roared at his own wit.

"What am I doing in this place, Mr. Reddish," I persisted. "There is nothing in here but psychopaths. Even Mr. Godwin agrees with me."

"Your transfer is up to the superintendent of *The Rock*, Mr. Sinclair."

"My wife has already talked with Mr. Sinclair," I fumed. "He said it was up to you, the classification officer, to transfer me. That he, Sinclair, had nothing to do with it."

"Like I said, forget it! You can go," Reddish ordered, dismissing me.

I slowly walked back to "U" wing and sat in the day room. I felt trapped, or maybe overwhelmed would be a better description, by superior forces. Somewhere, somehow I had to use the system itself to better my own conditions. I had to get out of the East Unit before my health completely fell apart, and before my underground medical clinic was discovered.

"Well! Well! Look who's here!" a voice sounded behind me.

I turned quickly and saw Floyd Holzapfel. "What are you doing here? And don't tell me time," I quickly added, thinking about Reddish. "I've already received that answer today."

"I'm the house man on 'U' wing."

"What happened to your job in the medical clinic? You know how much I rely on you as a contact for my clinic."

"Oh! There seems to be some irregularity about the amount of drugs and syringes. And I thought I'd better get out before the shit hit the fan! What's the matter with you, huh? You look so glum."

"I just came back from seeing fatso Reddish."

"Oh! That son-of-a-bitch!"

"Yeah! He wanted to know how come I keep insisting I'm innocent. On top of that, he won't transfer me to *The Rock*."

"Reddish is a redneck bigot," Holzapfel said. "Forget him! Let's play chess."

My underground clinic was booming during this holiday season. I found myself practicing psychiatry more than internal medicine.

Most of the men were suicidal at one time or another. When they weren't suicidal, they were directing their hostilities toward other men.

Some were looking for pain, or looking for ways to hurt themselves.

Then there were the self-mutilators. These men actually cut their wrists or sliced their legs until they were drenched with blood. One of them slashed himself every day of the week. Some walked down the corridor holding their bleeding arm in a dirty towel as they headed for the medical clinic in hopes of getting sutured. Others didn't. These were the ones I saw. They were loners. No family. No mail. No visits.

Why lie, they would ask me? These were the ones not too far gone to ask a reasonable question. Others would sit and sob, their cut arms wrapped up in toilet paper and hidden from the probing eyes of the guards.

In some way or another all of them were crying out: "I'm human! I'm a person! Look at me! Talk to me!"

I did the best I could. And in helping them, I helped myself by keeping my misery at a distance.

CHRISTMAS EVE, 1967

The night before Christmas, as the poem goes, the State passed out their presents to their indentured servants, the convicts.

I received my present that night, a brown paper bag that contained two apples, two oranges, six packs of free-world cigarettes, a handkerchief, a comb, and a bag of assorted nuts. Merry Christmas! Ho! Ho! Ho!

I had received two packages that night, one from Claire and one from Mary. I should say I received the remnants of two packages.

Under the guise of "security," each package that entered the institution was opened and checked for contents. When I say checked, I mean checked. The packages were pounded, squeezed, and shaken. The cookies Claire baked for me arrived at my cell reduced to crumbs, after the guards finished "inspecting" the package. Even the candy was smashed beyond recognition. My packages weren't the only targets for their sadism. All of the men suffered the same indignity. Why? Why should a convict be treated that way at a time of the year when love and good cheer ought to be the prevalent theme? It doesn't make sense, does it?

Of course it makes sense. It makes sense when you realize that: 1) the correc-tional officers are deathly afraid of the convicts, and 2) they hate the convicts because, on the average, the convicts are smarter, sharper, and have more money than the guards. And 3) of course, the guards are free!

There is no question that the convict's body is confined; but not his mind. In contrast, the guard's body and mind are trapped in his own hatred, bigotry, and the smallness of his world.

FEBRUARY-MARCH 1968

The State of Florida filed its brief in response to Bailey's attack against my conviction. The State's brief was a poor effort to plug up the gaping holes in my asinine conviction. The next step consisted of our response to the State's brief, and the court's setting a date for oral arguments. Meanwhile, prison life went on.

In March I was exposed to my first legalized or, better yet, condoned murder. There were two convicts involved: Bud Albright and Wayne Falk.

Albright and Falk were admitted as patients in the East Unit clinic. This was the same place known for those few hours after my episode of coronary insufficiency.

Albright had a history of mental instability and a long, long sentence. Falk was a violent individual. He had recently received a sentence of five years for stabbing another convict while in solitary confinement.

Henry Hull was admitted into the East Unit and placed in the same ward as Falk and Albright. Hull was a young man, a homosexual. Placing Hull with Falk and Albright was comparable to throwing a hunk of raw meat into a den of ravenous lions.

Within a few hours, Falk and Albright propositioned Hull. The young man turned down their advances and asked the two convict nurses on duty, Max Roberts and Bill Smith, to request the medical technician on duty to transfer him out of the clinic.

Roberts and Smith reported Hull's request to medical technician Harden, a crusty old Navy veteran who had worked in the prison for years. Harden dutifully reported the matter and request to tobacco-chewing Lieutenant Davis, the officer who was on duty that day.

Lieutenant Davis never came down to the clinic to investigate Hull's charges. He did what he was noted for doing. Nothing.

That night Hull was raped repeatedly by Falk and Albright. His agonized screams were heard by the medical technician on duty, but they were ignored.

Sobbing, Hull told Falk and Albright that when morning came, he would report them. Neither of the men could tolerate an official investigation. How could they stop Hull? There were only the three of them in the locked clinic ward. What could they do? Falk and Albright did the first thing that came into their diseased, warped minds. They strangled Hull.

An incident like this was not something new in the prison system. In 1962 a convict named Marc C. Garvin was deliberately murdered by the prison officials in charge of the East Unit.

Garvin died one day from what the coroner's jury said were natural causes resulting from acute hemorrhagic pneumonia. What the coroner's jury neglected to report was that Garvin had been locked in his cell in the closed wing and that his 9' × 6' cell had been pumped full of tear gas for over one hour.

Eight years after Garvin was murdered by society's representatives—the correctional officers—an investigation by the Florida Department of Law Enforcement concluded that the tear gas used on Garvin was far in excess of the "accepted" incapacitating dosage and was far in excess of the median lethal doses. In plain language, Garvin was executed, but then he was only a Nigger.

What happened to the murderers? What happened to the true representatives of law and order and justice? The report went on to say that manslaughter charges (not pre-meditated murder) would have been justified. But by 1970 the statute of limitations had run out and the officials involved could not be prosecuted.

APRIL, 1968

The letters I had received from Bailey in March and April became more and more threatening; if I didn't come up with the money, he wouldn't continue with my appeals.

Perhaps Lee realized that he went too far because I received the following letter:

April 16, 1968

Dear Carl:

There seems to be some confusion, generated from quarters that are somewhat murky, as to your continued representation by me.

I will, of course, appear and argue your case before the District Court of Appeal on May 14 as skillfully and forcefully as I possibly can. Naturally, I do not appreciate any of the suggestions implicit in Mary's recent letter to Jim Russ. Mary and I disagree as to the proper distribution of certain funds and she writes nasty letters about her position. This, of course, does little to improve the situation.

You and Mary would favor us greatly by being a little less suspicious and a little more realistic about what you asked as against what you are willing to give.

Very truly yours,
F. Lee Bailey

MAY, 1968

Oral arguments before the judges of the Second District Court of Appeals were held. Bailey argued my side; the suave Georgieff argued for the State.

The arguments took place in front of the same judges who gave Bailey such a rough time over my appeal for bond. I didn't have much hope concerning the outcome. There wasn't anything I could do but pray. Besides, I had a more urgent problem—my health.

I am a very restless sleeper (Mary says it's like going to bed with a windmill). This tendency plus my anxiety caused me to sleep in fits and bursts. Now this small amount of sleep was being threatened. I would wake up because I couldn't breathe. I felt that I was smothering. My only relief was to get up and sit at the edge of the bunk and pull in the air. Medically, this is called dyspnea (difficulty in breathing) and orthopnea (difficulty in breathing in a horizontal position). Both of these symptoms are cardinal signs of heart failure.

In addition, I had developed asthma (a wheezing, coughing, gasping for breath). This would occur sometimes at night but mainly during the day, so much so that it would slow my walking down almost to a crawl. I felt sure this was cardiac asthma, which is asthma due to fluid in the lungs because of a failing heart. I was plagued with swollen ankles, orthopnea and dyspnea, and cardiac asthma. Without any more history, such as my attacks of angina pectoris and my past history of a myocardial infarction, a third year medical student could diagnose that my heart was shutting down and that I was in congestive heart failure.

In desperation I sought medical treatment at the clinic and was given some antihistamine tablets and an asthma medication called "asthma bars." No matter how often I asked the medical technicians to let me see a physician (?) for treatment for my failing heart, the answer was always the same, No. I became desperate.

For some time now I had been impressing on Mary that I needed adequate legal representation. I felt that Russ was hamstrung by Bailey and that Red McEwen was kept in the dark by Bailey. And as far as Bailey was concerned, I felt that Lee was simply going through the motions, that he didn't really care about me (and I already knew his feelings concerning Mary!), that he felt peevish, like a child, because he lost the case and because I wouldn't give him any more money.

By this time I had been receiving one letter after another from Bailey, each one more threatening than the last. All the name-calling and threats were the same. I hadn't realized how serious my position was. If I didn't come up with more money, Bailey was going to drop me; he wouldn't proceed with the appeals, and then I would rot in prison.

It was psychological warfare on Bailey's part and, for all intents and purpose, it would appear that he had me on the run. After all, I was in a maximum security prison with a life sentence—and from the attitude of the prison officials, I would stay there for LIFE. Bailey had all of my records and files, and my health was failing.

However, I had a few things going for me. Bailey hated Florida and his professional competence was at stake. If he persisted in his threat to dump me, he would be on shaky grounds with the American Bar Association. No matter what his personal feelings were, he had to deal with Mary. She was free, and I was determined to survive, no matter what it took.

That was the position in which I found myself, and that was why I wanted *effective legal representation*. However neither Mary nor I really knew where to turn.

One name kept cropping up in conversations among convicts and it was also a name Mary had heard through her Sarasota-Tampa contacts: Henry Gonzalez, criminal attorney from Tampa.

In a very short time Mary spoke with Henry on several occasions about me, my health, our legal problems, especially the bond issue which Bailey felt was dead, but for which I still had hopes. Mary wrote me that Gonzalez wanted to see me. I agreed and one day in May, Henry Gonzalez rented a plane and hired a pilot and he and Mary flew into the East Unit to pay me a visit.

Gonzalez turned out to be a tall heavy-set Latin with jet black hair, a square head and a big smile. For all his size he was a gentle man.

The meeting took place in the conference room. After the introductions and small talk, Gonzalez got down to business.

"Doctor," Gonzalez said, "I can't see any reason why you should be denied bond. You are not a criminal and have no previous record. The law is very clear on these points."

"The law is clear? Then why did the Second District Court choose not to hear my bond appeal on the technicality of no transcript and no assignment of errors? If it's so impossible, what am I doing here, dammit?" I wasn't about to be spoon-fed.

"In a way, Doctor, they were right," Gonzalez countered. "I don't know how much damage Bailey caused you, but you and I know that it did do some harm." Gonzalez paused, choosing his words carefully. "I don't think the matter is closed, especially in the light of your medical condition. There is no doubt in my mind that keeping you in this prison is destroying your health and eventually may kill you. In addition, your wife told me about your broken nose and her fears for your safety."

I agreed with Gonzalez and liked what he had to say. I looked at Mary and could see that she was also impressed with Henry. Perhaps I was impressed that somebody thought something positive could be done, and we no longer had to carry the fight alone.

"That's all well and good, Henry, but there are no guarantees in this life. And I am sure you mean well, but how can you be that sure?"

Gonzalez laughed, tilted back in his chair, and clasped those massive hands behind his head. "I'm so sure of success, Doctor, that I am willing to do this for nothing, not a penny, not even expenses. Why do you say about that?"

Now I really was impressed. My information from convicts was that Gonzalez no doubt was one of the best attorneys on the west coast of Florida, that he was very successful in the causes he presented in front of the Second District Court of Appeals, and finally, that he was very, very expensive.

The fact that Gonzalez was willing to take on this challenge and was so sure of victory that he would forego even expenses had to weigh heavily in my decision-making process.

Cautiously, without seeming to agree, I questioned Henry about the mechanics of securing bond when and if the Second District Court set one.

"You leave that to me," Henry quietly answered. "Armando Arcus, a top bondsman in Tampa, will write your bond, no matter what it is."

I sat quietly for a moment, looking around the same drab conference room in which Bailey, Plaut and I had met that previous July, a lifetime ago, and I was no closer to getting out, to living my life at home with Mary and the children. This was it. Decision-making time.

"Okay. You have a client."

Henry Gonzalez exhaled, leaned back, and relaxed in his chair.

"What about Bailey?" I asked. "He is not going to like this."

"I'll take care of Lee," Mary said. These were her first words. She had left all the talk and decisions up to me. "I'll call Lee and explain the situation about Henry's representing you only for bond."

"He is still not going to like it, Mary," I persisted.

"Tough," she shrugged. "He's a big boy. He had his chance to get you out on bond and he dropped the ball."

I turned to Gonzalez. "What's your plan, Henry? How do you intend to go about getting me out on bond?"

"Let me think about it for a while, and I'll get back to you. All right?"

The meeting was over. We shook hands. I kissed Mary goodbye. Walking back to "U" wing, I felt very good. At last, Mary and I had a fighter in our corner.

JUNE, 1968

Henry Gonzalex was back, and not alone. Red McEwen was with him. So was Mary. And a new entry in this drama in the person of John Feegel, physician and attorney at law.

John Feegel, M.D.J.D. was, at this time, medical examiner for Hillsborough County and had testified as an expert witness for the State of Florida in many criminal cases. In addition, Feegel was a medical expert in civil and malpractice cases.

I liked John immediately when we met, and we have remained close friends throughout the years. Feegel would play an important part in my eventual release, eleven years later, but we didn't know it on that day in June, 1968.

We met again in the conference room. There was little small talk. We were dealing with serious business. My health was worse, much worse, if indeed it was possible to be in such bad shape and still be alive.

Feegel took over the questioning. He had a piercing wit and a brilliant legal and medical mind. He was interested in my daily activities, and the type of medical treatment I had received. He became paler and paler as my drama unfolded. When I reached the part about my attack of coronary insufficiency a year before, June 1967, and the extent of my medical treatment by Dr. Zaffke, I thought he was going to have a fit.

Feegel kept saying, "I can't believe it! I can't believe it! I know it's true, but I can't believe it!"

Turning to Gonzalez, Feegel said, "Do you know, Henry, that twenty-five percent to forty percent of persons who have heart attacks die before they can be brought to the hospital? In contrast, death from acute myocardial infarction in a patient already in a modern hospital is ten percent to fifteen percent. The prevention of sudden death in susceptible people like Dr. Copppolino necessitates therapeutic and prophylactic approaches, none of which he has received, nor from what I see and hear, will receive."

"What should have been done for Dr. Coppolino last June?" McEwen asked in a squeaky voice.

"Red, Dr. Coppolino should have had his heart monitored electrocardiograph-ically and any significant arrythmias treated immediately. (Instead I had to treat my own arrythmia with purloined Dilantin!) He should have had blood chemistries done to determine the extent of cardiac damage. He should . . . Damn! What's the use!"

"It's criminal! Absolutely criminal," Feegel shouted, pointing to me, "the way this man was treated! The immediate cause of sudden cardiac death is ventricular fibrillation preceded by ventricular premature beats. And Copppolino has a history of premature ventricular contractions. Doctors Sheehan and Kelly in New Jersey were treating him for that."

Gonzalez spun around to me. "Does Dr. Zaffke have those records?"

"Certainly he does. I signed the release for them. And I know he received the letter with details from Dr. Kelly."

"How do you know he's gotten a letter back from Kelly?"

"I can't tell you," I answered, thinking how Floyd Holzapfel saw the letter and told me about it.

"This is all very interesting, and I don't mean to knock any of it," Mary interrupted, "but I know all this. Carl knows all this. The question is, how are we going to use this material to get Carl out on bond?"

"John?" Henry asked, turning again to Feegel.

"First we will have to look at Carl's medical records here in the prison."

Turning to me, Feegel asked, "You said Zaffke took an electrocardiograph last year. Anything else?"

"Just my clinic visits when I pick up my three nitroglycerin tablets. My admission in the East Unit clinic is simply a note in the pink sheets. It is not officially classified as an admission."

McEwen took out a legal pad and wrote out a medical release for me to sign. "Sign this, Doctor. I will get copies of all your records."

"You're dreaming, Red," I answered, as I signed the release. "Once the prison officials suspect you're up to something, they aren't going to give you the records. They don't want you to see how little they have done for me."

"We'll see, all right," Henry said. "Right now, stay alive. Otherwise this whole operation becomes moot. Are you still writing?"

"Yes. I've finished a novel. I'll give it to you."

"May I read it also?" Mary asked, a pixie smile on her face.

I kissed her. "I wrote it for you, and I called it *Angelo Anena.*

A round of handshaking, another kiss from Mary and I was back on "U" wing. Things were finally happening!

JULY, 1968

My prediction to Red McEwen became true. The prison officials, including Zaffke, resisted Red's efforts to get copies of my electrocardiograph and medical records.

First Red tried to get the records by writing Dr. Zaffke. Zaffke, in turn, pushed the panic button and wrote a letter to Dave Bachman, Deputy Director of Inmate Treatment in Tallahassee, indicating he didn't want to send the records, only a summary. The superintendent, the predictably uncooperative Mr. Sinclair, also directed Red to Bachman in Tallahassee. He was running scared.

Finally, by August the first, Red McEwen was able to get copies of my medical records. I, in turn, was able to obtain the letter that Dr. Kelly sent Dr. Zaffke back in May of 1967 indicating to Zaffke the seriousness of my condition; proving that he knew all about it when I had my attack the following month in June, when he, Zaffke, did nothing.

AUGUST, 1968

The Florida Prison System has a grim fate in store for those men who break prison rules. This was driven home to me by my friend Santos. I had left him in the West Unit working as a clerk to Lieutenant Chambers, but we had kept in touch.

"Santos, what are you doing here in the East Unit?" I asked my friend this August night while sitting in the gym.

Santos was lifting weights. The sweat on his brown body poured like torrents of rain down the side of a barn. He pressed 250 pounds, released, and sat down beside me.

"*Amigo mío,*" he gasped, his breath rasping through his barreled chest. He wrapped a towel around his neck and smiled at me.

"Well?" I demanded. "I left you holding down a good job. Now you are here in this pig sty. What happened?"

"*Sí. Bueno.* I left the animal Chambers and started to work in the cateen, then . . ."

"Hold it!" I yelled. "I know a little bit more about things now. How did you get in the canteen?"

"The assistant superintendent of *The Rock,* E. Odell Carlton."

"*Carlton! No me gusta!*"

"Ha! You speak a little Spanish now, eh?!"

That was true. I had started a Spanish self-study course. Mary was supplying me with grammar books, and I practiced in school with my Cuban friends.

"*Yo hablo español un poco,* but continue my friend. What happened?"

Santos wiped his sweating hands and face on the towel. "I worked in the 'free man's' canteen. And you know how I am. Business is business. They pulled a sneak inventory."

"And you were short," I finished for him.

"*Sí.* They also found cash money. So here I am!"

"Did you come straight over from *The Rock?*"

"No. I went to D.R. court. Ha! They gave me thirty days in the flattop, then over here. Now I am a houseman and I'm eating to put back the weight I lost in solitary."

I shook my head in dismay. "This is a *muy malo* place."

"Yes. A bad place, Carl." His eyes darkened. "They fed me two bowls of slop—beans, carrots, peas, all dried up. It looked like vomit. I had nothing to read except the *Bible.*"

I laughed. "I'll bet you slept for thirty days."

Santos looked at me. "How could anyone sleep?" he whispered. "All I had was two blankets on the concrete floor." He shivered. "The man in the next cell tried to talk to me. They caught the poor bastard and sealed his cell tight." Santos' body racked with coughing. "He was only a kid, maybe sixteen."

"What the hell did he do?" I asked.

"Told the hack in charge of his work squad to drop dead!"

"That's all?" I shouted.

"That's nothing, *Amigo*. Did you know, Carl, that three months ago in May, around Mother's Day, they put a boy in solitary confinement because he cut some flowers and gave them to his Mother? But that's life," Santos added.

"How do you feel?" I asked.

Santos flexed his biceps and triceps. "Nothing can hurt a Chicano. But I'm hungry. When you come out of solitary, your whole system is fouled up. The first thing I did was go straight to the mess hall. I knew I was coming to the East Unit. So I ate and ate. Everybody does. Then I got sick. I vomited and vomited some more and pretty soon I had the dry heaves."

I playfully punched him on his arms. "Come on. Let's go to the latrine where the light is better. Let me take a good look at you."

"You still playing doctor?" he smiled. "Good! Let's go! My own private doctor! If *mi padre* could see me now!"

SEPTEMBER, *1968*

The unbelievable happened! I was transferred to *The Rock!* Right out of the blue! Not bad, I thought. There's room for miracles, even in maximum security.

I came into the wing from school at noon. The guard on "U" wing ordered me to pack my personal belongings. I was transferred to *The Rock!*

Within the hour I was in the back of the "bus" (station wagon), handcuffed of course, and driven by Mr. Stancil a distance of one and a half miles. He deposited me in front of the control room, the same control room that fifteen months ago ordered me to the East Unit.

I was marched down to the laundry to turn in my white uniform and to don the inevitable gray coveralls. On the way back, I passed a red brick chapel and whom did I see on the steps? None other than my friend, Jerry, the Dinger!

"How are you? You son-of-a-bitch!" he hollered from the chapel steps. Dinger had been transferred to *The Rock* several months before and he kept in touch by sending me messages by different convicts as they traveled from *The Rock* to the East Unit and back again.

I signalled that I'd see him inside. I was assigned a cell on "G" floor, the "bowery" of Raiford.

I dumped my personal property on the empty rack in the ten-man cell. It was dark and dreary on "G" floor. I said "hello" to some of the men I knew and nodded to others.

I left my cell and went out to the yard. The yard consisted of a large grassy area, hexagonal in shape, furnished with stone benches, a ball field, and weight-lifting equipment. It was teeming with black and white convicts, yelling, running, some fighting, others sitting on the stone bench gazing out into nothingness.

"Dinger pulled me aside. "You got any dough?"

"No. I haven't drawn canteen this week. I was supposed to do that tomorrow. So I'm broke."

"Fuck it. Come on with me. I got it made."

He took me to the window of the canteen and screamed, "Harry! You fat Jew bastard. This is my friend, Dr. Coppolino, only I call him the 'Schnozz' because his nose is so big!"

Harry came over and we shook hands.

"Look," the Dinger continued, "you Jew bastard, give Carl what he wants and put it on my bill!"

"Come on!" Dinger yanked on my coveralls. I waved good-bye to Harry.

I followed Jerry through a large gate into an office of broken-down furniture, a beat-up Underwood typewriter, and a fan. This was the Dinger's office. Actually it was at the office of *The Rock* lieutenant's clerk. A black convict sat in the corner, shining a pair of black boots that belonged to a guard.

"That's Tangalie," Jerry pointed to the black man. "He's my runner. He's good people."

Jerry wanted to know all about his pals at the East Unit, Floyd, Joe Peel, Pete and others. "Where are you locking?" he asked.

"'G' floor."

"Jesus! I got to get you out of there! A white kid was raped by three blacks last week right on 'G' floor, and emotions are running high."

"You don't say. Bullshit!" I spat viciously. "Emotions are always high for one reason or another. It took me three days to learn that and I've been here going on two years!"

"Got a little fighty since I saw you last, eh?"

I grinned. "It's called survival."

"In a week I'll make a move to have the Lieutenant ship you up to 3T. That's where I'm at. 3T-13. It's a half-ass trusty quarters. Not as good as 2T. But getting there. Where are you working?"

"I don't know. I don't know how I got here in the first place!"

"Don't knock it! Anyway, the East Unit is too crowded. Tomorrow you'll see Reddish."

The Dinger saw the look on my face. "Yeah! Fatso Reddish is on this side now. He is no tiger here. He is scared to death some convict is going to chop off his head. So he is *real* nice!" Sure enough Jerry was telling me the truth. The next day when I saw Reddish, he was polite, almost nice but hardly *real* nice, and assigned me to the easy job of checker on the West Gate. I worked from 5:00 a.m. to 2:00 p.m. every other day. My duties consisted of checking the men in and out the gate by moving pins on a large peg board.

In her next letter Mary had a few comments to make about an over-trained pin mover. In addition she told me that she had bought a bottle of champagne and opened it at the house in celebration of my transfer. "Now I can bring you some food and put the pounds back on you!" My parents were at my home at this time and joined Mary in the toast.

"G" floor! What a place! Like nothing you could possibly imagine! You built one day at a time there, slowly, oh so very slowly. It was best not to think or feel!

I lay in my bunk at night, listening to the snores of the other nine men. Suddenly one of them would scream in his sleep, "You son-of-a-bitch!" Another, a genuine Miami gangster type, would moan and mumble, "Momma! Momma!"

I stared up at the ceiling. There were reflections from the search lights on top of the gun towers. The bars on the door and windows cast a grid work of shadows on the cells walls and on the one porcelain commode, sitting in all its majesty along the far wall.

What a horrible feeling, being locked up and trying to hold down the panic, and knowing that tomorrow night, and the next night, and the next night, I would lie there staring at the same lights and same shadows, listening to the snores and screams of the men, trying not to think, not to think of home.

In the morning I could hear a metal key being dragged across the radiators in the hallway and across the cell bars. The redneck hack was shouting, "Aw right! Let's shake em!"

When the light came on, twenty feet hit the floor. Metal locker drawers were banged open and closed. The men took a turn pissing in the seatless commode. Water from different pocket combs splashed the floor as several men tried to use the one small ten-cent mirror.

The cell doors banged open and the filthy corridor was filled with gray, wrinkled shapes, shuffling and murmuring, pushing and shoving through the darkened courtyard into the mess hall.

I was one of them. A miserable, dehumanized shape.

In the mess hall I got what everybody else got: watery grits, dried eggs, powdered milk. I was hungry, but not that hungry. I threw it all in the slop bucket and settled for a cup of state coffee, black and cold.

When dawn broke and it was light enough to walk, the gates were opened and the men drifted out into the yard to stroll aimlessly around a circular path worn into the ground.

I liked this time of day. The air was crisp and clear. I could hear the birds, the swallows, sparrows, and sometimes woodpeckers. The mob of men were still sleepy, so it was always quiet. Mary's face was always before my eyes. It was our togetherness time.

An hour passed.

The work squads began to form in a double line. Here stood the men who worked in the tag plant, the furniture factory, the construction gangs, and horticulture. They were counted off and marched to the West Unit. All but one. I was unassigned until I started on the West Gate the following week. I reported to the yard officer standing at the foot of the prison flag pole, and I received my temporary assignment, which was picking up scrap paper lying around in the yard. I was lucky. I could have pulled kitchen clean up duty.

Then it was noon and the whole process was reversed. The population drifted back to *The Rock* from the factory, shops, and school. This moment was signalled by the noon whistle, a prolonged and piercing blast of the steam whistle on top of the power plant. It wailed, and wailed, and tore through my brain. I hated that whistle.

Noon chow consisted of black-eyed peas, collard greens, corn bread, and bologna. Then it was back out in the yard to make a few more laps around—please don't litter! I have to pick it up.

Instead of going to the yard, some men went back to their cells to sleep for twenty minutes and to check their lockers. Mutterings of "Who busted into my locker? My coffee's gone! I'll kill the son-of-a-bitch if I find him!" could be heard. Then the order was bellowed out up and down the corridors: "Outside! Outside! Everybody outside!" Cell doors slammed. The shuffling started again. It was back into the yard.

"Line up!" the microphone screeched. The 1:00 p.m. whistle joined the screech and I thought I'd go mad with the shrill, tearing, unrelenting noise.

Out the men mached again to make license plates and metal lockers or whatever else the State deemed necessary for their rehabilitation for the day.

I went back to picking up paper: Carl A. Coppolino, M.D.—sanitation engineer!

Supper time in the mess hall, officially called "Bulea Blitch Hall," provided us with collard greens, white beans, and greasy fried sausage with lots of bread.

At 6:00 p.m., the screaming order arrived: "In your hole! Everybody in your hole!" Cell doors rattled and clanged shut. "Count time! Everybody in your hole!" The last cell door banged closed.

The guard's cowboy boots clicked as he went from cell to cell. "Morgan!" the guard called. "00697" answered the well-tanned, wiry old convict with deep scars on his face.

"Hernandez! Coppolino!" The guard went through the ritual ten times, and simultaneously handed out mail. There wasn't any for me.

The cell door slammed behind him, and you could hear the clunk of the bolt. The guard's voice grew dimmer as he moved down the corridor from cell to cell.

The toilet flushed. My cellmates relaxed. Some lay on their bunks; others sat down on the edges and rolled cigarettes. I stood at the locked cell door, staring out through the bar at the canteen, the visiting park, the hospital, the gun towers, and the barbed wire fences.

Just outside the locked compound was an asphalt drive, a drivewalk, and a row of live oak trees. A few men in whites, trustees who lived on 2T, were sitting on the curb listening to the hundreds of birds that lived in those massive oaks.

"Lights out!" yelled the "G" floor guard. "Lights out!" The radio was turned off and cigaretes were lit. Bunks creaked and finally the snores began.

Mary burrowed her way behind my closed eyelids and I drank in her loveliness.

I moved up to 3T on the following Monday and started work on the West Gate.

NOVEMBER 1968

I woke up on November 8 to find out from the radio news broadcast that my appeals had been turned down by the Second District Court of

Appeals at Lakeland. I felt nothing, no sadness, no depression. Numb.

Many of my friends came up to me in the yard to offer their condolences. "That's Florida," they agreed. "There is no justice in Florida!" others murmured. The many jail house lawyers, some of whom had been attorneys on the street, were stunned that Florida could somehow justify the second degree murder conviction when there wasn't a shred of evidence.

Bailey's office sent me a copy of the written opinion out of the Second District Court of Appeals plus some caustic remarks and observations, which made me feel good, but did nothing to alleviate my situation. I might as well have been a "con" in a movie, with a tin cup to scrape across the bars. For this I didn't need Bailey.

Mary was concerned about my health in face of this denial. She knew how precarious was my cardiac situation. I spent our next visit trying to reassure her that I was handling it well, but it wasn't easy, and I don't think I was successful.

She knew too much about my medical problem for me to gloss over it. My treatment consisted of peritrate and nitroglycerin. I still had cardiac asthma and could sleep only at a forty-five degree angle, not horizontally. If I did sleep, I awoke with chest pain (nocturnal angina). My ankles remained swollen.

Now my appeal had been turned down, and I was thrust back that much further in my attempt to be free.

My hope for immediate release rested with Henry Gonzalez and his petition for supersedeas bond pending appeal. I didn't have long to wait.

Gonzalez's petition with affidavits arrived on November 13. Henry was concise and to the point in his pleading. There were eight parts that covered five typewritten pages. The "meat" rested in item #7 and item #8:

Item #7

That your petitioner, having a history of heart disease since 1962, is an extremely ill person suffering from severe coronary insuffuciency manifesting itself as angina pectoris. Said coronary insufficiency perists to date while petitioner is confined in the Florida State Penitentiary at Raiford, Florida. Said penitentiary having insufficient facilities to cope with this presently existing condition. The prognosis and future expectations of your petitioner's present condition are extremely grave, in that said condition will most probably progress to the incurrence of a myocardial infarction or "full blown" heart attack. The Florida State Prison facilities are likewise insufficient to cope with the eventuality of this prognosis. Petitioner's incarceration pending the appeal has had an injurious effect on his physical health and further incarceration pending the ultimate and final disposition of this appeal will, under such circumstances, substantially endanger the health, even life, of your petitioner.

Attached hereto and made a part hereof are the affidavits of Louis Lemberg, M.D.; John R. Feegel, M.D.; William A. Lemmert, M.D.; and Karl Rolls, M.D., all practicing medical doctors and licensed by the Florida Board of Medical Examiners; which said affidavits reflect your petitioner's present physical and medical condition, the prognosis for one afflicted with such condition, and the inadequacy of the prison facilities to properly care for your petitioner. Said affidavits are marked exhibits "D," "E," "F," and "G."

Item #8

Your petitioner has no criminal record, is an established resident of Sarasota, Florida, having married and lived there at his home with his wife and four children. Since coming to Florida, he has acquired property, and due to his heart condition, has engaged in his profession to a limited extent.

WHEREFORE, your petitioner, Carl A. Coppolino, most respectfully moves this Honorable Court that it consider this application made for Sueprsedeas Bail in accordance with the application law as presented in petitioner's brief filed in support of said application, along with the exhibits attached hereto, and thereafter, enter such order setting Supersedeas Bond as this court deems meet and just.

Respectfully submitted,

Henry Gonzalez of Counsel for petitioner

The affidavits that Henry alluded to in his petition consisted of twenty-seven pages from Dr. John Feegel in which he tore into my lack of medical care and Dr. Zaffke's ineptitude. In his conclusions, Feegel stated:

Conclusion: The analysis of the existing medical records of Carl Coppolino coupled with a personal interview with both Carl Coppolino and Dr. Zaffke, the prison physician, and supplemented by research into the nature of coronary heart disease, its prognosis and its modern treatment leads the Affiant to the opinion, based on reasonable medical certitude (a) that Carl Coppolino has severe coronary artery disease, (b) that such heart disease is expected to become significantly worse, (c) that a sudden, fatal outcome is anticipated, (d) that the medical facilities at Florida State Prison at Raiford are inadequate to treat both the present degree of heart disease manifested by Dr. Coppolino and the sudden cardiac emergency which probably will subsequently develop.

John R. Feegel, M.D.

The affidavits from Louis Lemberg, Karl R. Rolls, and William Lemmert were no less emphatic.

Dr. Lemberg's sworn statement read in part: "In light of his past medical history of coronary artery disease, the recent onset of 'asthma attacks,' and sudden awakening at night with ischemic chest pain and shortness of breath of which Dr. Coppolino presently complains, strongly suggests the onset of left heart failure. This latter complication would certainly indicate a more grave prognosis."

Dr. Rolls of Sarasota, Florida, in his affadavit went so far as to say, "It is my opinion that any person with the history and findings exhibited by Carl A. Coppolino, M.D. should have highly sophisticated treatment facilities (available) within a very few minutes at all times."

It did not take long for the State to respond. On the following day, November 14, I was called to the Lieutenant's office and told to pack "my shit." I was being moved back to the East Unit. I was stunned. "Why?" I kept shouting. I was told to go to the control room to find out.

Hurriedly I rushed up to my quarters on 3T and threw my belongings into a cardboard box. Then I went searching for Jerry.

I never had to leave the floor to find him because he was looking for me. We met at the head of the stairs.

"What the fuck's going on?" he growled, waving the white transfer sheet in my face. Mine was the only name, destination East Unit. "What the fuck's going on?" he repeated.

"I don't know." Frantically I ran my fingers through my hair. "It must be the bond appeal. All those doctors' affidavits."

"No! You are in trouble!" the Dinger said, pointing at my chest.

"I know! I know!" I answered in an agitated voice. My fingers were drippig sweat, and I knew I was pale.

"Look, Jerry! I don't care how you do it, but you have to get a telephone message to Mary!" I tore off a piece of paper and jotted our unlisted phone number.

"Sure, pal! Anything else?"

"No! Just make sure she knows where I am."

We shook hands.

I lugged my box of belongings down the metal steps, out the dusty courtyard, through the West Gate, along the paved sidewalk into the control room. I collapsed on a wooden chair. My chest hurt. I was exhausted.

At the control room desk sat short, fat Sergeant Smith, Snuffy Smith to the convicts, and tall, thin, leathery-looking Lieutenant Connors. His piercing eyes pinned me to the mahogany arm chair.

I was boiling, literally boiling with rage.

"What's bothering you, Coppolino?" Connors' voice grated on my ear.

"Why are you shipping me to the East Unit?"

Sergeant Smith waved a piece of paper at me. "Your transfer orders."

"That's no answer," I shot back.

A startled look crossed Lieutenant Connors' face. "Watch your mouth, boy!" he growled.

"Not unless I get some answers! Why are you sending me back?" My voice had risen three octaves.

Slowly, Lieutenant Connors rose from behind the control room desk. "The sergeant has already explained that. You have been transferred. Now if I were you, I'd sit quiet and wait for the bus."

"You're not me, Lieutenant," I snapped. "I'm not going to the East Unit until I get some answers!"

"What! You shut your mouth!" Connors roared. "You're an inmate and I tell you what to do! Don't you forget it!"

"You make me sick!" I exploded. I was on my feet, anger blurring my vision. "I'm not going to the East Unit until I find out why! I want to see Superintendent Sinclair or his assistant, Tompkins." I gasped for breath.

Connors opened and closed his fingers. Hatred twisted his face into a snarling and obscene thing. His short gray hair stood on end.

"You're going in the bus," he yelled, "if I have to throw chains around you and drag you by the handcuffs. Now sit down!"

"No! I won't! Chains, is it? Well, that's what you are going to have to do!" I accented each word by shaking my index finger in Connors' incredulous face. Out of the corner of my eye I could see Sergeant Smith speaking into the telephone. His eyes were wide with fear as he watched both of us.

They didn't expect me to fight, I thought. No. They expected that I would lie down like a dog because they yelled. No way! I was sick of them and their prison. And I knew that I was doomed in the East Unit with no medical treatment. I decided I had rather fight than die unattended and in agony.

Sergeant Smith broke the strained quiet that had fallen on the control room. "Lieutenant, I just spoke to Mr. Tompkins. He said to bring inmate Coppolino to the interview room at the old adminstration building."

"That's better," I muttered.

Connors snapped an order to the guard sitting nearby. "Go with

Coppolino to the administration building and stay with him!" The Lieutenant glared at me and picked up the phone.

My keeper and I walked along under the oak trees. Sunlight filtered
through the leaves throwing weird shadows on the wide cobbled walk. I
was blind to nature. Blinded by anger.

Tompkins reached the interview room at the same time we did. He
motioned to the guard to wait outside.

We sat in the barren office facing each other over a long, scarred
wooden table. Tompkins was a medium-sized man with a large head and
florid complexion. He had an ingratiating manner of speaking with a
trace of whine in his voice. If he could get away with it, he'd promise to make anyone President if that's what the poor jerk wanted to
hear. He was an empty man.

"Now, Carl," he began in his lilting voice. "You've created a racket out
there in the control room. I don't know what's. . . ."

"Cut it! Let's get down to business, Mr. Tompkins. Let's stop pussy-
footing. Why am I going to the East Unit?"

"Well, now, Carl, you didn't let me finish what I was about to say." He
paused, eyes darting around the room, never settling on me. "You have a
good record in the prison, up to now. I don't want to see you spoil it by
doing a foolish thing."

"Mr. Tompkins, why am I going to the East Unit?" I repeated loudly.

"Like I said, Carl," Tompkins droned. "You are doing so well. You
have such a good record that it is a shame that your lawyers didn't take
this into account when they filed that petition on your behalf."

I slumped in the chair, exhausted. There it was, out in the open at last.

"You mean the bond motion?"

"Yes. Now, we take care of you the best we can. We have good doctors
here. Dr. Zaffke is a fine man, the best doctor there is in this part of
Florida. I'm real proud that he is part of our team . . ."

I wanted to vomit. Preferably, on Tompkins. Then I wanted to scream.

"What can I do about it, Mr. Tompkins? My attorneys are only exercis-
ing my constitutional rights." I knew the words were meaningless to a
man like this, but I had to try.

"Well, Carl, if you could see a way of stopping this petition, I think we
could make things easier for you and your wife. Those trips to see you are
so long, aren't they? What is it, about four hundred miles round trip?"

"Five hundred miles round trip each week, that's how far Mary trav-
els," I answered in a dull voice.

"I see no reason why you can't be at Avon Park; now that's a nice place
and close to Sarasota. They have a small hospital with a fine doctor."

"I see." And I did see. I saw that I was supposed to believe that if I pulled the petition I'd get transferred to Avon Park. But I didn't believe him. Why should I? And I wanted to be free, not in another prison. Bond was my way out. Particularly since it looked as if the bond motion had hit a sensitive nerve.

"No, Mr. Thompkins. No deal. I'm going to follow exactly what my lawyers advise. And I'm not going to the East Unit!"

"I don't see that it's up to you. . . . Now, Carl, I'm sorry you have taken that attitude. Really sorry. There is nothing I can do for you now. Those men in the control room have their orders to transfer you. And they'll take any measure necessary to carry out those orders." His eyes, now, locked on mine.

"Then, I guess there's nothing more to say." I got up to walk out. Tompkins' voice stopped me.

"You go on over to the East Unit. It may only be for a few months until we get things worked out."

I walked out of the room. The guard and I returned to the control room. A surprise was waiting for me. The control room was crowded with guards. There were chains and handcuffs in plain view. For all my assurance with Tompkins, I was sick with fear now. Mr. Stancil stood by the door, ready to move. His bus was parked nearby.

I surrendered. Damn.

Stancil snapped the handcuffs over my outstretched wrists. I snatched up my personal property, left the control room, and entered the bus.

The ride acoss the river took about five to ten minutes. But the bus never slowed down. I had heard the crackling sounds of the two way radio, but paid no attention. I was tired and depressed after losing another battle with the State.

The bus made a full circle and I found myself back in front of the control room! Lieutenant Connors, all smiles, helped me out of the bus. "Mr. Tompkins called," he said as Stancil unlocked and removed my handcuffs. "Your transfer orders have been cancelled. You can go back to your cell on 3T."

Hurrah. Another miracle. I finally won a round.

Unstairs on 3T I related to Jerry all that happened. He shook his head. "The mother-fucking bastards," he said vehemently. He shook his head again.

"What's with you?" I asked. I was putting my personal property back in my metal locker.

"While you were gone, either with Tompkins or on the bus, a telegram arrived for you. It hit Captain Edwards' desk in the control room. It was from your lawyer, Henry Gonzalez."

I straightened up. "Do you know what it said?"

"Yeah! Our spy heard that the telegram read something about a hearing on your bond motion being set for December 3. That sadist Edwards got scared and called you back. I'll bet that's what happened, and I'll bet that he is checking with Tallahassee right now!"

I stared at the Dinger. "What's Tallahassee going to do?"

"They ain't going to give up. That's for fucking sure!"

"Tallahassee," I sighed.

"Sure. Your transfer orders came from Carlton, our glorious assistant superintendent. He received them from the Attorney General's office."

"Yeah! Well, I figured Georgieff had his hand in the stew. Christ, I wonder what their next move will be?"

It didn't take long to find out. I had completed unpacking my personal property, when the convict runner came and told me I was wanted in the Lieutenant's office.

Back I went. Again I was told "pack your shit! You're being transferred to the East Unit." Again I asked Dinger to make a phone call to Mary. Out in the control room, Lieutenant Connors showed me the new transfer orders. Quietly, I sat and waited for the bus. Cancel that last miracle. The bastards were too good at the game. It figures. They've had so many lives to practice on.

Ten minutes later I found myself in the East Unit in Captain Combs' office. Godwin had been transferred to Avon Park Correctional Institution. His sudden departure, it was rumored, concerned the death of a convict back in maximum security. Combs was now acting superintendent.

"What are you doing here, Coppolino?" he snapped. "I thought we had gotten rid of you!"

"You tell me, Captain. I can't get a straight answer out of anybody."

"Well, we'll see about that."

Combs picked up the telephone and dialed the administration office at The Rock.

"What's Coppolino doing here?" he asked his telephone contact. Combs sat silently, listening; anger crossed his face. He fiddled through my record until he came to a piece of paper. 'Yes. It's right here. They want him in max?" Combs' face darkened. "That's stupid!" He paused, then said, "I don't give a damn what the Attorney General's office wants!" And he slammed the phone down.

Combs looked up at me. "You heard? Carlton wants you in max; that's the request from the Attorney General's office. But Carlton doesn't run anything here. I do."

Combs leaned back in his chair. Every crease in his brown shirt was sharp and in the right place. He looked like a Marine Colonel. "The East

Unit, as you know, doesn't have any assistant superintendent. I'm acting in that capacity, and I'm not going to put you in max. There is no need to. But you can't go back in the school. It's too good a job." Combs leaned forward. "Get on down to 'T' wing. Tomorrow you report to the tobacco factory." He gave me a bleak grin.

It was a repeating nightmare, a walk through the double electric gates, down the long concrete and steel cold corridor to "T" wing, which was the exact duplicate of "U" wing and 'W" wing before that.

NOVEMBER 15, 1968

The tobacco factory was a large warehouse with plenty of windows and a fan. Depending on your job, you were stationed where the barrels of pressed tobacco were cracked open, or where the tobacco leaf was moistened, dumped on wooden tables, and hand stripped from its stem, then placed into smaller barrels.

I was assigned to the stripping table. The convicts assigned there had to strip tobacco and meet a quota of fifty pounds per man per day, under pain of a D.R. for unsatisfactory work.

I had been in the prison system long enough to know I was on a punishment squad. The tobacco squad, for instance, was where one was assigned after coming out of solitary.

It was the worst possible place for someone with asthma, like me. My coughing and wheezing became much worse because of the dense tobacco dust and dirt. My ankles looked like watermelons at the end of each day because I had to stand for hours at the stripping table to make my fifty pound quota.

Fortunately, I had friends to help me. Pete was there. So was Crazy Tony (the convict they moved out of "F" floor when I entered the prison). And there were others who gave me a helping hand, and Joe Peel sent me a cheery message.

Mary and Henry Gonzalez arrived the next day, the 16th. They had chartered a plane and landed at the East Unit airstrip. The prison officials were in a frenzy! Orders were issued that I was to be brought to the conference room immediately. My HELP had arrived! Nobody knew how Gonzalez and Mary found out I had been shipped back to the East Unit.

I must have looked terrible because Mary couldn't hide her tears as she held me in her arms. Henry clasped my right hand and held it for a long,

long time. They were shocked as I told them my story, especially when I came to Tompkins' attempt to have me pull the bond petition. Gonzalez's face alternated pale, in shock—then dark, in rage. He repeatedly smashed his fist into his open hand.

That's why Tompkins was so nervous when I called yesterday," Mary whis-pered.

"You called yesterday?" I asked in disbelief.

"8:30 in the morning. I got your message late the night before. In fact I received two phone calls saying the same thing, that you had been moved to the East Unit. I waited for morning before calling. At first Tompkins denied any knowledge of your being here. Then when he realized I knew he had talked with you, he admitted you were here, but gave me no reason."

"Did you roast him on the telephone?" Gonzalez asked.

"You bet I did." Mary's eyes blazed with anger. "I told him that he'd have to answer to the Associated Press, television and other media if anything, *anything* happened to my husband. That shook him. Then he kept pressing me about how I learned Carl was here."

"Let them sweat," I gloated. And they did. Carlton tried to find out from me. So did Combs. I referred Carlton to Mary. I was locked up in his maximum security prison, I told him. How would I know how she found out? Later that month Carlton showed his brutish mentality by calling Mary unprintable names in a conversation to Sheriff Ross Boyer at the annual sheriffs' convention.

After visiting about an hour, Gonzalez and Mary left. Henry assured me that the hearing on December 3 would go well.

On November 15 George Georgieff teletyped Florida State Prison for an up-to-date medical report. He was alarmed at the findings registered in the affidavits filed with the Second District Court of Appeals. Doctor Zaffke, by omission, did nothing to alleviate his apprehension.

Zaffke sent Georgieff a four-page report with copies to David D. Bachman in Tallahassee, which essentially said I had a cardiac problem by history, not by physical examination, despite the preponderous amount of evidence to the contrary.

On November 30, Georgieff struck. He filed a motion vigorously opposing the setting of a supercedeas bond. He played what he thought was a trump card: Georgieff demanded that I be examined by an independent agency, the J. Hillis Miller Health Center, University of Florida, Gainesville.

DECEMBER, 1968

On the night of the hearing, December 3, I was called to the control room where I spoke with Henry Gonzalez on the telephone. He was ecstatic over the hearing and thought that the court was favorably inclined. However, I had to be examined at Gainesville on the 6th.

I wasn't concerned about the upcoming examination. It was a nuisance. However, since I hoped it would lead to adequate treatment and freedom on bond, I welcomed it. My health had deteriorated with the stress of the tobacco factory. I was willing to grasp at any straw.

The morning of December 6 was unforgettable. There I was in pain, severely underweight, lungs filled with fluid; yet, that morning I was skin stripped, prodded and body-searched, and handcuffed. I left the prison and was placed in the right front seat of a State car. The driver was a medical technician. In the back sat two correctional officers holding .357 Magnums in their hands. A State car followed us with two more fully armed correctional officers. Later I was told that the sheriffs of the counties through which we travelled were informed that I was coming through! In addition, there was a State helicopter following our path! Unbelievable, you say? Yet I lived it.

At the J. Hillis Medical Center I was examined by Dr. Robert Eliot, Professor of Medicine, who at present is Professor of Medicine at the University of Nebraska.

Dr. Eliot's examination took six hours. During the total time a guard stood beside me. I wasn't handcuffed; Dr. Eliot saw to that.

After the examination was completed, Dr. Eliot took me to his office and closed the door in the guard's face. He told me that I was in congestive heart failure, and that I had two areas of permanent damage in my heart. The first was in the back of my heart (posterior wall) which showed the scar of an old infarct. The second area was a damaged muscle surrounding one of the heart valves.

I wasn't stunned by the news. In fact, I was relieved to have confirmed what I already knew.

"What are my chances, Dr. Eliot?"

Eliot rubbed his chin. He stared intently at me. "I have a series of ten patients who have . . . who *had* similar histories of heart damage. None of them lived past the age of forty.

Now that threw me! I was 36, married, with four children, the youngest six years old, and I was incarcerated with a life sentence. Now one of the country's leading cardiologists was telling me that four more years to live was my lot, maybe.

I shuddered. "That's hard to take."

"I did that purposefully, Doctor Coppolino. You are a physician with a family and legal problems." Eliot smiled as he said that! "So I felt you should know what's facing you. I will write a letter to Dr. Zaffke outlining my findings and stating what medication and treatment you should receive."

After I thanked Dr. Eliot for all his kindness, my guards escorted me out of the medical center. The procession was the same going back to the prison: armed guards in the back seat and a car following us.

Within the hour I was back in the East Unit and on "T" wing. No treatment. And to make it worse, the next day I was forced to go back to work in the tobacco factory.

Now I ask you, what would you do if a world renowned cardiologist had told you that you had four years to live, on the outside, and you needed particular treatment and medication and a normal environment, and you found yourself with no treatment and in an environment that would substantially reduce the time you had to live?

Well, whatever you decided to do, I couldn't. I was trapped.

My line of communication, my grapevine, was open between *The Rock* hospital and the East Unit medical clinic and then on to 'T" wing and me. From my brother convicts I found out that Eliot's letter to Zaffke arrived on December 13. The letter was three pages long and said essentially what Eliot had told me in person, leaving out my prognosis. Included was the treatment schedule that was so essential to my bare survival.

I told Mary that Sunday about the letter.

"Are you sure?" she said.

"Positive."

"I was at the hearing, Carl, and heard Georgieff promise those appellate judges that as soon as Zaffke got the report from Gainesville, he, Georgieff would submit it to the court."

"Zaffke has Eliot's letter. And it indicates how seriously ill I am. Georgieff will fight to keep that letter hidden," I reminded her.

We were sitting in the corner of the visiting room, away from potential eaves-droppers. I was under so much pressure that I was short and curt to Lisa's convict friends, Charlie and Bob, who ran the canteen.

I grabbed Mary's hand. "Look Sweetie! I haven't received any treatment. I'm still in the tobacco factory!" I was losing control.

"You're hurting my hand!" She winced.

I released her immediately. "I'm sorry."

She smiled. "That's all right. When you come home, I'll pay you back. I'll bite all of you, from top to bottom!" And suddenly we were off in our own world of love and foolishness again.

"I'm not going to send home for Christmas packages, since I'll be home soon. Tell Henry about the letter."

"Okay," said Mary. "I sent all your clothes to the cleaners and your shirts to the laundry. That's how sure I am you'll be home for Christmas."

My last words to her at the end of the visit were, "Tell Henry about the letter." The following week I was suddenly transferred from the tobacco factory to a quiet houseman's job. The prison officials were taking no more chances.

Christmas came and went. New Year's came and went. I was still in the East Unit. And I was still without treatment!

JANUARY, 1969

Mary spoke with Dr. Eliot on the telephone, and, of course, his hands were tied. He had done all he could by sending his detailed report and outlining the life-saving treatment schedule.

Meanwhile Dr. John Feegel and Henry Gonzalez were in a stew. Knowing that Georgieff was stalling both of them and the court, coupled with the fact that I was seriously ill and had received no treatment, Henry Gonzalez was about to blow up.

In what must be considered one of the most remarkable letters ever written to an appellate court, Gonzalez laid it on the line:

January 8, 1969

Honorable Woodie A. Liles, Judge
District Court of Appeals
Second District, State of Florida
Lakeland, Florida

Dear Judge Liles:

On or about November 12, 1968, your undersigned, in behalf of the the Appellant, Carl A. Coppolino, did argue a Petition to Set Supersedeas Bond Pending Appeal, an argument for said Petition was scheduled for the morning of December 3, 1968. In response to said Petition, George R. Georgieff, Assistant Attorney General, did file an "Opposition to Petition to Set Supersedeas Bond" containing therein an advisory to this

Honorable Court that the Appellant, Carl A. Coppolino, was to be examined or or about December 6, 1968, at the University of Florida Medical Center, Cardiology Unit, and that said arrangements were made by the Attorney General's office.

During the argument on said Petition before this Honorable Court, Mr. Georgieff emphatically advised orally to the Court of the arrangements that had been made relative to the Appellant's examination and, furthermore, advised the Court that upon the examination being made and a medical report being issued, he would see that said report would be immediately forthcoming to the Court and to the parties, and it be made a part of the Record in this cause. The Court expressed a desire to have the report.

The Appellant, Carl A. Coppolino, was on December 6, 1968, pursuant to arrangements made by Dr. Georgieff and Dr. Zaffke of the hospital at Raiford, Florida, examined by a Doctor Robert S. Eliot of the J. Hillis Medical Health Center, University of Florida, Department of Medicine, Division of Cardiology. Not having received a medical report as agreed to by Mr. Georgieff, I wrote Mr. Georgieff on December 20, 1968, asking that the report, if the same was available, be forwarded to the Court and to this office without delay. A copy of said letter is attached.
As of the date of this writing, January 8, 1969, I have not had a response to my request of Mr. Georgieff or a copy of the medical report issued by Dr. Robert Eliot. In view of the foregoing, I am most respectfully requesting that this Honorable Court issue a directive, through its Clerk, to the Honorable George R. Georgieff, Assistant Attorney General, Tallahassee, Florida, to forward a copy of the medical report of the said Robert Eliot to this Honorable Court and to me without further delay.

Respectfully yours,

Henry Gonzalez

Gonzalez wasn't the only one worried and upset. Bachman was the Deputy Director for Inmate Welfare and the evidence was persuasive concerning my illness. The State was in serious trouble. Bachman teletyped Dr. Zaffke for further follow-up information.

On January 7, 1969, Zaffke answered that he, Zaffke, officially indicated the existence of Eliot's report, that he, Zaffke, diagnosed my lung fluid as an upper respiratory infection and that he, Zaffke, by omission, admitted he hadn't started treatment for my heart disease!

In response to Henry Gonzalez's letter, the wrath of the Second District Court of Appeals fell on the head of George Georgieff. Georgieff quickly, with a letter of bluster and apology, submitted Eliot's letter to the Court.
On January 10 the Second District Court appointed Judge John J.

Crews, Circuit Judge of the Eighth Judicial Circuit, as Commissioner with directions to take such testimony as he deemed advisable and to make such findings of fact as to the adequacy of the medical facilities available at the prison for the proper treatment of my physical condition. The Second District Court specifically ordered Judge Crews to make such finding and recommendations promptly and render his report to the Court immediately.

J.T. Tompkins, the same Tompkins who tried to convince me to yank my bond petition by dangling a transfer to Avon Park, was now assistant superintendent at the East Unit. Tompkins became frightened over the facts concerning my health and ordered Zaffke to admit me to the hospital.

On January 14, 1969, I finally reached the hospital at Raiford. On approximately February 1, Eliot's treatment schedule was begun a full two months after it was ordered. Judge Crews set February 7 as the day he would hold his hearing at Raiford and requested the availability of Dr. Zaffke as a witness. The ball was beginning to roll.

FEBRUARY 7, 1969

What a glorious day! It was glorious, not only for me because I felt I was on the last legs of this long journey, but glorious because the patients in the hospital were treated to a bit of cleanliness.

The night before, squads of convicts had swarmed through the hospital washing floors, scrubbing walls. Of course, nothing could be done with the peeling paint and the cracked walls, but the roaches and their filth disappeared along with the rat droppings. Unfortunately the house flies, gnats, and mosquitoes flew in and out at will through the broken windows and torn screens.

Doctor Limcango, the Chief Medical Officer for the Raiford Hospital, was concerned that Judge Crews might hold an on-the-spot inspection of the hospital and its patients. Therefore, every patient received clean pajamas and the bed were stripped and made with clean linen.

On the morning of the 7th I stood by my hospital window and watched a State car pull up in front of the administration building. Mary, Henry, and Dr. John Feegel landed. They had flown into the East Unit airfield and were picked up by the prison officials.

At the same time Judge Crews and Dr. Eliot arrived in the same car. Although they didn't talk about my case, Dr. Eliot knew that Judge Crews had suffered a coronary very recently and Eliot described to the Judge in great detail the necessary modern treatments for a coronary patient. Dr. Eliot felt that the contrast that Crews would find existing at Raiford could only help me.

An hour later a guard came for me. I left the hospital in my pajamas, robe, and slides and walked down the road to the laundry. There I received a set of "blues."

The guard slapped handcuffs on my wrists and we walked out the main gate into the road in front of the administration building. The air did smell cleaner and fresher outside the barbed wire fence!

The first person I saw in the gleaming, spacious modern administration building was Mary. Despite my shackled wrists, we embraced. The guard became so embarrassed that he quickly removed my handcuffs.

I shook hands with Henry Gonzalez and Dr. John Feegel. "Who's representing the State?"

"George Georgieff and Frank Schuab," Gonzalez answered.

"Schaub!" I looked at Mary. "Do you know anything about this?"

She shrugged her shoulders. Her white A-line dress highlighted the red in her freshly coiffured hair. "I heard he wanted to get into the act. The poor man is hung up on the Coppolino case. It seems to me it's the only reason for his existence."

The hallway rapidly filled with people. I saw Tompkins walking around nervously, shoving his hands in and out of his pockets. The new superintendent, Don Hassfurder, stood on the side whispering to Georgieff. Hassfurder had taken over after Sinclair retired. Schaub, dressed in his drab blue suit, stood all alone. His battered brown briefcase rested between his legs.

Finally we were escorted into a large, airy conference room. The huge freshly polished table reflected the strain on my face. All of a sudden I didn't feel so confident.

Judge Crews arrived and we all rose to our feet. Crews was a venerable old man with a full head of white hair. His face showed signs of his recent illness, and his eyes appeared dim with pain. No doubt he wasn't feeling well. He was accompanied by a court reporter, Mr. Leo Powell.

The hearing. I was allowed to stay only for two hours.

The hearing lasted until 5:00 p.m. Doctors Zaffke, Eliot, and Feegel testified. All were questioned by Judge Crews, examined and cross-examined by Gonzalez, Schaub, and Georgieff.

After the conclusion of the hearing, Mary, Feegel, and Gonzalez came into the prison to visit with me for a few minutes in the control room.

Mary told me that Superintendent Don Hassfurder assured her I would not be going back to the East Unit, agreeing that it was no place for me.

Henry had that twinkle in his eye. John Feegel looked expansive and Mary beamed with joy.

"Well, Doctor," Henry said, "it looks like you are on your way home."

John and Mary nodded their agreement.

"Wait until you get the transcript of the hearing!" John added. "Eliot makes Zaffke look like a Nazi butcher!"

"What happens now?" I asked Gonzalez.

Henry paced the small room. He stopped and pointed his finger at me. "I requested that the court reporter, Leo Powell, who traveled here at the request of Judge Crews, transcribe the proceedings and submit it to Crews with a copy for us."

The meeting ended on the agreement that we had to wait for the transcript and Judge Crews' report to the Second District Court of Appeals.

That night, as I lay in my hospital bed, images of the day's events trotted past my shut eyes like soldiers in a parade: Henry's anger at Schaub's rudeness and uncouth manner; Georgieff's facial grimaces; Judge Crews' vacillation, perhaps because his recent illness had drained all the fire out of his judicial robes; perhaps he was afraid of the controversy surrounding me, perhaps . . .

I thought of other convicts with previous records, convicted of more serious offenses, being released on appeal bond. For example, John Sweet who was convicted of first degree murder, had gotten plenty of bad publicity, and yet was out on a $50,000 appeal bond. The bond was granted by the Second District Court of Appeal. Could these same men in black robes do any different for me?

While I waited for the transcript and ruling of Second District Court of Appeals, life—in this case death—went on. Freeman, a twenty-three year old Negro convict, a known asthmatic, died two feet away from me. And I could do nothing about it.

Freeman had been taking asthma medication, asthma bars, yet he progressively went in and out of status asthmaticus. He literally sat on the floor of the hospital gasping for air. Sweat flowed from every pore. His eyes were wide with panic. He knew and I knew that the time for pills had passed. The only medication that would help him now had to be given intravenously—adrenalin or aminophylline. If these medications weren't available, then aerosol therapy with a medi-haler was the next best approach.

The medical technican on duty was J.J. Murphy, a small, dried-up man with a pruney face. Murphy owed his job to his brother-in-law, Mr. Hitchcock, an ex-tower guard and now hospital adminstrator.

It was a well-known fact that Murphy hated black men and hated them with a passion.

Freeman begged Murphy. "Boss," he gasped, "the pipe. I need the pipe!" He was referring to the medi-haler.

Murphy stood there, watching Freeman as he sat on his mattress which was placed on the floor of the hospital room. I knelt beside Freeman sponging his sweaty face with a cool rag.

Freeman kept begging Murphy, as I took his pulse, which was an alarming 220 beats per minute.

"Aren't you going to give him the medi-haler?" I asked Murphy.

"Mind your own business," Murphy snapped. Then he turned to Freeman. "You get nothing, Nigger!"

Twenty minutes later, Freeman's heart stopped.

Word quickly spread throughout the prison. A memorandum notice directed to Superintendent Hassfurder mysteriously appeared on all the prison bulletin boards. The message was plain and to the point. It asked Hassfurder to remove Murphy before Murphy caused the death of other convicts.

The administration, of course, had no way of knowing that this was the opening salvo of a war. And, more importantly, it was the beginning of a movement of cooperation between black and white inmates.

Death had taken Freeman from us. Now it moved in to pay me a visit. On Sunday, February 9, Claire and Monica came to see me, or rather I should say Claire arrived. The prison officials wouldn't let Monica in, since I was under oxygen.

I had awakened that morning with nagging chest pain. It became progressively worse as I got up to go to the bathroom. I was becoming concerned because the same pain preceded my previous collapses and blackouts. I struggled back to my hospital bed. By this time I was drenched with perspiration and the pain was excruciating.

The medical technician on duty picked up the phone and called Dr. Miguel, a prison surgeon who had the weekend covered. Dr. Miguel ordered 75 mgs. of Demerol intramuscular, oxygen, and nitroglycerin tablets. That was it.

Claire found me in bed, pale and sweaty, with an old green oxygen mask strapped to my face. She broke into tears and told me the officials stopped Monica at the front gate. I mumbled through the oxygen mask that it would be better if Monica didn't see me this way.

Claire left after an hour.

I continued to lie there glued to the oxygen mask. The Demerol had eased the pain, but I had no idea how much more damage my heart had already received. Again I had to fight a sense of despair that threatened to engulf me.

Help arrived twelve hours later, at 8:00 p.m.

When Claire had left the hospital, she picked up Monica, found the first pay phone, and called her mother. Between her tears and sobbing, the child told Mary what she had seen.

Alarmed, Mary called Henry Gonzalez and then called J.T. Thompkins. Tomp-kins became alarmed and assured Mary that she would be allowed to enter Raiford at any time, day or night.

At 9:00 p.m., Mary was at the prison gates. She had made the 250 mile trip in three hours. Tompkins arrived and personally escorted her inside the gate. It was the first time a female had ever been allowed within the prison confines after dark. A correction officer escorted her to the hospital and to my room.

My eyes were at half-mast. My bed linen was filthy. I was grimy and unshaven. Worse, I was attached by the old rubber mask directly to the bottle oxygen without a humidifier. This was the picture Mary saw when she entered my room.

"Sweetie!" I mumbled from beneath the mask.

Mary came to my bed, sat on it, and put her arms around me, hugging me closer to her. I could feel the tremors rippling through her body as she fought for control. I patted her on the shoulder. She pulled awey and brushed the tears from her eyes. Before she could say a word, a medical technician, Linzy, stormed into the room.

"Get off the bed!" he snarled.

I tore the mask off my face and screeched, "Get out! Get out!" at the white-haired ex-tower guard. I raised up, struggling to get out of bed, when Mary forcibly threw me back onto my pillow.

She said, "Sweetie, he isn't worth it! He isn't worth it, calm yourself! You'll kill yourself and leave me all alone!"

I leaned back, gasping for air. Slowly I brought my right hand up and brushed the tears from Mary's cheeks. "I love you so," I whispered. "I can't stand to see you treated the same way I am, like dirt."

"Sh! Sh!" she closed my lips with a kiss. "Whatever happens to you happens to me."

She picked up my wrist searching for a pulse. It was irregular and I knew it, but I was curious to see what she would say.

"Doctor, your rhythm is out of kilter," she teased, trying to inject humor into a grim situation. "Who was the doctor who examined you?"

My cough came out as a gurgle. "What doctor? I'm the only physician that has seen me!"

Mary looked at me incredulously. "That's ridiculous!" I could see what was going on in her mind.

Now it was my turn to hold *her* down. "There is no point in your becoming more upset. We know what the State is trying to do. They'd love it if I'd die. No more Coppolino case. File closed."

"I won't let it happen," Mary cooed. Her hazel eyes blazed with anger at some private scene above my head.

I sank back in the pillow and closed my eyes. I heard no more. Later, Mary told me that I fell asleep holding her hands.

She reached home in Sarasota, at 2:00 a.m. on Monday.

The next morning, February 10, Dr. Zaffke came to the hospital and wrote in my medical jacket: "Had a fair night. States he still has trace dull chest ache— no sharp pains. Feels exhausted."

That was it. I didn't even receive the medication that Dr. Eliot ordered!

On February 24 I was discharged, having survived on my own.

On the following day I was called to Dr. Limcango's office. Limcango was chief medical officer for the hospital and a friend of Superintendent Hassfurder. He was worried.

He asked me if I had held any animosity over my care or lack of care. He indicated that he wanted a quiet "house." In the spirit of "making it up to me," he offered to have me permanently transferred to *The Rock* and assigned to the hospital.

I had nothing to lose. It would get me out of the East Unit and I could put my underground clinic back in action. Now I would be at a place from which I really could do some good. Freeman's death-etched face still haunted me.

I was back on "G" floor awaiting my transfer, and I was finally receiving the full medical treatment as outlined by Dr. Eliot.

Four weeks later I was still unassigned because Mr. Carlton was so incensed by my transfer that he refused to approve it personally. In addition, he was beside himself at the thought of my working at the hospital where I could see first-hand how horrible things were.

Eventually, it took a direct order from Superintendent Hassfurder to have me assigned to the hospital. But my troubles were far from over.

Each time I attempted to enter the hospital, I was stopped by Mr. Hitchcock, the hospital administrator, that monster of an ex-tower guard. One day he bodily threw me out of his office into the corridor, screaming, "I'll call you if I need you!" Dr. Limcango heard the ruckus and when I told him what happened, he stormed to the Adminstration Building to see Hassfurder. Twenty-four hours later a written order was posted concerning my assignment to the Raiford Hospital.

Meanwhile, Mary and the children were delighted I was again out of the East Unit and back at *The Rock* where they could bring me some home-cooked meals. I would constantly plague Mary with questions concerning the transcript. Had Judge Crews received it? Did he make his report to the Second District Court of Appeals? I began to have uneasy feelings about the situation. Rumors from convicts reached me that the Attorney General's office was putting pressure on Powell Reporting Service to not transcribe the hearing. Georgieff knew that once the judges of the Second District Court of Appeals read the facts, my chances for bond were very, very good.

Every time I would ask Mary about the transcript she, in turn, would call Harry Gonzalez. Finally, on March 5, Gonzalez called Judge Crews at the Alachua Court House to remind the judge that the court reporter had not submitted the transcript. Crews responded by saying that he didn't have it either and would need it before he could submit his findings to the Court.

On March the 7th, Gonzalez sent Crews a letter confirming their telephone conversation about the lack of a transcript. By this time Henry had developed the same uneasy feeling that I already had. Something wasn't right.

On March 31, Gonzalez sent me a letter saying he was still awaiting the commissioner's (Crews') report.

Life went on. Jerry had me moved from "G" floor to 3T into his cell, #13.

And what a cell! It consisted of four double bunks occupied by safe-crackers, armed robbers, burglars, jewel thieves, and a "murderer." Besides the four bunks there were eight metal lockers, any number of floor fans, and a kitchen table with two chairs.

Foolishness was the order of the day. The Dinger was a born practical joker and was constantly shorting sheets, putting salt in bed linens, doing a "Three Stooges" routine of one crazy thing after another. It was ludicrous, but it made the time pass by.

Chess was serious business with the men; Jerry or Dick would take me on, beating my brains in on the chessboard. Soon, instead of winning one game out of ten, I began to win one out of three or four. However, I never was able to beat Dick consistently. Dick was bright, intuitive, and blessed with a high I.Q. He had been a successful yacht broker before he became one of the country's most successful jewel thieves.

At other times they would take turns showing me how to cheat at gin rummy or how to pick a lock, or how to forge identification papers, pass phony checks, or embezzle. Eventually they gave up. I just didn't have a criminal mind and couldn't see the "edge," as they called it. I would look at any business problem honestly, which would make their heads spin in disbelief.

The barred windows of cell #13 faced toward the visiting park and across the street toward the parking lot. Each Sunday I would shower, shave, dress in my "whites," and stand at the windows, straining my eyes to identify the people arriving at the parking lot. My constant worry was that something would happen to Mary on the highway. After all, it *was* five hundred miles round trip. How many times can a person tempt fate and get away with it?

The Dinger fixed my problem. He used a couple of cardboard rolls from toilet tissue taped together along with some eye glass lenses we had on the 3T floor, and presto—a telescope! Now we could see our visitors!

Unfortunately, the guards heard about our invention, shook our cell down, and found and confiscated the telescope. The Dinger made another one. The guards found that one and took it. Jerry made the third one. That also went the way of the prison shakedown. Finally we ran out of lenses and had to give up.

JUNE, 1969

There still was no transcript, no finding of fact by Crews, and, therefore, no ruling by the Court. Anxiety never left me. I pushed Mary about the transcript. She pushed Henry. On June 17 the Second District Court of Appeals entered an Order denying my petition for bail pending appeal. It also entered an Order, on the same day, vacating the appointment of Judge Crews.

Mary came to visit me on the following Sunday to bring me the bad news. She knew how desperately I was counting on this bond. She knew that despite the history of failure
PART 2G—CRIME
Crime, Part 2, Galley 39

Mary came to visit me on the following Sunday to bring me the bad news. She knew how desperately I was counting on this bond. She knew that despite the history of failure, this time I had made no allowances for a denial. She was worried. How many blows could my feeble heart endure?

What a black Sunday! Mary held me while I ranted and raved, working myself into a rage, then despair. For five hours she pleaded with me to hold on, to do nothing foolish. She loved me and needed me. If something happened to me, she would be totally lost.

We were sitting at a corner table of the visiting park. Miraculously, there wasn't anybody sitting close by. We sat hand in hand, two forlorn people on a deserted island. "Mary, Mary, how could they?" I kept saying over and over and over again. "All the affidavits and testimony by the physician show how seriously ill I am—that further imprisonment would kill me!"

Mary kissed my lips, cutting off my moans of self pity.

"Henry told me," she said, "that he had lunch with one of Second District Court officials. He told Henry that the Appellant judges could not get Crews to move. He also said that the courts suspected the Attorney General's office told the court reporter to delay transcribing the hearing to force a denial."

"On top of that," Mary continued, "Powell Reporting Service sent Henry a bill for $162.00, for typing and preparing the transcript. Powell made out that bill June the 18th, the day after the Second District turned you down!"

"Now, Mary, what other disappointments are in store for me?"

"I don't know, Sweetie. But Henry will think of something. He plans to ask for a re-hearing and put everything that happened right in the record."

My Mary was right. Gonzalez struck swiftly and hard.

On the 18th of June he sent the following letter to Powell, the court reporter:

June 18, 1969

Mr. Leo Powell
Court Reporter
Jacksonville, Florida

Dear Mr. Powell:

On February 7, 1969 a hearing was held at Raiford State Prison on the above captioned matter. At the time of hearing you attended as requested by Judge John J. Crews. After the conclusion of the hearing the Court requested you to transcribe the proceedings so as to file with its findings. As you will recall, I also requested a copy of said transcript in the presence of Judge Crews and George R. Georgieff of the Attorney General's office.

On April the 30th, 1969, after sufficient time had passed for the transcript to be available, my secretary called to ascertain when we could expect our copy. She was advised that it had not been transcribed, but as soon as it was, a copy would be forwarded to my office.

On June 16, 1969, my secretary again called to ascertain when we would receive our copy of the transcript and this time she was advised that no one had ordered the original and until someone did, we, of course, could not receive a copy.

I have just received an Order of the District Court of Appeals which has vacated the previous Order appointing Judge Crews as jury commissioner. Undoubtedly, your negligence in not providing a transcript as directed by the Court on February 7, 1969, had a direct bearing on the action on the District Court of Appeals and unquestionably deprived my plaintiff, Carl A. Coppolino, of a fair determination of the issues. I do not know why Judge Crews did not pursue this matter with more diligence, but I certainly feel that my client's rights have been jeopardized and further action would be taken.

In view of the above I am especially requesting you to prepare the original and one copy of the testimony that was presented on February 7, 1969, in behalf of the Appellant, Carl A. Coppolino, *immediately* and have same sent to me. Any expense incurred shall be paid by this office. I am awaiting the original and one copy of the transcript.

Very truly yours,

Henry Gonzalez

On July 2, 1969, in his petition for re-hearing, Henry put the facts in front of the Court, and ended with point 23.

That your Petitioner has been denied a fair and impartial hearing on the issue of bail because of the negligence of the court reporter in not transcribing the testimony as requested and by Honorable Judge J. Crews not complying with this Honorable Court's order to submit his findings promptly. That because of the very nature of this petition and the basis upon which said petition is predicated, it is of utmost urgency that all of the testimony, especially the medical findings, be submitted to this Honorable Court for proper adjudication of this petition.
WHEREFORE, upon the foregoing reasons the Petitioners move this Honorable Court to reconsider its petition denying bail pending deposition of this appeal and that after consideration of same and the testimony presented in support thereof, that this Honorable Court direct the supersedeas Bond to be set in a fair amount.

Dated this second day of July, 1969.

Respectfully submitted,

Henry Gonzalez

It didn't do any good to petition, for re-hearing was denied in August. And to add insult to injury, the State took action to force us to pay the bill submitted by Powell Reporting Service!

Gonzalez, in a fit of anger, sent a stinging letter of refusal to Frank Schaub on September 24. In it Henry pointedly stated: "It was primarily because of the negligence of the court reporter and of Judge Crews that the petition for re-hearing was not considered by the Second District Court of Appeals."

The State again showed how strong it was. Gonzalez's letter was ignored and in April, 1970, Powell threatened to sue Gonzalez if he didn't pay the bill.

Mary and I paid.

JULY, 1969

The next step in my appeal was to ask the Florida Supreme Court for relief and Gerald Alch, Bailey's partner, wrote me a letter saying that Bailey had submitted an appeal to Florida's Supreme Court, but that they expected it to be denied. Alch went on to say:

"Upon our appeal's being denied by the Florida Supreme Court, which is not an unreasonable assumption, we shall then immediately bring the matter to the attention of the United States Supreme Court."

AUGUST—OCTOBER, 1969

I'm a grandfather! I received a telegram from Mary today. "Heidi delivered. Mother and child doing well, a boy."

Heidi had gotten married October, 1967, to a young Costa Rican named Juan Murillo. She was now living in San Jose, Costa Rica.

I wanted desperately to be with my step-daughter for the delivery of my first grandchild. Certainly there would be more since I have four daughters, but this was *the first!* There's only one first time. Nothing can replace those feelings of sharing and wonderment that it brings.

Mary went to be with our step-daughter and spent ten days in Costa Rica.

NOVEMBER—DECEMBER, 1969

Meanwhile, other things were happening outside of prison, in the family.

The Chief of Detectives of Monmouth County, New Jersey, John Gawler, committed suicide on the eve of a Grand Jury investigation into Mafia ties. Gawler was the detective who came to Sarasota County Jail and took me into custody to fly me to stand trial in New Jersey.

On top of this, the Monmouth County prosecutor, Vincent Keuper, was suspended, under the cloud of the same investigation. Keuper later on would be investigated by federal law enforcement officials for Mafia connections. After my acquittal in New Jersey, Prosecutor Keuper made a statement that even though he did not have enough evidence to pursue my case in court, he felt under the public pressure that he had to prosecute me!

Monmouth County jail warden, Earl Smith, who had made life miserable for Mary and me, dropped dead in the street during an argument!

The latter part of 1969 was a bad time for the Coppolino family. It was holiday time again, and I was still locked up in a cocoon of concrete and steel.

Mary had had several conversations with the director of the Division of Corrections, Louie L. Wainwright, in an attempt to have me transferred closer to home. Each time Wainwright said he had no objections, but each time nothing happened.

And the five hundred mile round trip continued taking its toll on her and the children.

My sole Christmas present was from the Florida Supreme Court—the quick decision dismissing my appeal. Finally, I was within striking distance of the United States Supreme Court. After all, that was what Bailey had been telling Mary and the media and using in his speeches—"Wait until we get to the Big Court!"

PART TWO

The Nightmare Continues

RAIFORD HOSPITAL

The hospital smell was easily recognizable; whether it was diluted by the size of the ward or concentrated around one bed, it choked the nose and throat, turned the stomach, and sickened the heart. There were many variations, and each told its own tale of gangrene, intestinal disease, abscesses, and putrefying flesh.

The convicts clothes were all impregnated with the smell. It went right under my skin and became part of my own breath. It stayed with me from one morning to the next as if I had never left the wards, and as if it would stay with me until the day I died.

Raiford Hospital would have looked the same in the Middle Ages: the peeling green paint, cracked riddled walls, the long rows of rusted metal beds covered with dirty linen and filthy patients, the weight of hot, fetid air bearing down upon me as soon as I entered the scarred and cracked front door.

All sense of place and time was wiped out for those men isolated by sickness. As soon as I came in each morning to help the patients, I had to close my eyes and ears to what I saw and heard; otherwise, I would become ineffective.

The story has been told and retold by thousands of convicts in hundreds of prisons across this land, in newspapers, and magazines, and sometimes on television.

Since I had first-hand knowledge that my health wouldn't be preserved unless I took my own measure of protection, I wasn't surprised to see the outright disregard of symptoms of illness by the prison doctors.

When a prisoner became ill, he became vulnerable. The sicker he got, the more vulnerable he became. As soon as the convict realized that no one cared—or worse, that things might be done to him that might kill him—he became first hopeless, then full of hate and rage.

Dr. Carl Menninger said it all when he wrote in his book, *The Crime of Punishment*, "thus, hidden from public gaze, with citizens enjoying a sense of security in thinking they are being protected from the lawless by modern, civilized methods, the terrible, dreadful prison regime grinds on, an endless contest between caged animals."

Whether he be in Attica, San Quentin, the state prison in New Mexico, or Raiford, a physician who is also a convict has a 360° view of prison life. Working in an atmosphere of bitterness, hate, and distrust takes its toll.

Many physicians have become involved in prison work because they couldn't make it any other place. This was the problem at Raiford. What we had were ill-trained, out-of-date physicians who would have been thrown out of any medical society and "free world" hospital. There were many examples of medicine practiced "Raiford style". Four come immediately to mind:

SEPTEMBER, *1969*

Wendell Smith, a while male, forty years old with only two and a half months left on his sentence, came to the hospital complaining of severe arthritic pain affecting all his large joints. After a cursory examination, Smith was admitted to the hospital and treated by the prison doctors with aspirin and prednisone. Smith's condition remained the same with swollen joints and complaints of pain. Naturally, the prison doctors wrote him off as a "chronic complainer."

After two months of this "treatment," I couldn't stand by any longer and do nothing. I arranged with a convict who operated the x-ray equipment to take Smith's chest x-ray. Naturally, this had to be done underground. After the chest x-ray was taken and dried, I read it. The diagnosis was obvious—cancer of the lung.

Unfortunately for Smith, his cancer had been ignored for two months, and even *worse*, it had been fed and fueled by steriods. And his prison doctor still didn't know about the cancer.

There wasn't a thing I could do; his cancer had spread too far. On the day Smith should have walked out of prison a free man, he lay on a slimy mattress in Raiford Hospital in a coma. Mercifully, he died shortly after that.

OCTOBER, 1969

Green—a huge, well-built black male, came to the hospital complaining of chest pain. The prison doctor on duty was of the opinion that the man was faking. He received no treatment.

Quietly I ran my electrocardiograph. It showed marked changes in all the leads, suggesting coronary insufficiency. Green kept complaining of intermittent chest pain. The prison doctors ignored him. Green died at 2:00 a.m. of an acute coronary occlusion, a heart attack.

NOVEMBER, 1969

Orville Platt was confined to maximum security in the East Unit on "N" wing for months of solitary confinement. He was brought to the hospital in a coma. He weighed ninety pounds. His clothes were caked in filth. He had long fingernails and matted hair. The stench from his body made me gag.

I started an intravenous of five percent Dextrose and water, 1,000 ccs.

Four days later Platt was dead with no diagnosis, no treatment—except for the I.V. I had started and kept running.

DECEMBER, 1969

Albert broke his leg in a very mysterious manner and was admitted to the hospital where he had his leg put in a cast by the prison surgeon.

During application of the cast, Albert was very nervous, with facial twitches and muscular tremors.

Later the same day, while I was making my hospital rounds, I found Albert unconscious. Spirits of ammonia and painful pressure stimulus failed to revive him. I called the prison surgeon. Hours later, when the surgeon finally arrived, Albert has slipped into a deeper coma. By this time I had started an intravenous, on my own say so, and made sure Albert's airway was clear.

The prison surgeon arrived and started to punch and slap Albert. At the same time he was screaming at the top of his lungs that Albert was faking! Getting no response, the prison surgeon walked away. Into the room walked the prison psychiatrist.

The prison psychiatrist ordered Thorazine 50 mgs. t.i.d. In other words, he ordered that Albert receive a potent tranquilizer three times a day when Albert was already in a deep coma! The prison psychiatrist also ordered a Levine stomach tube and a Foley bladder catheter.

Later that night, Albert was still unresponsive. I took his temperature which was 102°. Here was my chance to do something to save him. After I ordered a portable chest x-ray, the convict took the plate, developed it, and dried it so I could read it. The x-ray showed that Albert had pneumonia of the right middle and lower lobe of his lungs. By stethoscope, I could not hear any breath sounds over the involved area. The diagnosis was obvious: pneumonia of the right lung.

I went down to the antibiotic room and made a 3,000 cc. solution of dextrose and saline to be administered intravenously and put in bicillin 1 1/2 million units. I started the I.V. and asked the convict ward nurse to keep Albert's temperature down with cool towels.

Albert never received any official treatment while he was in the hospital. The medication he did receive, he received from me and his brother convicts. We did all we could to make sure he did not receive any of the "thorazine." It would have killed him.

The prison officials knew full well what conditions prevailed at Raiford Prison Hospital in 1969.

Dr. Kenneth Babcock, retired director of the Joint Commission on Accreditation of Hospitals, was retained by the state in 1968 for a report on the medical services throughout the prison system. His report concerning Raiford Hospital read in part:

a. Obsolete building—too many people in the building, too little space for things to be put. On any given day there may be as many as 130 patients in a hospital designed to serve 75. Sick calls average 400 visits a day.

b. Insufficient insect control—no screens on windows, window panes broken— signs of rats and mice.

c. Sanitation at Raiford Hospital, as compared to the cells, lavatories, and kitchens in the prison proper, is worse.

d. An archetypal obsolete physical plant suffering from an extreme shortage of competent personnel.

e. Hospital rooms contain four double deck beds crammed into less space than the United States Public Health Service considers the minimum for only two patients.

f. Physiotherapy facilities are pitiful, with no equipment and no therapist.

g. Treatment facilities for chronic asthmatics and men with emphysema are inadequate. The men with these diseases, under the tension of prison life, really suffer.

As if the hospital conditions weren't bad enough, we also had a drug ring working right out of the hospital. Anybody, but anybody, could buy any drug —and amphetamines, heroin, pot, LSD and cocaine.

Since the convicts did not have a manufacturing plant, and since the hospital pharmacy did not stock these drugs, the question arose, *where did they come from?*

The answer was simple: the employees of the Divisions of Corrections who worked as symbols of law and order brought them into the prison, right into the hospital.

Some eventually got caught: medical technician Green, June 29; medical technician Houlahan, June, 1970; medical technician Wilcox, May, 1972; medical technician Browning, August, 1970. However, most of the employees weren't discovered and continued to reap huge profits.

The problem became so wide open that the convicts came on sick call just to buy drugs from the medical technicians, whose prices were cheaper than street prices! More and more men were showing up in their cells overdrugged, while other convicts were dying from overdoses of illegal drugs.

At this time Wainwright was making his visits to Raiford, receiving reports in his office at the Administration Building, but life and death went on at Raiford.

My experience with Albert, the persistent useless death, made me embark on a dangerous course of action. I decided to expand my underground clinic to include diagnosis and treatment. This was dangerous because if I were discovered, I would be sent back to the East Unit immediately and placed in solitary confinement.

Fortunately, there were some very good convicts in key positions in the hospital. By good I mean good medical technicians, interested in the welfare of their fellow men, able to maintain complete secrecy and not afraid of getting caught.

The convicts I worked with were placed in the x-ray department, laboratory, central supply (in order to obtain medication), and the operating room (to have access to the autoclave so I could sterilize syringes and needles.) I had made up two complete medical kits: one was secreted in the hospital proper and the other hidden on 3T.

My practice was extensive and didn't cost my patients one penny since I had no overhead! I felt that I was doing the job the prison doctors should have been doing. More importantly, I saved lives.

I performed minor surgery: lanced boils, extracted cysts, incised and drained abscesses, and sutured wounds that occurred during night fights.

I examined the lungs of those men who were told by medical technicians and/or the prison doctors that they had colds. But the *rales rhonci* I heard through my stethoscope told a different story. I would send these men for chest x-rays and blood tests, to confirm the diagnosis of pneumonia, and then would institute antibiotic treatment.

Despite my efforts, the butchery at the hospital didn't stop.

FEBRUARY 13, 1970

Tiger Taylor, a while male, swallowed three tablespoon handles. This was Tiger's way of seeking attention. One time he swallowed parts of a transistor radio. This time it was the spoon handles. The prison surgeon decided to teach Taylor a lesson. The prison surgeon operated on Tiger Taylor. He cut open Taylor's abdomen, cut through the skin, connective tissue, musculature, peritoneum, and then stomach. Finally, he extracted the spoon handles. Technically, it was an adequate performance. Unfortunately for Taylor, it was done WITHOUT ANY ANESTHESIA!

Taylor's pitiful animal screams could be heard, not only throughout the hospital corridors, but even outside the buildings.

FEBRUARY 16, 1970

Dykes, a white male, swallowed a pen and pencil. He was operated upon by a different prison surgeon. He was strapped down to the operating room table. His surgery was done WITHOUT ANESTHESIA! Dykes' blood-curdling screams would have made you retch.

FEBRUARY 16, 1970

Rayls, a white male, was a very depressed convict. He swallowed a piece of wire. The unfortunate man was operated upon by two prison surgeons WITHOUT ANESTHESIA! Rayls wailed horribly, endlessly, in torment. Pretty picture? Right?

FEBRUARY 20, 1970

Burk, a white male, had swallowed a spoon handle in November, 1969. At that time he was operated upon by the prison surgeon. Now in February of 1970 he had swallowed two more spoon handles. At this time the prison surgeon decided to teach him a lesson. Yes, you can guess what happened, he was operated upon WITHOUT ANESTHESIA!

APRIL 15, 1970

Richard Walls, Sr., serving a twenty-five year sentence, came to the clinic complaining that he "felt weak and dizzy" and had shortness of breath. He was admitted for observation. No electrocardiogram was taken even though Walls was fifty-one years old.

The records showed that he was given an injection of Coramine, a stimulant, and an appointment was made for a physician to see him nine days later on April 24.

Walls didn't live to keep it. He didn't live out the day. Shortly before 11:30 p.m., he collapsed complaining of severe pains in his stomach and chest. Minutes later he was dead.

Eleven days before his death, Walls had visited the clinic to complain of chest pains, but had received no treatment.

APRIL 23, 1970

Jack Reynolds, a white male, came to the hospital complaining of chest pain. He had a history of congestive heart failure; therefore, I ran an electrocardiograph on Jack which showed an anterior wall infarct. Unfortunately, I couldn't get the prison doctor who was on duty to come in to see Reynolds. All I was able to do was to give Jack some oxygen.

14 hours later a prison doctor did arrive to see Reynolds. In the interim, Jack's electrocardiograph showed paraxismal ventricular contractions, artrial flutter, and atrial fibrillation.

On April the 25th, Reynolds had more chest pains; again I ran an electrocardiograph which showed me an extension of Reynolds' myocardial infarction. He still did not receive *any treatment* until two days later, the 27th. On April 27, Reynolds was placed on the critical list. He died the next day.

Around this time another incident occurred, showing the general contempt and disdain prison officials had for convicts.

Milton Frank, a convicted forger, tried for days to get treatment for an injured hand, but a medical technician told him, "Don't bother me, you Jew bastard; get out of here!" Finally, gangrene set in, and Frank's hand had to be cut off.

MAY, 1970

Besides trying to fight the irresponsible medicine practiced by ignorant prison doctors, I continued to pray for my own release from prison.

Bailey filed my printed brief with the United States Supreme Court and sent me a copy. I went over the detailed brief line by line. This was supposed to be my ticket to freedom.

After reading the brief and discussing it with some friends whose opinions I valued, I felt that I was, at long last, about to enter the "Promised Land."

Unfortunately for me, at this time Bailey was having problems in Washington. Lee was Executive Director of the Professional Air Traffic Controllers Organization (PATCO) and that organization and its members were engaged in a "sick-out." The Federal Aviation Administration were incensed at Bailey since they felt he was very active in this "sick-out." They had a psychiatrist put together a profile of F. Lee Bailey. The FAA's panel of doctors came to the conclusion that Bailey was "dangerous" and "not responsible." To tell you the truth, their findings didn't take me by surprise.

In addition PATCO was maneuvering to have their famed attorney fired. Bailey was claiming that he had received no pay from PATCO and even suffered financially for his services to the Controller's Union. To dispute this, PATCO Board members gathered up more than $90,000 in cancelled checks that had been paid to Bailey.

With the national airways paralyzed, the Secretary of Transportation, John Volte, former governor of Massachusetts and no friend of Bailey, came down hard on Lee.

Newspaper articles were referring to Bailey as "Little Caesar" and other people began to question Bailey's mental processes.

Finally Lee was subjected to a disbarment proceeding which ended up in a censure.

This was the climate in Washington that greeted my brief at the United States Supreme Court, a brief that had on its front cover the name of F. Lee Bailey.

JUNE 1, 1970

Barwick, a twenty-three year old white male, was found unconscious in his cell (#6) on 3T at 4:00 p.m. The men came to me in cell 13 to get me to look at him.

My examination revealed that Barwick was bleeding from his right ear; he had a broken jaw and discolored, puffy eyes. I placed him on the push-cart that was our ambulance and wheeled him to the hospital where he was seen and examined by the prison surgeon, Dr. Miguel, at 5:30 p.m.

X-rays were taken which showed a fractured skull and a jaw fractured in three places.

A tracheotomy was performed and I.V. started by me. Dr. Limcango refused to send him to the hospital in Gainesville. Instead, Dr. Limcango ordered 75 mgs. of demerol and 50 mgs. of thorazine! This medication was given to Barwick, a patient who was unconscious with a head injury!

JUNE 2, 1970

Barwick stopped breathing at 6:00 a.m. I gave him artificial respiration with the Ambue. Barwick's blood pressure was 80/60; his pulse was 140 beats per minute. Barwick's pupils were fixed. I was the only physician present. Finally, the prison doctors arrived at their regular working time, 8:00 a.m.

Superintendent Hassfurder arrived at 9:00 a.m. I talked with Hassfurder and begged him to send Barwick to Gainesville. Hassfurder agreed with me. Four hours later Barwick was transferred to the Gainesville Hospital at the University of Florida Medical Center. Barwick died at 8:00 p.m. on June 3, leaving his parents, a wife, and a child. He had served half of a six year sentence.

Now came the big investigation. Why wasn't Barwick's skull fracture properly treated? According to Dr. Carlos Hernandez of the prison hospital staff, nobody knew he had a fractured skull because of inadequate x-ray equipment. Yet the x-rays clearly showed the fracture!

The heat on Raiford Hospital continued to build.

JUNE 3, 1970

Remember Tony Gentile, tough Tony on "F" floor? Gentile collapsed on the ball field. He was carried to the hospital by a few of his convict friends. The medical technician on duty, Green, did not treat Gentile. I ran an electrocardiograph on Tony which showed unmistakably that he had suffered an acute myocardio infarction. Tony died a few hours later. He'd meant a lot to me. And I had to watch him slip away because they just didn't care.

Medical technician Green was subsequently fired, not because of the Gentle incident, but because he was caught sleeping on the job.

JUNE 23, 1970

William Lester, a white male, appeared at the Discipline Court in the East Unit. Poor, thin, insipid Lester had made a "threatening gesture." So the guards in the Discipline Court room smashed his face, stomped on him, and broke his right arm. The prison surgeon "repaired" the arm.

On June 23, 1970, a bombshell finally dropped on Florida State Prison Hospital at Raiford. Nationwide attention was finally focused upon conditions at the house through a series of columns written by Jack Anderson, the Washington columnist.

The material that appeared in the columns was gathered by Les Whitten, Anderson's chief aide. Les was no stranger to Mary and me. He had been with the Hearst papers during my trials and eventually would write a biography of F. Lee Bailey.

This is how Anderson's June 23 column started—"Chilling tales from inside the United States penal system . . ." It went on to describe some of the atrocities I've related among others. One paragraph of the column read: "The main section of the prison where the report tells of these atrocities was run at the time by Captain J. E. Edwards, described as a "sadist alcoholic."

On the heels of this column, Hassfurder immediately transferred Edwards from the main section of the prison to a smaller housing area.

Mary started to get calls from The Press regarding my welfare, as Anderson's columns detailed the horror I dealt with daily at Raiford.

JUNE 29, 1970

The United States Supreme Court refused to grant certiorari. My direct appeals had come to an end. I had no idea what to do or where to turn. My health was holding its own, but I was approaching my third year in prison, and the situation at Raiford was at an all-time low.

JULY 4, 1970

There was no question that tension was building among both convicts and guards. Little incidents of friction were blown way out of proportion. The guards overreacted to the slightest real or imagined provocation.

At this time Raiford had a very small cadre of Black Muslims. These poor guys were vilified by the prison officials in every possible way. They were given no literature and no newspapers; they received the worst prison jobs and constant harassment by the guards, who forced the convicts to wind up in Discipline Court, and solitary confinement. Since they were blacks, they also received the worst medical care. There developed deep feelings of hatred by the Black Muslims for the whites, not only for the white prison officials but for *all* the white population. A plot was hatched by the Muslims, a plot that would definitely end in a blood-bath. I found out about it because one of the leaders, whom I'll call Elijah, took me into his confidence. It wasn't a break of their security at all. I was deliberately told because Elijah knew I had something they needed—my underground clinic. Elijah wanted to know if I could and would get involved to the point that I would take care of their wounded, no matter what!

Elijah and I had met in the yard after the mid-day chow. Walking along the "track," I asked the tall, well-developed convict about the plot. His shrewd eyes coolly appraised me. "Can't tell you, Doc."

I shrugged my shoulders. "Then I can't help you."

We walked several hundred feet more. Elijah moved slowly, but with infinite grace. His eyes were now covered by sunglasses. My eyes checked the gun-towers, the fence, the position of the rest of the men. Was anybody overly curious about the two of us? Anybody? Guard *or* convict?

Elijah broke the silence. "Can't do it, Doc."

"Look," I said, still darting my eyes around our environment. "If I'm going to patch up the wounded, I've got to know what I need. I have to know how bad this jump off of yours will get! After all, I can't call an order in to our friendly local drug store! I'll have to be prepared. Or some of you will die needlessly, with or without my cooperation."

Elijah sighed and scratched his head. "Today is June 27, right?" he plunged on without waiting for an answer. "Okay, we may jump off on the fourth. We have weapons. We have gasoline. And you know what?" Elijah grabbed my shirt sleeve.

"What?" My eyes kept up their relentless vigilance.

"You're walking on our arsenal!"

I stopped dead in my tracks.

Elijah jerked my arm. "Not now!" he hissed. I had stopped by the third base of the ball field.

"We've got the knives and gasoline right here." Elijah grinned. His pearly teeth gave his sombre face one thousand watts of light.

Wow! I thought. Gasoline burns! My mind ticked off what I would need: furacin dressings, sulfonyl bandages, and a way to get at the place where they were located in the hospital.

"I have seven days to get ready, right?" I asked.

"Maybe."

We kept walking. "What do you mean, maybe?"

Elijah was quiet. I peeked at his face. From behind the dark sunglasses I could see unmitigated rage.

"I think we have a leak, Doc, a rat. I think the hacks are suspicious. We may have to postpone it."

"Okay! No problem." If Elijah suspected a leak, I thought, then a lot of people in cells were in for a severe shake down. That definitely was enough to postpone the blowoff.

"But we've got something else in mind in case we get ratted out, Doc." Elijah paused. "Let's sit down on the grass." He led me to the middle of the field. There wasn't a soul within fifty feet of us.

"Look!" he began. "You get visits, right?"

I nodded, wondering what the hell Elijah was getting to. "You know my wife and children come to see me every Sunday."

"Right. Well, I think you'd better write to your old lady and tell her to cool it for awhile."

Now he was going too far. No way. "What the hell are you talking about?" I spat angrily.

"We're going to take over the visiting park."

Elijah saw the look on my face and smiled. "Yeah, man! the visiting park. You see, the brothers feel that unless the world knows what's going on in here, we are all going to be murdered, slow but sure."

I couldn't argue there!

"So," Elijah continued, "we take over the visiting park on a Sunday. We snatch all the visitors. What are the hacks going to do? Shoot? Naw! We'll kill a few if they mess with us! And they can't wait us out since we got broads and kids. You see?"

I saw all right. I saw screaming children and hysterical mothers! Their fathers, the convicts, would be just as frightened.

"Where are the weapons?" My throat was dry. The words came out muffled, but Elijah didn't seem to notice. He was caught up in the excitement.

"The knives are buried in the park under the bushes and flower beds."

Elijah got up. He stood towering over me. "Remember, Doc, tell your family to cool it. I would hate to see you and yours get it. Besides, we need you." He turned on his heels and walked away.

I mailed home two letters that night. I couldn't very well explain to Mary what I had learned. The mail was censored, but I had to be sure that she and the children stayed home for awhile. So I wrote: "The bees and wasps are stinging all the visitors. It is better if you and the children don't come to see me for awhile."

Needless to say, Mary ignored both letters and was at Raiford that Sunday, bright eyed and bursting with curiosity. The only concession she made was to come alone. She urged me to try to stop Elijah. I shook my head and told her that things had gone too far.

"Mary, they don't care if they live or die!" We clung to each other and found a quiet table in a corner of the visiting park. It was a grim, gray day. "You know what's going on at the hospital! In addition, the men and guards are ready to jump at each other's throats." I took a deep breath. "That's what makes the situation so dangerous. These black people want to be treated like human beings. They want better medical care and more paroles. They're willing to pay the price to get it, even in blood and lives."

We ended our visit with my promise to keep trying to get Elijah to change his tactics.

It turned out that Elijah's suspicions were well-founded. The administration geared up for battle. All shifts of officers were called in and *The Rock* was taken, shaken, and every cranny combed. Hundreds of knives and glass jars, plastic buckets, and metal cans filled with gasoline were confiscated.

Next came mass arrests, lockups and dispersals of convicts, white and black, involved or not involved. It was a good time for the correctional officers to square away all grudges.

At 5:30 a.m., streams of convicts, handcuffed or chained, were whisked away to other institutions like the East Unit.

Miraculously, Elijah wasn't discovered. Later I learned that the Black Muslims decided to hold off their secondary plans concerning the visiting park until a more propitious time. They would wait less than one year before becoming involved in violence. As far as I know, even at this writing in February, 1980, those weapons and gasoline are still buried under the flower beds in the visiting park!

JULY—OCTOBER, 1970

It seemed to me that every newspaper sent a reporter to Raiford to examine the hospital and talk with the convicts. I spent more time ducking the media procession than taking care of my patients. I didn't need the publicity even though the reporters particularly asked to see me. One reporter from the *Medical World News* was so miffed when I refused to talk with him, he threw a tantrum directed against me on the editorial page of that magazine!

There was one investigator I wanted to talk with, Les Whitten, Jack Anderson's aide, and a friend. The Tallahassee prison officials, Wainwright and Company, challenged Jack Anderson to come into the prison system without escort and see what he wanted to see and talk with whomever he wished. Anderson took up the challenge and planned to send in Whitten.

Meanwhile, hospital deaths continued.

JULY 8, 1970

Amos Jackson, a black male, aged 50 to 55, was admitted in good health and scheduled for a hemorrhoid operation under spinal anesthesia.

He was operated upon July 9. On July 10 the prison doctor diagnosed Jackson as having a cerebral vascular accident despite the fact that Jackson could move both arms and legs and his blood pressure was only 120/80.

On July 12 Jackson stopped breathing twice. On July 13 at 6:10 p.m. Jackson died. The death certificate was signed out as CVA. In actuality, there was sufficient evidence available to suspect spinal meningitis caused by Jackson's receiving contaminated spinal anesthesia.

SEPTEMBER 10, 1970

The medical technician in charge of the N.P. annex was constantly drunk and often slept on the job. On this particular day, a convict patient named "Red" Barber, a white male, was clammy from perspiration, extremely pale, and horribly nauseated; he was having chest pains.

I examined him and made a snap diagnosis of acute myocardial infarction. The medical technician at first ignored my pleas to get Barber into the hospital proper. After an hour or so of pleading, the technician strolled Barber to the main hospital. The prison doctor on duty diagnosed Barber as suffering from anxiety. End of diagnosis. Shortly after that Barber died.

SEPTEMBER
END OF THE MONTH

David Rich, 24, a hemophiliac, had been writhing in his encrusted hospital bed in the hallway, screaming with pain for four days. His knee was swollen with blood. Rich threatened to stab himself in the knee to relieve the pressure of the internal bleeding.

At this point, Les Whitten arrived. At first he was surrounded by correctional officers, but Whitten complained bitterly and the officers disappeared into the woodwork, like roaches.

Whitten arrived at the hospital that morning and we greeted each other warmly. He told me that my friends in the media were concerned about me and that he had spoken with Mary.

I gave Les what infomation I had, including the incident about Rich and his suffering. When Dr. Limcango learned that Whitten was headed for Rich, he rushed up and ordered the demerol to kill his pain—and keep him quiet.

Jack Anderson's article came out on October 1, 1970, and was as hard-hitting as any piece of writing I have ever seen. Part of the article read:

> The most depressing place was the hospital where Whitten saw patients lying in the hall like beggars in Bedlam, trying to get a doctor's attention. Cockroaches skittered up walls, and ants filed busily to food spots on the floor."

The article also detailed the horrors committed by medical technician J.J. Murphy, the same man who had allowed Freeman to die.

Wainwright was quick to deny the charge, and attacked Jack Anderson as being unqualified to judge the professional ethics and the decisions made. However, I was qualified and had names, dates, and primary documentation.

DECEMBER, 1970

F. Lee Bailey was unusually silent after the denial of our apeal by the United States Supreme Court. After all, Lee had maintained loudly to all the world that the "Big Court" would be the shining beacon of justice to set me free.

Gerald Alch, Bailey's associate, told Mary that if by faint chance the United States Supreme Court failed to hear the case, the firm would proceed by filing a petition of habeas corpus with the Federal District Court in Tampa.

It was December. Almost six months had passed since the United States Supreme Court denied our petition, and Bailey had not filed the petition for habeas corpus. Mary wanted to know from me whether she should call Lee. I advised against it. Hadn't Alch said specifically that Bailey would file? Yes. Then there wasn't any point in calling. Either Bailey would file or he wouldn't. I knew that PATCO was still giving Bailey trouble. In fact, they eventually fired him.

Finally I heard from Bailey indirectly. Terri Plaut was now no longer a secretary-investigator, but an attorney. She wrote me asking if I would like to confer with her about the petition.

I answered by saying that according to Alch, Bailey was going to file, and since I didn't know a thing about law, I saw no point in our meeting.

I had a fairly good idea why things were not happening. It concerned money, naturally. Perhaps this was the reason Plaut wanted to meet with me, under Bailey's urging.

In addition, I had come to the conclusion that unless some new evidence came to light, I wasn't going anywhere with my appeal.

Henry Gonzalez had promised that he would keep close tabs on Tallahassee to see what course I should take in my efforts to be free.

Meanwhile, another event occurred that almost cost me my life—a riot!

FEBRUARY, 1971

The bitterness of the men over the lack of paroles, the despicable medical treatment, the legal murders in the hospitals, and the crowded and obscenely dirty living conditions set the stage for an explosion.

It came on Thursday, February 11, 1971. The East Unit witnessed a bizarre phenomenon that eleventh day of February. Almost one thousand men refused to leave their cells and report for work or go to the mess hall for their meals. Tompkins, the assistant superintendent, frantically called Tallahassee, informing Wainwright of the situation.

Urgent meetings were held between the administration officials and correctional officers. The one thing Wainwright didn't want was a full-scale riot. Being a successful politician, Wainwright was afraid the resulting publicity would push him right out of his job.

While these things were happening at the East Unit, I received a report at the hospital from sympathetic correctional officers, confirmed by the convict "grapevine." I learned that Wainwright had met with my good friend, Judge Joe Peel, in an attempt to defuse the building fury.

By early Friday morning there still was no settlement of the unrest at the East Unit. The news had spread throughout the compound. And there was a sit-down at the East Unit!

Elijah and his Black Muslim group held a secret meeting with the leaders of several white factions and they made their peace. White and black now joined hands. The plan? A peaceful sit-down at *The Rock!*

On Friday afternoon the usual 1:00 p.m. call went out for the squad to line up to go to work on the ball field. Nobody made a move. Blacks and whites, several hundred strong, sat down. Just like that!

The correctional officers were in a complete panic. There was an element of humor in their reactions. They were stumped. Captain Johns gathered together his goon squad. This was the same Johns who, as a lieutenant, had been implicated in the mysterious death of an inmate at the East Unit. At that time, he had been reprimanded, then subsequently promoted to captain by Wainwright.

Johns and his men forced some of the convicts back from the yard and into their cells, leaving about seven hundred to eight hundred men still sitting on the ground on the ball field.

By this time all shifts of correctional officers had been called in, armed with shotguns, machine guns, tear gas, and rifles. They surrounded the ball field fence.

Wainwright and Attorney General Robert Shevin were on the scene. Shevin was perched in a gun tower, so he could have a better overview of the field. Wainwright was closeted with Superintendent Don Hassfurder trying to figure out the best way out of a disaster rapidly heading for chaos.

Finally, twenty-one black and white convicts acting as spokesmen and a negotiating team met with Wainwright and the other prison officials.

The convicts demanded better medical care, inmate counsels to represent the prison population with the prison officials, reorganization of the parole commissions system, and fairer practices in the canteen.

After three hours of discussion, an impasse was the only result.

Small groups of men were sitting on the ground, huddled together against the cold February wind. Others were standing in the center of the ball field, smoking and talking. Still others were singing "peace songs" in chorus.

As dusk approached, the field remained surrounded by the armed guards. Loud speakers kept blaring commands that the men move off the field to their cells, but not a man moved.

The protest singing continued. Some of the men broke wooden benches into pieces and set them aflame along with other scraps of wood. The small blazes kept some of the cold away from the huddling convicts. Some of the men were dressed only in shirt-sleeves; others were fortunate to be wearing their blue windbeaker jackets.

Trouble suddenly erupted. Prison Inspector McLendon fired three rounds of tear gas at the inmates. It covered the whole field. Some of it blew into the windows of my cell. I started to cough and sneeze and my eyes were smarting from the gas. The men on the ball field were lying down in a desperate attempt to avoid the fumes.

Next, the air was filled with sounds of gun shots as shotguns, rifles, and machine guns were fired at the convicts lying down on the field. It was the old proverb come to life—like shooting fish in a barrel. The cries of the wounded men could be heard over the firing.

I ran down the stairs out into the road and over to the hospital. Somebody would have to take care of the wounded. At the hospital, I found two nervous medical technicians and some of my convict nurses. No prison doctors were present.

The wounded arrived. Scores of helmeted, fully-armed guards dragged and kicked about 75 bloody convicts into the Out Patient Clinic.

I grabbed a suture set, Methiolate, sterile forceps, and bandages, and began to pick out birdshot from the less severely wounded. There were two seriously wounded men in the corner. One convict, black, had a pellet in his eye. Another had a .45 caliber bullet in his abdomen.

Some of the men were milling around, wide-eyed, obviously in shock. Some were mumbling, "They shot us! They shot us!"

Others sat on the cold floor, backs propped against the wall, staring out at nothing.

I started intravenous fluids on some of the more critically wounded and tried to reassure those convicts that I knew. Some of the men were old like Radio Joe, a man in his late sixties. He aged right in front of my eyes.

Superintendent Hassfurder came limping into the OPC. I was the only physician on the scene at the time. Hassfurder came over to me and asked me how badly the men were hurt. I described all the wounds as best I could, including the two seriously wounded.

The superintendent seemed to listen to me. He had deep black rings under his eyes, and weaved when he walked, and slurred his words.

"The crazy bastards!" Hassfurder complained. His breath caused me to take a step backwards. For some reason he seemed compelled to explain what happened. "Carl, we only used the weapons as a last resort, and then only after the inmates had been warned four times to get back in their cells."

He gaped at me, his eyes glassy. "They thought we were going to fight with them with billy clubs and sticks! We sure surprised the bastards when we started shooting!"

"Any of the officers hurt?" I asked.

"No. There were no physical injuries to the staff, just verbal abuse. It looked as though the inmates were about to throw rocks," Hassfurder said.

I swallowed hard. The smell of blood permeated the very air we were breathing. The moans of the wounded assaulted my ears; yet here stood a man who condoned this senseless shooting because his men were verbally abused!

By this time some of the prison doctors arrive. Dr. Carlos Hernandez began to make sketches of the wounds of the prisoners. Ten of the convicts were admitted to the prison hospital. The black with the buckshot in his eye, Peoples, was sent under heavy guard to the University of Florida Medical Center. There he would lose his eye. On Saturday morning the newspapers covered the "riot" in banner headlines. At first the State claimed that the convicts were shot because they were storming the fences surrounding the ball field. Later, the State had to retract that story. The false story was the first mistake. The second mistake was allowing visitors to come into the institution on Sunday, February 14.

Sunday morning was the mob scene. The telephone lines to the prison had been jammed by calls from loved ones who were horrified from reading and listening to the media description of the full-scale shooting of convicts who had only been lying down on the ground.

The visiting park was jammed. Some of the wounded, in bloody bandages and arm slings, told their visitors in great detail what happened.

Letters splattered with blood, screeching for help, were smuggled out of the prison and sent off to Jack Anderson and Les Whitten. Other letters went to editors of other Florida newspapers like *The Miami Herald*.

Mary arrived bright and early. She was relieved I wasn't hurt and proud that I was involved in healing the men wherever I could. I warned her that things were going to get worse and they did.

FEBRUARY 15, 1971
MONDAY

The grounds of Raiford Prison were under heavy guard by the state Marine Patrol. At approximately 2:30 p.m. I stood at a window on the second floor of the hospital, trying to take care of patients. I watched the comings and goings of the guards. My friend, Santos, was standing beside me. I could see the Marine Patrol guards armed with helmets and shot guns under the orders of the assistant superintendent of Raiford, R. V. Turner, who was marching a group of convicts toward the flat top solitary confinement. I recognized Lieutenant Griffis, Lieutenant Barton, and Sergeant Harris, who were carrying shot guns.

As the group walked along the hospital, the men on the second floor, both patients and workers, cat-called and hooted at Turner and the Marine Patrol.

"Stop!" Turner shouted to his squad.

The heavily armed patrol came to a halt.

"Up there!" Turner pointed toward the general direction of the second floor windows and me. Turner shrieked, "Shoot! Shoot! Shott!" The Marine Patrol hesitated. Turner, eyes wide—I was approximately twenty feet away from him, looking down—screamed "Shoot the bastards! Shoot the bastards!"

Shot guns fired into the second floor window and Santos knocked me off my feet. As I lay on my back, stunned, I saw a shot gun blast take out the window where I had stood just a fraction of a second ago. A second volley of shot gun blasts ripped through the second story windows. The sick patients in their hospital beds were moaning, trying to crawl out of their beds and onto the floor.

I peeked over the sill and saw Wainwright and Hassfurder standing together on the grass about fifty feet away from the firing Marine Patrol. Calmly watching the proceedings. Like a picnic.

Suddenly the front door of the hospital smashed open and Turner, completely out of control, stormed in accompanied by some of the helmeted armed guards.

They ran up the stairs onto the second floor and screamed at the convicts and medical technician, McBride. Turner ranted that if he saw us looking out of the windows again he would *kill all of us*.

Then he turned and left.

At this writing, February, 1980, R. V. Turner is Superintendent of Glades Correctional Institution of the Florida Prison System.

FEBRUARY 16, 1971
TUESDAY

Reports were coming to me from my friends in the East Unit. Armed troppers were beating the convicts. At least twenty-two men were forced to run a gauntlet of armed guards and were systematically beaten with billy-clubs.

Governor Askew had sent in a team of investigators and had heard the facts from my convict friend, Joe Peel. According to Peel, the victims were called out of their cells after the armed officers entered each of the eight wings of the maximum security prison to warn the prisoners that "from here on out there will be no more strikes." The prisoners were assembled on the bottom floors of their respective wings for the display of force which included guards and state Marine Patrol.

Investigators found out that this occurred within the sight and approval of J. T. Tompkins, Major McKenzie, R. V. Turner and J. C. Combs (Tompkins is now Superintendent of Polk Correctional Institution of the Florida Prison System; McKenzie is now head of the Florida Prison System Juvenile Program.)

The national media had a field day. There were charges and counter-charges. The ACLU attorneys filed petitions in Federal Court in an attempt to have the federal judge issue an injunction to halt the State's continuing brutalization of its prisoners.

Jack Anderson wrote another column on February 19, based on the letters and documentations smuggled to him and Les Whitten. Mary was very instrumental in this maneuver.

The Anderson column shook up Governor Askew. The Governor refused to allow Whitten or Anderson to tour the prison.

Wainwright, meanwhile, had been pinned down by the media because of the differences between the stories he had released and the actual facts. The media turned on him.

The Federal judge in Jacksonville ordered a rapid hearing on the ACLU petition. The petition itself, as reported in *The Times Union*, Jacksonville's newspaper, was a litany of horrors:

PRISON SEEKS FEDERAL TAKEOVER

Charging that inmates are being subjected to shootings and beatings, a suit filed here is asking that Raiford State Prison be placed under Federal authority.

The suit, filed on behalf of two named inmates and thirty-four who are unnamed, charges that forty-three prisoners have been wounded by gun fire and that more than three hundred have been placed in maximum security and beaten by prison guards.

It charges also that since last Friday, the prisoners have been harassed, beaten and tear-gassed without being formally charged with any offenses and without access to legal council.

Named plantiffs are James Peoples, who the suit said is believed to be confined to Shands Teaching Hospital in Gainesville, and Alfred St. Laurent confined to the main unit at Raiford State Prison. The other plaintiffs are listed as "John Doe" on behalf of thirty-four other inmates.

They demand a temporary restraining order against further action by the prison administration.

Listed as defendants are Louie L. Wainwright, Florida Director of Corrections, Don Hassfurder, Raiford Prison Superintendent, R. V. Turner and J. T. Tompkins, Assistant Superintendents.

A charge that these officials and others are violating the civil rights of the inmates as guaranteed under the first, sixth, eighth and fourteenth amendments to the United States Constitution. These cover free speech, right to counsel, cruel and unusual punishment and due process and equal protection of the law.

The suit also cites the 1964 Civil Rights Act.

The suit charges that on February 12 about 7:30 p.m. about five hundred inmates were fired upon by other prison officials "at point blank range with automatic weapons and shot guns with lethal caliber buck-shot." It charges the shots came without warning as the prisoners were gathered peacefully on the athletic yard.

These same guards and officials immediately after injuring forty-three inmates on the field, fired into windows of adjacent occupied cells of the main housing unit. Some of these inmates were later confined to maximum security cells in the "flat-top" and beaten with billy-clubs and other riot weapons, the suit charges. Last Saturday it charges, the flat-top area was filled to capacity.

More beatings occurred on Monday, it charges, and says the prison personnel released tear gas in the confinement area, and that the guards had to leave the area because of the density of the gas.

While marching a line of inmates past the east side of the prison hospital, the suit charges, the guards or other officials fired buck shot into the hospital windows and that on Monday the guards entered the prison school and intimidated the teachers and threatened inmates with arms. It charges more beatings occurred on Tuesday.

As of Wednesday, it charges further, more than two hundred inmates had been confined and beaten in the flat-top area and more than one hundred in the East Unit. It claims beaten inmates were being denied medical treatment.

It claims the actions against the inmates are taken without formal charges and with minimal investigation hearing or chance for the inmates to face their accusers or to rebut any charges.

The suit says the actions constitute cruel and unusual punishment contrary to established practices in penology.

For the next month, there were hearings held and legislative committees formed to find out what happened and why it happened and what could be done to improve the prison situation.

Wainwright found himself grilled by the media and legislative committees. He replaced Hassfurder as superintendent and gave "medical reasons" as the basis for his decision. Marvin Davis, and an NAACP field secretary said, "They're using him," meaning Hassfurder, as a scapegoat. We insist that Louis Wainwright be the first to go. The whole rotten prison hierarchy must go!"

Meanwhile Assistant Superintendents R. V. Turner and Jim Tompkins and Chief Correctional Officer Curtis McKenzie were accused by convicts and a prison guard, named Roberts, at the Federal Court hearings of leading the guards who beat prisoners with clubs, slugged them with rifle butts, and punched and kicked them without provocation.

At first Wainwright refused to take any action against these three men; however, he finally relented and suspended or demoted some of his prison officials. Later, Wainwright promoted or rehired them.

By September, 1971, it was obvious that nothing significant had happened with the Florida Prison system.

APRIL, 1971

Henry Gonzalez was still trying to help me with the parole commission. The February riot brought some changes on the drawing board. Two of the present sitting commissioners resigned and it was hoped that their replacement would be more humane.

My health continued to improve. However, since the state through Georgieff had made such a determined effort to keep me in prison by changing I was a "phony," Gonzalez said it would be best if I could get an updated report on my medical health sent to the Parole Commission.

Dr. Carlos Hernandez was now medical director at the Raiford Hospital. Because of my professional help during the February riot I was able to prevail upon him to send a detailed report to the commission. His report coupled with Professor Eliot's stand was in stark contrast to Assistant Attorney Georgieff's allegations.

This was Dr. Carlos Hernandez's report to the Parole Commision:

Medical report on Carl A. Coppolino, M.D.

This thirty-nine year old patient has a history of heart disorder going back to 1962. At that time at the age of thirty he first noted retrosternal pain radiating to his left and right arm with nausea and diaphoresis. It happened one day while walking. Electrocardiogram taken within twenty-four hours was found abnormal. He had a bygeminal rhythm and was placed on quinidin and later Procaine Amide for this arrhythmia. This medication was continued for about three and one half years. Subsequently he had multiple occasions of similar symptoms until the present with at least six or seven episodes with syncope associated with these episodes.

Patient has been examined by numerous internists and cardiologists during the last six years and was told he had coronary insufficiency and an anginal syndrome.

In December of 1968 patient was evaluated in the Cardiology clinic at Shands of The University of Florida at Gainesville by the Cardiologist, Dr. Robert S. Eliot, Associate Professor of Medicine. Prior to this time patient experienced coughing spells with wheezing mostly at night. He had nocturial and minimal ankle edema. Chest film with barium at that time revealed a normal heart size and no abnormalities of the lungs. Electrocardiograph was consistent with posterior inferior myocardial infarction.

It was determined that Coppolino has ischemic heart disease manifested by an old inferior myocardial infarction, and anginal syndrome and dysfunction of a papil-lary muscle with mitral reflex. This was suggestive of minimal ventricular failure and it was recommended that the patient be digitalized. He was admitted to the hospital 1/14/69 and released a week later improved. Diagnosis at that time was status post myocardial infarction and anginal syndrome. Patient was followed up with Puro-digen 1 tab daily, Isordil 10 mgm 1 tab t.i.d., and was medically regraded #3—capable of light physical activity.

Patient experienced anginal episodes again in June, 1969, and admitted to the hospital June 23 in 1969 because of dull chest pain. He was discharged one week later with medication unchanged from the puri-digin and isordil. In addition he received nitroglycerin tabs p.r.n. as needed. Patient has been maintained on this medication without any major difficulties. He is fully ambulatory and works at Raiford Hospital as instructor for the hospital nursing staff.

Since July, 1969, his nitroglycerin medication has been replaced with nitrospan capsules. With this regimen of purigidin and isordil, and ni-trospan, the patient has been maintained in excellent condition. He was practically asymptomatic until January, 1971. At that time he noticed nocturnal chest pain with increase of his heart rate. Pulse was up to 110 beats per minute without clinical evidence of nocturial or ankle edema.

On February 8, 1971, inderal was added to his medication beginning with 10 mgs. 1 tab twice daily. He responded well and his spells of nocturnal pain and pressure and fast heart rate disappeared completely. Patient was finally stabilized on inderal with a dose of 40 mgs. daily besides his purodigen, isordil and nitrospan. It can be said Coppolino improved considerably with the addition of inderal to his regimen and he has stayed asymptomatic until the present showing no evidence of anginal syndrome or any clinical findings of cardiac failure. He has maintained his weight ideally around 150 to 155 lbs. (5'11"). Electrocar-diogram on April 2, 1971, showed a definite improvement compared with the previous tracing.

Final diagnosis: 1. Ischemic heart disease with status post old inferior myocardial infarction, and 2. anginal syndrome, improved, asymptom-atic at present.

MAY, 1971

On May 4, Governor Askew's investigating team submitted its report to the Governor.

In addition to what I know and have written, the investigators learned that Major McKenzie at approximately 7:00 p.m. on February 16, 1971, on

"P" wing in the East Unit, did the following: maced five inmates directly across the eyes, although he knew that mace might cause blindness; employed a tear gas grenade to quiet the wing when noise resumed; and employed pepper fog gas throughout the wing to quell the disturbance. All inmates, at the time, were locked in individual cells.

The report goes on to say "the testimony and facts summarized above suggest that the employees involved in the inmate beatings may well be subject to prosecution in the state courts for crimes against the person of inmates . . ."

The Governor's investigating team's report focused upon Assistant Superintendent R. V. Turner and Major I. C. McKenzie as those responsible for participating or aiding and abetting the use of excessive physical force and/or the infliction of corporal punishment.

As I wrote earlier, not only was nothing done, neither firing nor prosecution, but Wainwright promoted McKenzie and re-hired and promoted Turner.

JUNE, 1971

The prison officials at Raiford showed signs of softening their attitude toward me. I had a progress report, and for the first time the classification committee hinted that soon I would receive a recommendation for parole!

Henry Gonzalez felt that I was making progress and thought that I should get together as much support as I could prior to being seen by a parole commissioner.

Because of the February riot, legislation had been passed which mandated that the Parole Commission interview each inmate at least once a year. I thought that my turn would come in November or December.

Newspaper reports pointed out the benefits to inmates because of the new law on parole interviews, benefits to other inmates, not to Carl A. Coppolino. In the July 29, 1971 issue of the *St. Petersburg Times*, Parole Commissioner Francis Bridges said that I would be interview sometime in the next six months; however, Bridges explained that I would receive only a "therapeutic interview." When questioned by The Press for a definition of therapeutic interview, Bridges said "A therapeutic interview means that the man is interviewed so he can't complain that he hasn't been seen by a member of the Commission. In other words, it doesn't mean a thing."

So I could only watch as Parole Commissioners came to Raiford and began handing out paroles. Convicts with second degree murder convictions were being paroled after serving three years to five years, even though the averae time spent in prison before parole was usually seven years.

After much discussion, Mary felt the time was ripe for her to go to Tallahassee to see the chairman of the Parole Commission, J. Hopps Barker, and report back to me.

AUGUST, 1971

The meeting with the chairman of the parole commission, J. Hopps Barker, turned out to be a bitter experience for Mary.

From conversations she had with Sheriff Ross Boyer prior to meeting with Barker, Mary knew that the chairman was opposed to my release on parole. Sheriff Boyer, who was instrumental in securing Barker's appointment to the Commission, could not get the chairman to listen to attempts to "mitigate" my conviction. Boyer's approach was the following: a. Boyer was the chief law enforcement investigating officer in the Coppolino matter; b. his investigation never turned up any concrete evidence against Coppolino; c. he was suspicious of the nature of the medical test as testified to by Umberger and Helpern; d. I was not a criminal nor the criminal-type and e. the conviction, although legal in his opinion, should be mitigated by early release.

In addition the Commission had received positive input concerning me from state legislators, religious leaders, and businessmen of Sarasota County. Also, as a further sign of softening by the prison officials, several Florida State Prison employees has written favorable letters to the Commission on my behalf, no doubt in response to my care and treatment of the wounded convicts during the February riot.

Barker's response to the information contained in my record and to Mary's pleas was violently negative. He told Mary that, although he sympathized with her plight of trying to reunite her family, he had not planned to interview me until April, 1977! Ten years after my conviction he planned only to interview, not grant parole!

However, Barker went on; since the legislature saw fit to change the law, he and the other commissioners were now compelled to interview me at least once a year, and my turn would come by November or December.

Mary tried to show him that I was a burden on the taxpayers; that all that was being done was "warehousing me"; that prison offered nothing for a man like me, no education, no skills beyond one in crime, no goals, no dignity. She asked him how long he thought I could survive in a closed society, a society predominately homosexual, a society built on hate, run on fear, without being totally destroyed. Barker's answer was that he didn't know, and his attitude indicated he was unconcerned.

Again Mary pleaded that besides her need for me, for her emotional support, financial help, our children were being raised in a broken home. They were the real losers, and that all we wanted was a chance to pick up the threads of our lives and try to live productively.

Despite paroles being given out indiscriminately in an attempt by the commission to remove public pressure from its record of inactivity, to minimize the pressure in the prison by reducing the population, and to short circuit a legislative move to vote it out of existence, Mary's pleas fell on Barker's deaf ears.

I had been prepared for the worst, but was shaken when Mary told me what the commission had originaly planned: to interview (not release) me in 1977! Six years away!

Frantically, Mary and I sought some way to break through Barker's obvious antagonism. Despite letters, phone calls, and personal contact by Henry Gon-zalez, I was left with the prospect of trying to convince whatever Commissioner came to interview me, to give me a parole.

NOVEMBER, 1971

Two members of the Parole Commission had resigned under the weight of the legislative investigation in the February riot, and two new men were appointed, Ray Howard and Armond Cross. I would be seen by Cross.

I tried to find out as much as I could about Cross prior to the interview. I learned he was about forty years old and had been appointed to the Commission the previous month. He was born in Bristol, Florida, the state's smallest county. He joined the Commission in 1957 and served in Bartow, Quincy, Tallahassee, Marianna, and Pensacola offices until he was named Area Supervisor of the mid-Atlantic coastal area in 1967.

After a nerve-racking one week's postponement, Armond Cross called for me, that bright, chilly, November 10 morning. I went to the classification offices to see him.

Sergeant Norman, one of the best correctional officers at Raiford, had been in the office and had spoken to Cross on my behalf. Norman told me later that Cross sat there behind the desk impassive, expressionless, as Norman outlined my excellent prison record.

Next, Dr. Carlos Hernandez entered the room and spoke with Cross in his official capacity as medical director. After about fifteen minutes, Hernandez came out and told me not to expect any favorable action.

Now it was my turn. I took a deep breath, thought of Mary and the children, and entered the office. Cross sat behind a battered wooden desk, his elbows propped on the table, my file opened in front of him. His brown suit jacket complimented his reddish-brown hiar.

"My name is Armond R. Cross; I'm a parole commissioner." His voice was heavily accented and sing-song.

"Congratulations on your appointment, sir."

He smiled.

I occupied the chair directly in front of him.

"I am here to interview you about a possible parole plan. Now you understand," Cross hastened to add, "that this doesn't mean you will be given a parole." He wiggled in his chair, leaned forward and said, "Tell me all about it."

I took a deep breath and began. "About five years ago I was convicted in Naples and sentenced to life at Florida State Prison where I have remained. Since that time I have keep a good record, taking care of my wife and children . . ."

I continued like this for about twenty minutes, emphasizing that my marriage had become stronger, my four children (two of Mary's, two of mine) had welded into a complete family.

"Why did you stop your appeals?" Cross interrupted.

I explained that I couldn't drain the family emotionally, physically, and financially with incessant appeals. "What would it accomplish?" I asked Cross. "The same people who believe I'm guilty will continue to do so even if I win my appeal, and the people who believe I am innocent will have been justified. It would be useless."

"So," Cross interjected, "despite the fact that you had one of the country's best lawyers defending you, that a jury of your peers found you guilty and your appeals have been denied, you still maintain your innocence?" His voice ended on a note of incredulity. I felt as if I had been kicked in the chest.

"Certainly. But," I hastened on, "I don't blame the jury for coming up with a compromise verdict. After all, Judge Silvertooth admitted to Schaub, Bailey, and me that he was totally confused by the medical evidence and couldn't understand it. If the judge couldn't follow the case, what can anyone expect from a jury?"

"Well," Cross said in a sonorous voice, "we can't make a mockery of justice and turn you loose." As I listened to Cross, I thought about two men just released on parole, one who had served five years on life for second degree murder and the other who had served four years on life for armed robbery, but I knew I had to keep my mouth shut! "Normally," Cross continued, "your past history and perfect prison record would be enough to recommend parole. But, in your case, I feel you haven't been in prison long enough and I believe prison acts as a deterrent." Cross paused, "Therefore I am going to recommend to the Commission that you be interviewed by another commissioner next November."

Despite my control, my face must have reflected some measure of despair, because urgency crept into Cross' voice.

"There is no question that you'll be paroled some day. So continue the good work. Keep up the good prison record!"

Cross beamed. It was over. I mumbled my thanks and left the office. Another year . . . next November? Suppose I blew my good prison record by not living that long? Would my family *ever* have me home?

Later that evening I was granted permission to telephone Henry Gonzalez. I gave Henry the bad news. He assured me that he was still trying to break through the impenetrable wall of the Parole Commission.

That Sunday Mary arrived for her visit and I told her what had happened with Cross. We didn't kid each other. After all, Barker had already tipped the Parole Commission's dealings in his conversation with Mary. Despite our feeling of gloom, Mary decided to see if she could put some pressure on the Commission.

Over the next 30 days, Mary sought the support of Governor Rueben Askew, Representative Quillian Yancey, Chairman of the Criminal Justice Committee, Representative Jim Tillman, Chairman of the House Committee on Prison Reform, and Sheriff Ross Boyer.

Nothing positive came of her efforts. In fact, Chairman Barker sent Mary a stinging letter in response to her letter to Governor Askew. He put his hard-nosed attitude in black and white.

January 5, 1972

Dear Mrs. Coppolino,

Your letter to the Governor has been taken up with this office.

What I told you on August 3, 1971, when you came to my office, was that under the old system, we had not planned to interview your husband until April, 1977, but under the new law requiring us to interview everyone annually, we had scheduled him for an interview in October but that an interview did not mean a parole in many cases. You will recall that I had the conversation recorded.

Your husband was interviewed on November 10, 1971, and he was continued. This interview, too, was recorded. He is now scheduled to be seen again in November, 1972.

Very truly yours,

J. Hopps Barker
Chairman

CHRISTMAS, 1971

The holiday season was here again and I could feel the tension building up among the men. Fights and knifings became commonplace. The February riot had in actuality accomplished nothing. True, two members of the Parole Commission had been replaced, and true, more men were being paroled, but the backlog was so huge that it would take some time to see any positive effects.

Medical care at Raiford was still of the same category, little or none; however, money had been allotted by the legislature for a new hospital and qualified personnel. I hoped that in short order there would be a dramatic improvement.

I had my annual progress report and lo and behold, I was formally recom-mended for parole! In addition, my custody was lowered to minimum, so that I could be transferred to a lower custody prison.

Naturally I was pleased with the Division of Corrections' formal recommendation for my parole. However, I felt, in view of the attitude of Barker and Cross, that it was a futile maneuver. In my judgment, the Parole Board would file the report and my record and accomplish nothing. They would have achieved as much by sticking a gold star on my forehead.

The only recourse Mary and I felt might work now was a move for a transfer to another institution closer to home.

JANUARY, 1972

Keeping this decision in mind, I decided to look for a law firm that could allow Mary and me to deal with Louie Wainwright and ultimately with the Parole Commission. Henry Gonzalez still had no results, and it was from obvious speaking with him that he felt he couldn't do a thing for me. He told me on the telephone, "Doctor, I can do a lot of things for a lot of people, but when it comes to you, I can't do a thing!"

It was a time to reach out for a new face, a new law firm, somebody who could get results. But who?

There were certain criteria that had to be met; first, it would be a Tallahassee law firm, an established firm, not one trying to make its name on my name through the media. I had a bellyful of that with Bailey. And I wanted a firm with clout and an impeccable reputation.

My choice was narrowed to one firm, the law firm of John Madigan and Julius F. Parker. John Madagin was the registered lobbyist for the Parole Commission and for the Florida Sheriffs' Association. In addition, the firm has associated with the former chief justice of the Florida Supreme Court, Millard Caldwell. Justice Caldwell had been sitting on the Florida Supreme Court when my appeal reached that court. Therefore, he was well aware of all the ramifications in my case.

Mary spoke with Parker by telephone, since Mr. Madagin could not actually represent me in view of his relationship with the Parole Commission.

Parker told Mary before he or Mr. Madagin accepted my case that they wanted to see if they could be effective in my immediate transfer to a prison closer to home, or parole. They would investigate and be back in touch with her. Meanwhile, I became more and more bitter and depressed as each agonizing day marched off into oblivion to be replaced by another. Try as I could, I could not shake it.

By this time I had a good staff of convict nurses working with me at the hospital. My underground clinic became "visible" but the prison hospital employees turned a blind eye as I continued to practice medicine.

Naturally, problems still existed. On January 5, Mr. Todd Baden, medical technician, was arrested for dealing in narcotics, syringes, and needles. In addition he was caught bringing in a pistol with fifty rounds of ammunition and selling it all to a convict named Kirby.

Despite the progress I was making treating my patients, I felt essentially useless. I really had no value, I told myself. The children didn't need me. They had their mother. Mary didn't need me. She was quite self-sufficient. The Parole Commission was never going to let me go, and unless I could prove the State used falsified medical evidence, I never would get out of prison through the courts. In sum, I felt as if I were an albatross weighing heavily on the family's neck.

Of course, the love of my wife and children, their support, and the gratitude I received from the families of the convicts I had helped caused me to pick myself up and strive to make each day better than the day before, and to hope tomorrow might be better than today.

Then a little ray of sunshine peeked into my darkened room. Representative Jim Tillman came to visit me.

Representative Tillman was minority leader of the Republican Party, Chairman of the Appropriations Committee for Criminal Justice, Chairman of the Committee for Prison Reform. He was at Raiford making one of his periodic tours and asked to see me.

We met in the Conference Room of the old administration building. I had on my mind the fact that Tillman had championed my cause with J. Hopps Barker.

Representative Tillman was a big, beefy individual and looked like a cattle rancher—which he was, in addition to being a legislator. That day he wore a checkered sports coat and cowboy boots. His face was full and his sandy hair was flecked with gray. We shook hands, sizing up one another.

"Doctor, what a pleasure," Tillman said softly and slowly.

"My pleasure, sir."

We occupied a pair of comfortable wooden chairs beside a well-polished table. The smell of leather and tobacco filled my nostrils. It became easy to forget this was still prison.

Tillman started talking about Mary. He mentioned how fortunate I was to have her "out there," what a fantastic woman she was, and how everybody who knew her liked and admired her.

"Everybody but Hopps Barker," I snapped.

"Seems that way," Tillman shifted in his chair. "Can't say I understand Hopps. Worked with him many a year. I always thought him to be a fair, practical man." His voice drifted off.

"Except when it comes to the Coppolinos," I prompted. "What's his problem?"

"I don't rightly know. He wouldn't say anything about you; he just asked if I would be willing to be treated by you. And I'm sure Hopps meant it very sarcastically." Tillman shifted his gaze to the other side of the room. "I told Barker quick enough that if I needed medical attention and you were in the vicinity, you'd get a call."

"Well, thank you, Jim." Tillman's sincerity deeply affected me. "Do you have any suggestions about parole?"

"First, I'd get transferred from Raiford. This place means one thing to the public—vicious, mad-dog criminals. Can you get a transfer?"

"I had a progress report last month and the prison officials lowered my custody and recommended transfer. But it really is up to Wainwright."

"I have a meeting set up with Louie Wainwright next week. I'll ask him about moving you closer to home, say Avon Park or DeSoto Correctional

Institution. It certainly would make it easier for Mary, and after five years of traveling five hundred miles round trip each week, she needs a break. Besides, that would put you under a different Commissioner, Cale Keller." Tillman crossed his legs. "If there is anything like a liberal on that Parole Commission, Keller fits the description. You would have a better chance for parole with Keller next time around."

"Fantastic!" I exclaimed. "But Jim, Mary has spoken to Wainwright all those times, and couldn't get him to budge."

Tillman held up his hand, "I know. I know. She told me. However, I think Louis will listen to me."

Tillman looked at his wristwatch. We had been talking for over thirty minutes. "I have to go, Doctor."

We stood up and shook hands. "I promise to talk to Wainwright about trans-ferring you closer to home. Don't give up," Tillman smiled. "We'll keep working on Barker."

Later that night in my cell I wrote what transpired with Representative Jim Tillman and sent it to Mary. I knew she needed a lift as much as I did.

Mary again tried on her own to have me moved. On January 31, she received her answer from Superintendent Dugger:

January 31, 1972

Dear Mrs. Coppolino:

This will acknowledge receipt of your letter, dated January 14, 1972, in reference to a transfer for Carl.

The matter has been discussed with other authorities; however, we will be unable to act favorably upon your request at this time.

Sincerely,

L.E. Dugger,
Superintendent

FEBRUARY, 1972

Mary met with Julius F. Parker in Tampa and immediately sent me a note, short but containing her excitement. She promised to tell me everything on Sunday.

I was up early Sunday morning and sneaked into the visiting park long before the guard arrived. I found a corner table and covered it with a tablecloth made out of disposable paper towels. In its center I placed a bouquet of roses, sitting in a plastic disposable urine cup. I had plucked the roses from the rose bush in front of the hospital, all the while keeping in the back of my mind that poor kid who wound up in solitary because he gave his mother a rose on Mother's Day!

Mary arrived wearing a stylish new outfit with a high neck and straight skirt. She has even frosted her hair! She still amazed me—and does to this day. Even in little details, she always went all-out to lift my spirits.

She took one look at the table and burst into laughter. She started to unpack what she had cooked for our Sunday meal—roast lamb basted in wine; apple, raisin, and lettuce salad; and chilled strawberries soaked in brandy. We sat at our table, ate, and held hands. Mary told me what Parker found out. We needed to file for petition of habeas corpus in Federal District Court in Tampa based on two points, insufficient evidence to sanction any conviction, never mind second degree, and that premeditated murder by poisoning has to be first degree or nothing. Reading the lesser included offenses allowed the jury to come in with a compromise verdict.

I wasn't pleased. As far as I was concerned, it was old material rehashed. Bailey appealed on the same points, and the Florida Supreme Court had made ruling after ruling requiring the judges to read all the lesser included offenses. As far as the medical evidence was concerned, everybody concerned could say the judge had wide latitude. No, I wasn't happy with the advice and said so.

Mary insisted that Parker knew what he was talking about. Parker felt absolutely certain that the federal judge in Tampa would overturn my conviction.

Even if that did happen, I argued, the Attorney General's office wouldn't give up. They'd appeal the reversal to Fifth Circuit in New Orleans. This would mean more delays, more money.

"You would be out on bond," Mary said, brushing a frosted strand of hair away from her hazel eyes.

I took a deep breath, the scent of Shalimar perfume filled my nostrils. I kissed her gently on the lips.

"He or John Madagin or both talked with Sheriff Ross Boyer and Representative Jim Tillman. They also talked with Roy Russell, the parole commissioner. Fred Parker said he thinks they can help you with parole."

I looked at her. Her eyes glowed and sparkled with happiness. It was obvious she felt good about Parker and had confidence in him. I still felt uneasy. It sounded too good to be true. But then again, I had been pushed around so long. Maybe it was true!

"Tell me about the children," I asked, deliberately changing the subject.

For the next few hours we discussed Claire, Monica, and Lisa. Heidi, of course, had her own life now with her own husband and child in San Jose, Costa Rica.

Claire had had her adventures in college, The University of South Florida. She didn't like her apartment nor her roommate. She moved to an apartment all alone and didn't like that, and now was in another apartment with several roommates.

Monica was engaged in what fifteen-year-olds do, band practice, chorus, and a wide range of school events.

Lisa? Well, Lisa was Lisa, bright, pretty, spoiled, and very southern. "I'll bring them up to see you next Sunday for their monthly visit. They miss you so!"

A sob escaped before I could control myself.

"Sh, sh!" she whispered, holding me and blowing into my ear.
3:00 p.m. It was time to leave.

In the aftermath of the February riot and the screams of outraged citizenry, the 1971 Florida legislature had passed a law creating the furlough program.

This program allowed inmates who were minimum custody, had good prison records and family ties, to be picked up by a family member and to leave the prison for a prescribed period of time.

Several days after Mary's visit, I received a letter from her which made me laugh until tears literally rolled down my checks. She had made an appointment to speak with Mr. L. E. Dugger who was the superintendent at Raiford, having relieved the dismissed Hassfurder. Dugger had been working for the prison for over 30 years. He was a small, rotund, gray-haired man—the grandfather type.

Mary had sought Dugger to ask him to put me in the furlough program. I had been minimum custody since December, had a perfect institutional record, had a family; therefore, I was eligible for furloughs. Of course, the problem was that my name happened to be Coppolino!

Dugger hemmed and hawed with Mary for over an hour. No, he couldn't approve a furlough for Carl. Yes, certainly the doctor deserved one. Yes, certainly Carl was eligible. No, he didn't have any worries about the doctor's escaping or any of that nonsense.

"Then what is the difficulty?" Mary asked.

"Suppose the newspaper found out about it?" Dugger said agitatedly. "Suppose he gets hit by a car on furlough? I'd have a lot of explaining to do!"

Mary laughed at him. "You can't be serious?" she asked.

"Definitely," Dugger replied.

Finally Mary and Dugger struck a bargain: if she didn't press the furlough issue, Mary would receive special passes to visit me during the middle of the week, not only on Sunday. This was a great help since she was working weekends at Sarasota Memorial Hospital, and it was difficult for her to switch schedules.

Meanwhile Dugger promised he would talk with Wainwright and have me transferred to Avon Park or DeSoto Correctional Institution, where furloughs might be easier to achieve.

MARCH, 1972

Racial tensions had reached the incendiary point at *The Rock*. It wasn't only the Black Muslims pushing for their share of human dignity; it was all the blacks.   My friend, Elijah, had left on parole, but I still had strong contacts with the black convict leaders. It wasn't difficult to see the rampant racism being prac-ticed at Raiford.

For example, take the assignment of jobs, with blacks assigned to the most menial and filthiest. If there were a white redneck illiterate and a black convict with a highschool education, the black man would wind up on the latrine detail.

Black nationalists and Black Muslim literature and religious services were often barred, or made so difficult as to cause any service to be ineffective. Individual guards who were racists or sadists or both had ample opportunity to abuse black prisoners. Blacks who were affirming their cultural and racial identity were likely to be singled out. Those men who showed signs of becoming convict leaders or who challenged prison practices through law suits wound up in Discipline Court, solitary confinement, and eventually the East Unit.

The racism at Raiford was consciously encouraged by the prison administration and work supervisors. When the black convict rebelled by seeking relief through courts, appealing to the superintendent and through newspapers, the work supervisors would become enraged and agitate the white convicts under their charge to "fuck up that black nigger bastard," promising the white convicts that there would be no repercussions and even offering them better work conditions!

I knew it was only a matter of time before the explosion. My hope was not to get caught in the middle. Some men were going to get killed out of the build-up of hate. Again, I warned Mary not to come until the situation cooled down.

My black friends kept telling me that they couldn't hold still any longer. Growing numbers of blacks were openly passed over when paroles were considered. They felt their only prayer rested in resistance. After the newspaper coverage of the February riot, the black leaders learned that resistance could achieve results. Most of the blacks I knew felt they were the most abused victims of the racist prison system.

How could I argue with them? Didn't I see racism practiced at the hospital in every aspect of their desecrated lives?

I was in my cell on 2T looking out the window onto the yard. Incongruously, the late afternoon sun sparkled off the gun towers and bathed the electrified fence with rays of gold, giving an aura of wonderland to the penal fortress. In the face of such beauty it took some minutes before my brain registered what my eyes were witnessing.

Black convicts were running down white convicts with clubs, stones, and chains. In another area of the yard, mobs of blacks were beating and stomping on trapped groups of whites.

I saw two convicts, one black and one white, who had known each other for years, beating each other sadistically. Sylvester Williams (black) was pounding Andy King (white) with a brick. King, with a lead pipe in his right hand, struck back.

The sunlight reflected off upraised knives as cuttings, slashings, and stabbings increased in fury. The screams of the wounded pierced the air. Full-fledged military battles couldn't possibly sound more terrifying.

I ran out of my cell, down the hall, into the hospital. The scene there was tranquil, almost bucolic. Nobody knew about the holocaust at *The Rock*. Until I told them!

By the time the alarm had been given by the control room, the Emergency Room and Operating Room at the hospital were fully activated.

Dr. Carlos Hernandez called in all the prison doctors and ordered me to examine the wounded as they arrived and to divide them into categories; those that needed immediate surgery, those that needed minor suturings, and those with minor cuts and bruises.

The wounded arrived accompanied by guards. Some had to be carried in on stretchers. The worst were:

Jackson (black)—multiple stab wounds of the back and abdomen.

King (white)—head battered, semi-conscious. Possible brain damage.

Regan (white)—severed radial nerve of the left arm and multiple stab wounds.

Chambliss (black)—throat cut from ear to ear. Severe loss of blood.

For the next few weeks it was the repeat of the February riot. The hospital and *Rock* compound were hosts to swarms of Tallahassee prison officials and investigative committees.

And as in the wake of the February riot, nothing positive came out of this tragic violence. A few men were punished in solitary confinement, and soon the incident was forgotten.

So much for "change."

APRIL-JUNE 1972

On April 5 I received a letter from my new attorney, Fred Parker. It was the first piece of good news in many a Sunday!

April 5, 1972

Dear Dr. Coppolino:

My law partner, Mr. Madagin, and I had lunch yesterday with Roy Russell of the Parole Commission. I think Roy will vote for and advocate your parole. I also had a short talk with Hopps Barker and have an appointment for more lengthy discussion with him next Monday. Unfortunately, my impression is the same as Mary's, Sheriff Boyer's and Jim Tillman's. I don't think we'll get any place with Mr. Barker.

I am also going to see Mr. Keller next week and Mr. Cross the week after and I am hopeful we can persuade a majority of the commission to vote for your parole at the earliest possible date.

In the meantime, I'm also working on a possible Federal petition for the writ of habeas corpus but I'm holding up filing that petition until we see where we are on the question of parole.

I'll try to keep you posted as well as possible on our progress and we'll do everything possible to secure your early release, either on parole or habeas corpus.

If we are successful, it will be largely because of Mary. She is a remarkable woman. With kindest regards, I am

Sincerely yours,
Julius F. Barker, Jr.

Roy Russell in my corner? Mr. Conservative himself? Maybe this *is it*, I thought.

Mary was not as enthusiastic as I. She vividly remembered the words and attitude of Barker. She repeatedly warned Fred Parker that the Parole Commission couldn't care less about the Coppolino family, and that he and Mr. Madagin had better utilize extraordinary measures in their efforts to secure me a parole.

To re-emphasize her point, Mary wrote Parker on May 22:

"You realize I tried to tell J. Hopps Barker that my children were the real losers, being denied a balanced home as well as their father's love and support. He (Barker) told me while he emphasized, my children and I were not the Parole Board's problem."

Meanwhile my medical clinic continued to flourish, and the needless mortality continued its senseless pace!

JUNE, 1972

Larabee—Viral hepatitis with jaundice and enlarged liver and spleen. Despite the obvious diagnosis, the prison surgeons performed a laparotomy! A useless piece of complicated major abdominal surgery! And Larabee went into partial liver failure, post-operatively.

McGuirty—Complained of right upper quadrant pain associated with burping and belching. All he needed was some antacids; instead he wound up on the operating table. The prison surgeon performed a laparotomy and found nothing.

King—Had a diagnosis of viral hepatitis made at the reception medical center in Lake Butler. He was sent to solitary confinement. He didn't have a physical examination, and received no treatment. After several days in solitary confinement, he was sent to the Raiford hospital. I examined him and found that he had an enlarged liver with a huge palpable mass. King had a tumor of the liver. A hepatoma for which no treatment was given. He died.

Bighem—Fifty years old, obese with hypertension. He had a B.U.N. of 59-86. No other work-up was done. No attempt was made to find out if he was a candidate for the kidney machine (dialysis). He lay in bed for four weeks with no treatment. Finally, the prison doctors realized he had Veterans Administration's benefits and made arrangements to have him moved to a VA center. Two weeks later Bighem was transferred to the VA in renal coma!

Chapman—an air compressor had blown diesel oil and steel filings into his right eye. The prison doctor called it conjunctivitis. He lay in the hospital bed in severe pain with no treatment. Eventually Chapman recovered with partial loss of vision of his right eye.

About the middle and end of June, things started to break. A letter from Parker on June 14 read:

"I don't think there is any chance of parole prior to your next scheduled interview in October. I think the chances of parole at that time are reasonably good . . ."

Then on June 20 Parker sent Mary the following letter:

June 20, 1972

Dear Mary:

Assuming the airplanes are flying, I'm leaving the country today for about a month. We have a rough draft of the petition for habeas corpus, but it still needs work. My plans are to file it at either Tampa or Jacksonville shortly after my return, during the week of July 17. We will have three principal grounds, of which the first is the strongest:

1.   Carl has been denied due process of law because he has been convicted of a crime for which the state produced no evidence, and of which he cannot be guilty.
2.   He has been denied due process twice because his conviction was based entirely on circumstantial evidence, which in turn was based on expert testimony of untried and unproven chemical tests and theories.

3.   He was denied a speedy trial and directly prejudiced by the fact that the state obtained the bulk of its evidence long after he should have been brought to trial.

In my absence, Jack Magadin will attempt to persuade Wainwright to transfer Carl to Avon Park, and we will also be preparing for Carl's next scheduled parole hearing in October. With any luck, he could be a free man before then.

Take heart.
Best regards,
Julius F. Parker, Jr.

I still had considerable misgivings concerning this petition. It seemed that I was making progress concerning parole and a transfer, and I wondered if taking action would in fact hurt me.

Then on June 29 I received the best news yet in a letter from John Magadin:

"I do not want to raise your hopes unnecessarily, but I did talk with Mr. Wainwright last week about your possible transfer, and he indicated that a transfer might be arranged to the DeSoto Prison in Arcadia, rather than Avon Park. As a practical matter this would be closer to Sarasota than Avon Park. Keep your fingers crossed!"

JULY 10, 1972

I'm on my way! Good-bye, Raiford! Hello, D.C.I.!

My good-byes were short. Jerry, Dick the Miami jewel thief, Dominic the Miami armed robber, Lou, and many others of my closest friends had left Raiford long ago for other institutions.

Santos was the only one left whom I genuinely regretted leaving. He didn't need to be in prison any longer, and I hoped he would be paroled before bitterness destroyed him.

The trip down to D.C.I. was an adventure for me. I rode in a State station wagon with two other convicts without handcufs. Our driver was a lieutenant who had spent many years with the prison system. He entertained us with stories about Louie Wainwright, about the time that

Wainwright was captain of the guards at Raiford, and stories about Godwin as a child growing up in the prison playing cards with the convicts.

The greatest pleasure for me was seeing *OUTSIDE*, the highway teeming with cars, the small towns with trees and people and children.

We traveled through towns like Lowell, Bartow, and Arcadia. Finally we reached D.C.I.

As I got out of the station wagon, I was met by Mr. Godwin.

"Hello, Carl!" Godwin said. He wore a pale blue short-sleeved shirt that groaned under the pressure of his huge bulging muscles. His face was unlined and smiling. He hadn't aged a day since the last time I had seen him some four years earlier.

"Mr. Godwin. Nice to see you, sir. Congratulations on your appointment as superintendent."

"Thank you." Godwin nervously straightened his deep blue tie and then thrust his hands into the pockets of his blue slacks.

"Carl, take your personal property and come with me into the control room." He looked at his wrist watch. "I expected you much earlier than this," pointing to his wrist watch which was almost covered with thick hair. It read 3:00 p.m. "What took you so long?"

I laughed. "My driver was telling stories about you and Mr. Wainwright, and I guess he lost track of the time."

Once we entered the control room, Godwin became serious. "Carl, when Mr. Wainwright called me and asked if it was all right with me to send you here, I thought immediately that it was an answer to my prayers." He cleared his throat and looked around. I could see a captain and lieutenant behind the wooden table that stretched like a barrier from one side of the room to the other.

Godwin turned to me. "I want you to live at the hospital and to work there. Most important, I want you to take over the medical problems that I have there."

"Okay, Mr. Godwin. But don't you have a doctor?"

Godwin made a face. "You might call him that. His name is Anderson, Jewel Anderson. I have been on the telephone to Dr. Hernandez practically every day because Anderson has been creating problems. All I want you to do, Carl, is to keep him out of the difficulties he has been getting into lately."

"Oh!" I murmured. This turn of events didn't sound good to me. It looked as if I was getting into a no-win situation. Since I was a convict, I would have to lose any time that push came to shove.

"See you later, Carl," Godwin said and walked out of the control room.

I turned and found two sets of curious eyes riveted on me, the captain's and the lieutenant's. I braced my shoulders and smiled. "Hello, I'm Coppolino 018591." I had my work cut out for me. None of these guards knew me. So there would be problems and some surprises.

The lieutenant was a short, bald-headed man. He said, "My name is Earnest, Lieutenant Earnest. This," pointing to the man along side him, "is Captain Carter." Carter nodded. He was about 6'2", weighed 250 pounds and had close-cropped hair.

"I'm putting you in 'D' dormitory, Coppolino, until you get classified," Earnest said.

I kept my mouth shut. Earnest had heard Godwin tell me that he wanted me to live at the hospital. There was no point in saying a thing except, "Yes sir!" I walked to the laundry which was a small, squat, white brick building situated on the left side of the compound. I picked up a bedroll and turned in my white uniform for a set of "blues."

"D," dormitory like "A," "B," "C," "E," "F," "G," and "H," was a long concrete block building. The dormitory was divided into cubicles that contained five or six single beds plus wooden lockers. Lavatories with two commodes, two sinks and a shower were situated between cubicles. Each dormitory held approximately 50 to 60 men. In the middle of the building was an all-purpose recreation room which contained a television set.

The beauty of the grounds, for those who wanted to "see," was everywhere. Hibiscus bushes lined the dormitories. Towering palm trees split the skyline of the compound into different geometric shapes. Here and there throughout the meticulously kept grounds I could see clusters of gardenias and wild roses.

There were many Australian pines and wild oak trees which shaded the compound buildings. In the trees I could see hundreds of home sites for meadowlarks, blackbirds, woodpeckers, and sparrows.

However, what struck me most was how quiet and clean D.C.I. was compared to the filth and noise of *The Rock*. Even the air smelled better. I felt good, really good. I was close to home.

Mary arrived the following Sunday. It was her first pleasant trip and visit to prison. First, travel time was less than one hour compared to four and one half to Raiford. Second, there was no rudeness and unpleasantness at the gate. She gave her name, asked for me, and walked in. No shakedown, no ugliness.

The visiting area consisted of a long tile and concrete building similar in design to the dormitories. Inside there were clusters of tables and chairs. Outside, in front of the building, was a sloping lawn with chairs and lawn furniture. In the middle of this grassed area was a concrete open air structure that contained concrete tables and chairs. It was a peaceful scene. From that Sunday on, Mary and the children would visit each and every weekend. Our family grew stronger and closer together.

On the following week I was assigned to the hospital. The hospital was a sprawling one-story concrete block building painted white that sat in the back of the compound, close to the posterior fence.

It contained a spacious waiting room with plastic aluminum chairs, two examining rooms, a doctor's office, a kitchen, spacious 20-bed ward, and a private room that contained two hospital beds. This room was obviously sleeping quarters for the convict staff; a black convict nurse and lab technician occupied one bed, I occupied the other.

The staff consisted of a black physician named Jewel Anderson and a competent medical technician staff headed by Joe Spears.

After getting settled in my quarters and introducing myself to my roommate, Ed, I sought out Anderson and Spears.

My name and reputation from Raiford Hospital had preceded me. Spears took me on a tour and showed me the equipment, facilities, and supplies. I was impressed by his smooth operation.

There were several patients admitted and I went over their charts. In addition I asked Spears for the out-patient clinic notes on the men that Dr. Anderson had seen recently. After reviewing these, I had a better conception of Godwin's problem. The men at this prison were in deep trouble as far as adequate medical care was concerned and Joe Spears knew it.

As chief medical technician, Spears thought the best way I could be utilized was at sick call. At 7:30 a.m. and 5:30 p.m. the men would come to the hospital with their complaints, and either Spears or I would examine and treat them.

Those men who were seriously ill, in my opinion, were kept at the clinic to await further examination and treatment by Dr. Anderson. However, it soon became apparent that the men did not want Anderson. They wanted me.

Within a few days I was running the sick-call clinic solo. Spears was delighted since he was overloaded with work in other areas.

The afternoon medical technician, Mr. Dolloff, was pleased to have as he put it, professional medical help on a twenty-four-hour basis!

However, Dr. Anderson became more and more agitated and he noticed he had fewer and fewer men waiting to see him when he arrived at the hospital.

I tried to keep an open mind about the situation, but it was difficult. Anderson claimed he was a graduate of medical school in Mexico City, Mexico, yet he spoke poor, very poor, Spanish. When I would question him about this or that (wrong) diagnosis of a medical condition, he became vague. He had little knowledge of drugs and tended to use the same ones over and over again, no matter what the patient's problem. Both Spears and Dolloff were deeply concerned over the men's welfare and had complained repeatedly to Godwin about Anderson.

In addition I was being put in an awkward position. I was a convict, a convicted murderer with a life sentence, taking over the medical care of men despite the presence of a prison doctor!

The situation was critical: Anderson was treating epileptics with amphetamine type drugs! These drugs could easily kill them. Others with simple colds were pumped full of penicillin until they had reactions to the antibiotic to the point of laryngospasm; wounds were not cleaned, yet they were sutured by Anderson. The results were fulminating infections!

The conclusion by Spears and me was obvious: Anderson was going to kill somebody because he didn't know what he was doing. Wrong diagnosis, wrong medication, over-medication, all pointed to the doctor's appalling incompetence.

I had a meeting with Mr. Godwin and outlined my findings. I also told him, if he hadn't noticed, that there was tension in the air. He assured me that he and the correctional staff were well aware of the problems with Anderson. However, short of calling the chief medical officer, Dr. Hernandez, there was little he could do. We ended our meeting on a somber note; I hoped I could prevent a needless death.

AUGUST, 1972

I had written Fred Parker and outlined my new situation. I hadn't heard a word about my parole progress, but felt that it would come with Parker and Magadin now at the helm. After all, I did get transferred!

On the 16th of August I received a reply to my letter from Parker which reiterated his positive feelings about parole in October. In addition, he was working toward the filing of a petition for a writ of habeas corpus in Federal Court in Tampa.

AUGUST 27, 1972

Sunday, Arcadia had its usual cloudburst at 3:00 p.m. and left the air smelling clean and fresh.

The visiting area had been crowded that Sunday because of the good weather. Mary did not come, since she had been with me for two hours on the previous Thursday, courtesy of Mr. Godwin.

I was working with Ed, my roommate at the hospital, stocking up supplies in anticipation of sick-call the following morning, when word came from the lieutenant's office: Bring a stretcher!

Ed and I pushed a gurny (stretcher) through the compound and the muttering groups of convicts. It didn't take a genius to see something was radically wrong. Oh Christ! I thought, the last time I saw these looks on convicts' faces was just before the February riot.

As we walked through the compound, some of the men came up to me and said that they suspected the shift lieutenant had beaten up one of the convicts. That was the reason I had been called. Others hooted at me, "Fix 'em up good, Doc! We're going to get us some ass!"

When Ed and I reached the lieutenant's office, we found the convict, nicknamed Cowboy, handcuffed on the floor and having one seizure after another. The room reeked of bad buck, a substance you'd call home-made prison alcoholic brew.

I began my examination: pupils dilated, abdomen rigid, feeble and thready pulse. He looked as though he had been poisoned, either on the buck, or drugs, or a combination of both. I asked the Lieutenant to call DeSoto Community Hospital to alert them and to take Cowboy there immediately.

The lieutenant grabbed the telephone and made the necessary arrangements. Meanwhile, Ed and I put Cowboy on the stretcher and wheeled him to the front gate, through the gate, and into a state car.

I stood there outside the prison and watched the lieutenant drive down the highway. It was the first time in five years that I was alone, outside the gate.

Ed and I rolled the stretcher back to the hospital. As I passed each group of convicts, I told them what I found in the lieutenant's office. I emphasized that Cowboy had not been beaten. In fact, he hadn't a mark on him, not even a bruise. They didn't believe me. Worse yet, they didn't want to believe me. We hadn't reached the hospital steps when Ed and I heard the smashing of windows coming from the direction of the dormitories.

From then on until approximately 8:00 p.m., D.C.I. had a mini riot. I walked out of the hospital to watch. The men tore out windows, light fixtures, destroyed television sets, and set fire to mattresses in the dormitories. Dormitories "G," "H," and "C," looked gutted.

They broke the windows in the library and machine shop. The electrical shop was set on fire and looted. They hated the grounds shed building so they tore it apart: every lawn mower was destroyed, picks, shovels and other equipment burned. The canteen was raided by a mob, not once, but on four separate occasions. It was stripped clean. By this time, the men were running and screaming throughout the compound. They were completely out of control.

I could see J.B. Godwin, huge in shirt sleeves with a shot gun over his shoulder. He walked up to the group of screaming inmates, alone. He pleaded with the men to go back to their dormitories.

The men in turn yelled their demands at Godwin. They wanted better food. The food was atrocious. During the past week the hamburger had been rancid and so foul-smeling that the compound dog refused to eat it. We had several cases of food poisoning, and I had admitted one man because of severe dehydration. There was censoring of the mail. Items and reading material permitted at other institutions were banned at D.C.I. Despite the fact that all minimum custody men were eligible for furloughs, only a handful had been permitted to participate. They also asked for medical care. "Get rid of the witch doctor, Anderson!" The men kept chanting at Godwin: "We want Coppolino! We want Coppolino! We want Coppolino!"

I went back to the hospital. I had seen and heard enough. Experience taught me that it wouldn't be long before the hospital would be jammed by hurt convicts.

Sure enough. For the next several hours I was busily treating smoke poisoning, cuts, bruises, stomach cramps from bad buck and engorgement on canteen candy. Thank God, no gunshot wounds. Godwin had ordered his men to fire into the air.

AUGUST 28, 1972

I got about two hours sleep and the dawn brought to me a sight I'll never forget. D.C.I. looked like a hamlet in Viet Nam after a hard infantry battle. Dormitories were burned out. Some had no windows or doors. The ground was littered with broken chairs, benches, tables, broken televisions, glass, and torn light fixtures. The riot squad from Raiford with their electric prods, helmets, visors, and protective jackets were marching up and down the compound.

On the way to lunch I met a lieutenant I knew from Raiford. He asked what was troubling the inmates here. He describes D.C.I. as a motel, and much too good for inmates. He asked if these men realized that all the ring-leaders and their accomplices would now be shipped to Raiford's solitary confinement center?

What could I answer? Could I tell him that he'd been in the system so long that his humanity had given way to some brute perception that equated fresh air with nice treatment? Could I tell him that iron bars didn't make a prison, but that lockup, harassment, tainted food, and brutalized medical practices gave D.C.I. the odor of a concentration camp?

The men at D.C.I. and in all prisons wanted to regain their freedom. Yet the prison staff was determined not to facilitate their ceaseless, unrelenting, very human ambition. Convicts and prison officials were in a perpetual cold war, which at times warmed up notably, especially in the case of a riot.

Many prison superintendents lived in dread of a riot. Superintendent Godwin was no exception. Uprisings by convicts for whatever cause frightened the public, and greatly alarmed the politicians. A riot was taken to be prime evidence that the system had broken down. Since Godwin was appointed by Wainwright, he was nervous about this public exhibition of chaos.

The roundup of the convicts started that morning of the 28th. Before it was over, alleged ringleaders, accomplices, and general troublemakers, 75 men in all, were sent to Raiford in chains and handcuffs.

Godwin told the rest of the prison population to get to work and make the compound livable again. He warned that if there were any more disturbances he would order his men to shoot, and not in the air.

The estimate of damage ran to $80,000, all of it as a testimony to pure rage and frustration. I walked up and down the compound urging the men, both black and white, to forget it. Nothing they could do would help. If they did continue, knowing Godwin as well as I did, I knew there could be bloodshed.

The officials had arrived from Tallahassee that afternoon. I met Bachman walking with Godwin. It was the first time. From his appearance, it seemed that the job of deputy director, second only to Wainwright, was wearing Bachman down. He had a middle-age spread and belly, his eyes were bagging and puffy, and his hair was peppered gray.

"How is Mary?" Bachman asked. For five long years Mary had been pounding on his door through letters and telephone calls when she couldn't reach Wainwright. Five long years, asking for release.

"Fine." I answered. "Better now that I am closer to home."

Bachman smiled. "She fought long and hard to get you moved here;

she is quite a woman."

"Yes. She is. But why did she have to struggle so hard to achieve something routinely given to others?"

"You know the answer to that," Godwin interjected. He turned and surveyed the scene of destruction. "How do you see the situation, Carl?"

"Bad. Very bad." I quickly answered. "Unless there are changes, especially in the medical department."

"You mean Anderson?" Godwin asked.

"Yes."

"I talked with Hernandez about him. And Hernandez still insists that Anderson's qualified."

"Hernandez doesn't see what Anderson is doing. Suppose he was made to see? I have a list of names of convicts that have been brutalized by Dr. Jewel Anderson."

"Fine. Send them to me." Godwin said. "I'll call you out and talk with you sometime at the end of the week. Something has to be done." Bachman and Godwin continued their inspection tour.

That night I tossed and turned thinking of my patients. Should I talk with Godwin? Why should I get involved, I kept asking myself? I couldn't keep my conscience still. It was bad enough being in prison. It was worse if the hospital became a "morgue."

I got up and went out to the nurses' station and wrote down the list of approximately 15 names and sent them off to Mr. Godwin.

AUGUST0 29

Mary received a letter from Parker about my parole:

I have now talked to all the parole commissioners and have an acute awareness of the brick wall you and Carl have been pounding your heads against for five years. I am assured that the question is not whether Carl will be paroled, but when. I am also assured, however, that there is virtually no chance for a parole following Carl's next interview in November . . .

Needless to say this was the heaviest blow I had received since my conviction. Parker and Magadin's previous letters had sounded so hopeful, yet here it was in black and white, no parole in November!

Parker went on in his letter to say that he was preparing the petition for habeas corpus and would file it by the coming Friday. That meant nothing to me because I had no faith in anybody or anything now.

SEPTEMBER, 1972

On my own.

Dr. Jewel Anderson left for Raiford. Whether to be fired by Dr. Hernandez or shoved off to another institution was unimportant as far as I was concerned. The total responsibility for proper medical treatment of my fellow convicts was mine and mine alone now. I had graduated from clandestine medical practice to one in the open, approved by the administration.

In addition, Godwin asked me at our meeting if I would be interested in working for the Division of Corrections as a physician on parole. He would like me to take over the medical department. Naturally I was surprised and delighted. I mentioned to Godwin that the Florida Medical Association had no interest in whether I practiced medicine or not, since I didn't need a license, and that I had a letter from them to that effect. Godwin explained that he would speak to Mr. Wainwright and that for the time being I should work with Spears. Finally, he promised he would personally speak with the parole commissioner who would come to interview me in November.

Joe Spears was extremely enthusiastic about the idea. He was so excited about having good medical care available for the men that he sent his own letter to Mr. Godwin:

September 1, 1972

Dear Mr. Godwin:

As you know, Dr. Anderson is scheduled to leave this week for U.C.I. to assist in clearing the overload.

With Dr. Anderson's absence and in line with our previous conversation, I suggest we utilize Dr. Coppolino's medical knowledge and experience in my department.

Naturally, because of technicalities, Dr. Coppolino will work under my direct supervision. In the time I have been working with him, I am impressed by his attitude in all areas. Certainly, there is no question that he is a well-qualified physician.

Dr. Coppolino's years as an inmate have taught him the particular problems we face in a prison setting. Therefore, he handles the men with the greatest of ease. Perhaps more or equally important, the inmates respect and trust Dr. Coppolino. This leads to a quiet, smoothly operating department.

Sincerely yours,
Joe R. Spears
Hospital Supervisor

Since Carlos Hernandez was the chief medical officer for the Florida State Prison System, I thought it best to inform him of Godwin's plans. On Septemer 5, I wrote Hernandez:

September 5, 1972

Carlos M. Hernandez, M.D.
Medical Director
Raiford Hospital
Raiford, Florida

Dear Carlos:

I had a long talk with Mr. Godwin about my future plans on parole. He has revived the idea you originated last year: namely, my working for the Division of Corrections as a physician on parole. He is very enthusiastic about it, especially in the light of recent events. And, Mr. Godwin would like me placed right here at D.C.I.

Carlos, I filled in Dr. Godwin on what you accomplished up to the time you spoke to Mr. Armond Cross about me. In addition, I told him about the letter from the Florida Medical Association indicating no opposition to my practicing medicine for the State.

Mr. Godwin will speak to Mr. Wainwright about his plan and he suggested that you also indicate to Mr. Wainwright your approval.

As far as the parole commission is concerned, Mr. Godwin will be with

me when the commissioner arrives. Hopefully we will be successful,
and I will receive my liberty . . .

What a hectic month! It seemed that every convict on the compound
came to see me. Some had long-standing medical problems that had been
ignored by Dr. Anderson. Others had minor surgical problems, cysts,
abscesses, etc.

I cancelled all Anderson's standing orders and instituted proper therapy where indicated. In other cases I simply stopped the drugs. They
weren't needed.

The true nature of my success was the arrival of prison employees
seeking help. It was obvious from the tremendous rapport I received from
the officers that they had gotten the official word: I was the medical officer
and it was just a matter of time before the Parole Commission made it
official!

About this time I found out that Sheriff Ross Boyer was seriously ill
with cancer of the liver. I was sorry for him and sorry for me, and
wondered if he had done or would do something about the knowledge
he possessed concerning the falsification of the medical evidence by
Helpern and Umberger. I thought that the best approach would be the
most direct: I wrote Ross Boyer a letter.

Ross responded immediately and went into great detail concerning his
illness which gave him four to six months to live at most. On my own
situation, he thought that the best he could do was write the Parole
Commission a letter with the strongest recommendations for my release.

Armond Cross was the chairman of the Parole Commission and had
told Parker that there was no possibility of my being paroled. Still, with
Godwin's offer, the many letters of support from responsible people, and
now this latest revelation from Sheriff Ross Boyer, I hoped there would be
a change in the outcome of November's interview.

I wrote Parker about Godwin's offer and Sheriff Boyer's letter. Parker's
response indicated that he was convinced that I would not be paroled.

OCTOBER, 1972

I was happy, as happy as any convict could be in prison. For the past
month I had been doing what I knew best: taking care of sick people. I

began to book appointments for the prison employees, just like a physician with an office on Park Avenue:

Lieutenant Smith brought his eight-year-old son for suturing of a laceration.

Sergeant Dorrance had severe cellulitis of the leg. I instituted proper antibiotic treatment.

Lieutenant Williams had conjunctivitis of both eyes.

Mr. George LeQuere suffered from severe bronchitis involving both lungs.

Mr. Thomas had severe episodes of paroxysmal auricular tachycardia which I treated with Quinidine.

Mr. Franklin had a severe case of ringworm.

Captain Carter needed heat treatment for muscle spasms.

With the help of Mr. Spears, I ordered numerous drug supplies and a great deal of medical equipment. Slowly but surely, D.C.I. dispensary was beginning to look and be staffed and equipped like a hospital.

As I planned to take over the Medical Department as a prison doctor on parole, Mary, on her visits, kept reminding me that Chairman Armond Cross was against my release and had told Fred Parker that I was to receive no parole.

And on the same Sunday visits, I kept telling my beloved wife that at D.C.I. it was obvious I had the support of not only the convicts, but most important, the administration.

Suddenly my bright sunny days turned to midnight darkness when the assistant superintendent, Rankin Brown, called me to the lieutenant's office.

It was a beautiful day, a classic warm Florida day. My step was springy. I was pleased with myself. *What did Brown want?* I mused as I hurried down the walk toward the lieutenant's office.

Brown had on a pair of brown slacks and a brown and white shirt. "Sit down, Carl," he said, gesturing to a hard-back wooden chair. We were in a small, gray, cheerless office. A steel desk, a desk chair, and the hard wooden seat were the only furniture.

Brown avoided my eyes. *This is it!* I thought. Trouble. Now what? Suddenly my hands were clammy.

"How long have you worked in the hospital?" Brown asked. "Since I arrived at D.C.I. in July." *What the hell is going on?* I thought. Brown knows the score.

Brown stirred in his chair. He stared across my left shoulder. "How long have you worked in a hospital since your imprisonment?"

"Oh, about three years."

Brown nodded his head. "Time for a job change, don't you think?"

There it was. Flat and to the point. I was finished at the hospital.

"Now wait a minute, Mr. Brown!" Anxiety entered my voice. "I don't understand! Have I done something wrong? Have there been any complaints that I'm unaware of?"

"No! No! Nothing like that!" Brown hesitantly assured me. "Mr. Godwin thinks that it would be better for you to be out of the hospital when Dr. Anderson returns on Monday."

I sank back in my chair.

Brown continued, "We want you to continue to live at the hospital and lend a hand when you can. But don't get caught in the middle with Dr. Anderson."

I began to relax. "Now I see. You and Mr. Godwin are afraid that Anderson will try in some way to jeopardize my parole chances."

"I can't answer that," Brown said. He stared at the gray steel desk. Then he rose from his chair. I remained seated.

"Where do you want me to work?"

"The library."

"What about my special progress report prior to my parole interview? Will this job change interfere with the timing?" I stood up.

Brown walked toward the closed door. He reached for the knob. Without looking back at me, he turned it and answered over his shoulder. "I don't know anything about your special progress report. Remember you don't work at the hospital any longer!"

I made my way back to the hospital. Joe Spears was as upset as I was over the turn of events. The idea of seeing Anderson again and trying to pick up the pieces behind him was more than the chief medical technician could bear.

About three days later I started work at the library, in the law section. I had gone from physician to lawyer. I was making the rounds.

Meanwhile the *Sarasota Herald* newspaper interviewed Mr. Godwin about me. The front page headlines read: "Coppolino Home by Christmas?" In the interview Godwin hinted on both furloughs and parole. He said that I would "soon" be able to participate in weekend visits home.

Mary sent me a photo copy of the interview with a note urging me to disregard it. She was convicned that I would not be paroled and as far as furloughs, she took a "wait and see" attitude.

On the following Sunday, I told Mary about my job change from physician to lawyer. We were sitting at our favorite table in a corner of the visiting park. Monica and Lisa were with us. While the children played cards—500 rummy—Mary explained to me how she was always fearful that I would wind up as a scapegoat because of my difficult position of convict yet medical officer.

"How do you think this job change will affect your chances for parole?" she asked. I sat back and drew a deep breath, not because of the question, but because it had been preceded by a long wet kiss. Oh yes indeed, Mary still knocked me off my pins.

I took her hand in mine. "None. In fact I believe Godwin pulled me out so that nothing could possibly interfere with the parole plan. He doesn't want anybody rocking the boat."

Then I reminded her, "Anderson is on his own. I am not going to be there to field his errors. And I know the men in this prison are going to put up one hell of an uproar!"

I was right.

For the next three weeks, Godwin had from three to ten daily complaints about Dr. Anderson. What made the situation so bad was the sharp contrast between my brand of medicine compared to Anderson's.

Soon the officers, lieutenants, sergeants, and even the captain began to manipulate and maneuver events so that I could examine and treat their favorite convicts. It was a treacherous, difficult time for me.

On October 26, 1972, I had my special progress report as promised by Mr. Godwin. The institutional classification board recommended that: *a.* I receive a formal recommendation for parole to work as a medical officer for the Division of Correcitons, assigned to D.C.I. and to live in Arcadia; *b.* minimum custody, (my custody had raised from minimum to medium on my transfer to D.C.I. from Raiford) and eligible for furloughs in thirty days; *c.* maximum gain time of six days a month. Actually the gain time was useless to me with a life sentence, but nevertheless a nice gesture.

I was delighted and wrote Fred Parker the good news. Now the Parole Commission had no excuse, I thought. This was the third official recommendation for parole!

NOVEMBER, 1972

It was the beginning of the month and I had an interview with Mr. Godwin at his request. At 8:30 in the morning he took me into an empty room at the lieutenant's office.

Godwin came immediately to the point. He had been in Tallahassee and had gone to the Parole Commission with Mr. Wainwright. They had spoken with Chairman Armond Cross about my parole. I could hardly believe my good fortune.

"What did Cross say?"

Godwin squirmed in his chair. The morning light brightened his pale blue short-sleeved shirt. "Cross didn't say anything; he simply sat there and listened. Mr. Wainwright and I asked that you be paroled to the Division of Corrections, particularly here at D.C.I. We went on to explain that we needed your services as a Medical Officer."

"That was more than I could hope for, Mr. Godwin. Thank you so much!"

Godwin leaned back in his chair. "I don't see why it wouldn't happen. Cale Keller is the commissioner coming to see you. I'll talk with him. He is a reasonable man. You will never have a better parole plan. So if the Parole Commission is going to let you go, this is the perfect time." His smile was contagious. He grinned, I grinned.

A thought came to me. "Mr. Godwin, suppose I don't make parole. What about furloughs?"

Godwin put up his hand. "One thing at a time. I don't think we have to worry about furloughs. You're going to be paroled."

"But . . ." I began.

Up went the hand again. Godwin continued. "However, if you don't get paroled, I will put you on furloughs to Lake Placid in the Holiday Inn. I spoke with Mr. Wainwright, and he has no objections."

I lit up like a Christmas tree. Even if the worst happened, I thought, I would still be with the family on furloughs, and later we could try again for parole.

"Thank you so much, Mr. Godwin, for everything. Most of all for your confidence in me."

Jim Brown Godwin smiled. "You and Mary deserve a break."

I walked away from that interview and went back to the hospital to "tally up the ledger." Parker had written at first that Roy Russell was receptive to my parole. Then Parker wrote that he learned through Chairman Cross I wouldn't be paroled, that Cross and Barker were definitely against releasing me. Now I had the weight of the Division of Corrections supporting my release and a "liberal commissioner coming to see me, Cale Keller." Most of all, I had been imprisoned five going on six years. Long enough for "society."

On November 16 I sent Superintendent Godwin a letter which read in part:

November 16, 1972

Dear Mr. Godwin:

Mary visited me today and I'd like to bring you up to date on the status of our parole plan:

Dr. Hernandez has assured Mary that he is keeping the position as staff physician open pending action by the parole commission. In addition, John Magadin sent me word that Mr. Wainwright will help all he can.

Now it is up to Mr. Keller and the rest of the commission. In view of the pressure they are under, perhaps we will be successful . . ."

NOVEMBER 21, 1972

The call came at 11:45 a.m. I had left the law library early and walked down toward the hospital. It was a bright sunny day, but a bit nippy in the shadows; therefore, I had worn my prison-issue blue jacket.

Hands thrust in my white slacks, I stopped at my favorite hibiscus bush to check on those gorgeous red-leafed yellow-throated flowers. This particular bush acted as a temporary home for a family of blackbirds. With their flaming red wings, they had given me much pleasure over the past few weeks.

When I reached the hospital, Spears told me I would be interviewed at 1:00 p.m. by Mr. Keller at the classification office.

This was it. Despite my mental preparation, my hands literally dripped with perspiration as I slowly paced my room waiting for the one o'clock count to clear. Ed, my roommate, took out one *Playboy* magazine after another, showing me the centerfolds. Incredible! It was his way of trying to ease my anxiety. Well, it might have worked for him but. . . .

I didn't go to lunch. No appetite. I sat on my hospital bed in my room and waited.

As soon as the count cleared, I raced down the walk to the classification office. There I met my classification officer, Mr. France, and asked him to inform Mr. Godwin of Keller's arrival since the superintendent wanted to talk with the parole commissioner before I did.

Keller would be arriving at any minute. I paced up and down the sidewalk in front of the classification office. I was oblivious to everything —sun, birds, trees, flowers, everything.

From the corner of my eye I spotted two men approaching along the walkway. Both men were dark business suits. One man had gray hair and was obviously older than the other. The classifiction office door closed behind them. I continued my pacing.

Next, Mr. Godwin came down the walk. He stopped at the door to the classification office and gave me a blank look.

Ten minutes later Godwin emerged and caught my eye. His face broke into a grin and he winked. My hopes soared. I was on my way home!

Keep calm, Carl! I cautioned to myself. No false hopes! Remember what Mary said! Remember Parker's letter! Think about Keller and the interview!

What would he want to talk about? Would he want to talk about rehabilitation? What answer would I give to Keller? Would I say that rehabilitation in our prisons is not rehabilitation at all but tokenisms, vague attepts to deal with criminals as humans, really motivated by a desire to designate scapegoats for all crimes committed by society so that citizens will not feel their own guilt? We try to ignore and forget what happens when the gates of prison clank shut, when a man is cut off from society he has offended until such a time as an arbitrary decision says he has "paid his debt." In order to know what our prisons are like, we must either be in them or listen to the men who are. What does a man feel when he is locked away from the rest of society, his friends, his children, his wife?

Would Commissioner Keller ask me about the more than five years I had spent in prison, about prison life and reality?

Prison life, I would answer, is like smothering to death in a powdered sea of self pity, like bleeding to death on a concrete plate. The moods are anger and bitterness. Prison is a monotonous bleating of bells and buzzers, a symphony of clanging doors and clicking locks. It's an exercise in patience, chastity, and despair. It is a perpetual musing of hope, life, and love. It is a goading reminder of innocence. It is a taunting desire to death, misery, and above all, self-pity.

Prison is the distinct moon perched on the barb of a chain link fence or the strip of sunlight across your bunk. It is the blaring of a radio or the incessant, non-sensical chattering of a cellmate. It's a birthday card from someone who didn't forget, a memory of someone you will never forget, a taste of life you will have to forget. Prison is watching the world march by while your mind keeps cadence.

And the reality of life in prison? It's waking up in the morning and discovering that all the water has been turned off again; it's waiting in line in the mess hall for grits and black-eyed peas, and green beans. Reality is being sick in a cell at night without anybody's caring.

Reality is a shakedown and the confiscation of a couple of slices of bread you tried to sneak out of the mess hall so you could have a snack before hitting your bunk at night. It's the faint glimpse of a car on the other side of the triple fence, or a perfumed letter dropped on your bars at count time.

Reality is knowing what your food is going to taste like before you eat it. It's memorizing your number and forgetting your name, shining your shoes when there is no place to go, and drinking bitter instant coffee made with lukewarm tap water.

The door to the classification office jerked open.

"Okay, Coppolino," a voice called. "Come on in!"

I made my way to Chief Classification Officer Reynolds' room. I could hear the lilting voices of the secretaries and the smell of perfume in the air. Reynolds' office was typical of the rest—gray walls, gray metal desks, and gray chairs.

A white-haired, red-nosed individual sat behind the desk. The prominent veins turned his flushed face into a multi-laned road map.

"Sit down, Mr. Coppolino," the individual rasped. "I am Cale Keller, a parole commissioner, and this is Mr. Ott." He gestured to a young black-haired man with a friendly smile which not only lighted up his face, but also his eyes. Ott sat to the left of Keller, almost in the corner.

"Hello, Dr. Coppolino. My pleasure in meeting you, sir," Mr. Ott said, as he stood up and shook my hand.

Keller had not budged from his seat nor did he offer to shake hands. The contrast between the two men was striking: Ott, warm, friendly, addressing me by my proper title, Dr.; Keller, cold, distant and showing his prejudice (ignorance?) by calling me "Mr."

The interview lasted ten minutes and was anticlimatic. Keller went over the D.C.I. parole plan and admitted that Wainwright and Godwin supported my immediate parole. Keller said the commission would inform me of their decision in two weeks. Ott wished me luck again, shaking my hand. Keller still had not budged.

It was over and I was numb for the rest of the day. One part of my mind said the interview seemed perfunctory, as the Commissioner already knew I would be turned down for parole. Another part of my brain screamed that the interview was exactly the kind I would receive when paroled.

Parker had sent me another letter on November 3 which indicated he had done all he could with the commissioners, but the tone of the letter was not optimistic.

That night I asked for and received permission to make a telephone call to Mary. I told her about my interview and she was pleased, but cautious.

"Remember, Carl," she said, her electronic voice grating on my ear, "Fred Parker told us point blank that Cross said 'No!' and there hasn't been any change in that decision."

I tried not to become exasperated with Mary. She was right, of course.

But I felt things *had* changed.

"By the way," I said, "will you be here for Thanksgiving?"

"I'm working at Sarasota Hospital that day."

My jaw tightened. I hated the idea of Mary's working. She had been working at Sarasota Memorial for some time now, and I still couldn't get used to the idea. Perhaps it was an unreasonable feeling, but that did not change my thinking.

"But I can be there at 1:00 p.m. . . .," she continued.

I breathed a sigh of relief. "Thanks, Sweetie, see you Thursday."

THANKSGIVING, 1972

What a beautiful day! I was on Cloud Nine! Everything looked good! I was going home! There was no doubt in my mind!

Mary arrived at 1:00 p.m. She was dressed in her hospital uniform and aquamarine slack outfit. Since it was a bit chilly, she wore Heidi's brown fur coat.

No doubt about it, looking back I was in a manic state. I gave Mary a complete rundown on my interview with Keller including Godwin's efforts. I ended my machine-gun delivery by saying, "It looks good, Sweetie. Real good!"

Mary clutched my arm and kissed me, "Even if it doesn't work out, remember, I love you!"

"Oh! I feel great! Confident! What the hell could go wrong? Everybody is in my corner!"

Mary dug out a newspaper clipping from her purse. "This came out on Monday in the *Sarasota Journal*."

The clipping was a write-up of an interview with Mr. Godwin. The tone was strictly reportorial in nature. Godwin indicated I had a good chance for parole, but if I was denied parole, I would be able to leave on furloughs. I interpreted the article as positive. Mary disagreed.

"Like I said, Carl, no matter what happens, I love you. As soon as I find out the decision of the Parole Commission from Fred Parker, I will call you."

"Okay, let's have our Thanksgiving dinner." I went to the canteen window and purchased two cups of hot coffee and two Cuban sandwiches. Our Thanksgiving dinner. We had a lot to be thankful for. We had each other and four wonderful children.

DECEMBER 8, 1972

Mary telephoned me later that night. The lieutenant's office called the medical technician on duty and asked him to send me down to the office. It was 9:30 p.m.

I knew it had to be Mary. A great weight lifted off my shoulders. No more uncertainty. No more sleepless nights. No more second guessing, rumors, conjectures, possibilities. No matter what the verdict, good or bad, at least the agonizing wait would be over.

It was chilly that night. The black curtain that covered the evening sky obliterated the stars. My steps echoed mournfully as I made my way toward the lieutenant's office.

The phone rang as soon as I opened the office door.

"Okay, Doc!" said the lieutenant as he picked up the extension in the other office and monitored my call.

My mouth was dry. Despite the best of intentions, my left hand trembled as I took the black-scuffed telephone receiver from its dirt encrusted cradle.

"Hello!" I whispered huskily.

"Carl," the flat voice came across the wire from Sarasota. Mary didn't have to spell it out. Her voice said it all.

"Is it yes or no?" I asked.

"It's no."

"Ah, hmmm," I swallowed hard. "Is this a temporary delay? Or is it final?" I squeezed the receiver until the fingers of my left hand ached.

"It is not a temporary delay," the flat voice from Sarasota continued. "It is final." The voice drilled into my head, which ached.

"Well, that's that. Will you be here Sunday?"

"I wouldn't miss it for the world," Mary answered.

"Thanks for calling." I hung up the phone, softly. The lieutenant hung up the extension. He didn't say a word. For that I was grateful."

SUNDAY

Even these many years later, I cannot put into words that horrible emotional Sunday. Mary came, alone. It was a beautiful sunny day. For once, neither one of us noticed.

What could we say to each other? What more could we have done to be successful? How much stronger a parole plan and support could I have had?

What we did was lean heavily on each other. I was shattered. It was a miserable Sunday.

Later on I received a letter from Parker that said it all:

December 18, 1972

Dear Carl:

Needless to say, all of us up here are equally disappointed at the arbitrary and purely political decision of the Parole Board. I've talked to each of the commissioners. *All of their remarks show the concern that your parole would result in unfavorable publicity for them.* None of them is able to cite any reasons to me for keeping you in custody other than the political questions.

I have also found out how the Board took the vote on your parole this year. Cale Keller, who interviewed you, reviewed the entire file and then noted on it his recommendation that you not be paroled. He then circulated that file to other members of the commission. As soon as there were three votes against parole, the file was returned to storage. Thus, Ray Howard and Roy Russell never saw the file. The vote would appear to have been three to zero, and since even if Russell and Howard had voted for parole, the votes still would have been three to two against; they didn't circulate the file to Howard and Russell. It's a hell of a way to run a railroad.

I needed to gather my emotional and physical resources. I needed time to stabilize my emotional climate before I could think clearly and come up with a workable plan for my family's future. On the following Sunday I talked over my idea with Mary.

SUNDAY, DECEMBER 17, 1972

It was 9:30 a.m. Mary and Lisa arrived to visit. Mary wore a beige slack suit; Lisa, a canary yellow pants and jacket. Both were pretty as pictures.

"Did you call Mr. Godwin on Monday?" I asked Mary.

We were seated at one of the tables in the visiting park, sipping black coffee. Lisa was making hot chocolate—a glass of hot water and a packet of instant hot chocolate.

Mary nodded. "He was very upset about your turndown. In fact, he said the Parole Commission were a bunch of bastards."

"He's right, Sweetie. Here I am with no previous criminal record, with family ties, recommendations for parole, and a Tallahassee jacket loaded with letters from responsible people. Add to this the support of the Superintendent of an institution plus the director of the Division of Corrections, and still no parole! Then I think that the residents of the State of Florida deserve to reap the wild wind of hate and violence that convicts carry out with them when they finally are released!"

"We love you, Daddy!" Lisa piped up. I reached over and put my ten-year-old on my lap and kissed her.

"What about the furloughs, Mary?"

"Mr. Godwin said he would do all he could to help. That it was up to Wainwright."

"Did you . . ." I began to interrupt.

"Sh! Sh! Love-lump! I told him that Wainwright had told Magadin and Parker that he would go along with what Godwin decided."

The words sounded nice, but I didn't have any faith or hope in anything or anybody.

I turned to Mary. "I'm going to ask for a 72-hour furlough over Christmas and see what happens. Perhaps we can spend Christmas as a family at the Holiday Inn in Lake Placid."

"Okay."

"Let's eat!" Lisa said, running to the canteen window.

DECEMBER 18, 1972, MONDAY

The circle is complete. Jerry The Dinger arrived today. I was standing in the doorway of the library, when his loud rough voice reached my ears. There he was, in a blue sweat shirt and white pants. His hair was flecked with gray. It had been more than a year since we had been together, and I hadn't realized how much I missed him until then.

"What doya' say, Schnozz!" Jerry pumped my hand like an oil well drill.

"What the hell are you doing here?" I let go of his hands and threw my arms around him.

"Wow! Do I have a story to tell you!" Jerry's hand whipped the air like a windmill gone wild.

We spent the entire afternoon alone as the Dinger told me his story: "Remember Reddish?" Jerry started. "How I fed the bastard every day? Breakfast, lunch, and for free? I gave him a diamond ring, wrist watches, pieces of jewelry?"

We were sitting on the back steps of the hospital. The afternoon sun threw its shadows across the double fence immediately in front of us.

"Well, it paid off, Schnozz. I got my custody lowered to minimum and got myself transferred to Lowell, and me with 90 years! Ha! Ha!"

"What did Mrs. Annabel Mitchell do when you arrived there? Ding, I can't believe as superintendent that she would want you?"

"Hell, no! She didn't want me! In fact, she tried to get rid of me. On top of that Major McKenzie and Lieutenant Griffis were calling Captain Collins, who runs Lowell, to have me sent back! But Reddish is chief classification officer and he knows where the bread's coming from. So no dice! I stayed!"

"So what happened, Ding?"

"I wanted furloughs. Every time I put in a request, Mitchell knocked it down. I tried to get a job change from pumping gasoline at the garage to work release driver for the van at Lowell. Superintendent Mitchell said, 'No!' That woman was driving me crazy! She couldn't get rid of me, but she wasn't making my life easier! I screamed for Reddish. What the hell, I was sending his old lady plenty of gifts!"

"Did he come to see you?" I asked.

"Does a bear shit in the woods? Of course he came! And you know what Mitchell did? She got on the telephone and called Bachman to ask him what connection Reddish had with me, and called me a hoodlum!"

Jerry stuck another wad of Red Man chewing tobacco in his jaw. He told me he had stopped smoking and took up chewing. Looking at the mess he was making out of a tin can plus the splotches of tobacco juice all over the hospital steps, I ardently wished he would go back to smoking.

"So what happened?"

"The heat got so bad, Reddish had to get me out of there! He sent me to Avon Park. I couldn't stand the place. It's got old barracks and the latrine is on the outside. Schnozz, I'm a city boy! Who the hell ever heard of taking a shit, shave, and shower in an outhouse in 1972? Crazy! Naw! I screamed at Reddish! Get me out of here!"

I thought how hard it was for me to get transferred from Raiford to D.C.I., and here my friend, Jerry, was going from place to place, like a catering service. "How long did it take you to get out of Avon Park?" I asked.

"Eight days," Jerry answered. "Eight days later I was at Tampa Work Release Center. Did you know that?"

Mary had told me Jerry called several times, and she and the children had gone down Buffalo Avenue in Tampa to visit with Dinger. Mary had described his place to me and it sounded like a brand new motel. The head man was Captain Chesser, the same Chesser that was a sergeant working with Lieutenant Chambers at the West Unit in 1967.

"You shouldn't have had any trouble with Chesser, Jerry. You knew him like I did from the West Unit!"

"That prick Chesser wanted to know if I was on furloughs! How the hell could I be on furloughs when Mitchell wouldn't approve them? And I didn't stay long enough at Avon Park to get into the program!"

Splatt! Jerry gave another donation to his tin can spittoon. The afternoon sun had almost touched the horizon, and the air became chilly. We moved back inside the hospital. I showed Jerry my room and introduced him to my roommate, Ed.

"Well, what happened at Tampa? What did Chesser do?"

We were sitting in my room. Actually, I was sitting; the Dinger was plopped in my bed, feet on the footrail.

"Chesser called Hassfurder. You know, don't you, that after Wainwright moved Hassfurder from Raiford after the riot, he brought him to Tallahassee? Now Haffurder sits like God over the furlough program. You need his say-so before you can get approved. Well, anyway, Chesser called Hassfurder and asked what the hell was going on? Why was I at Tampa? Well, Tallahassee started to dig, and that's when the shit hit the fan!"

Jerry went on to explain that his record showed him transferred from Raiford to Lowell, authority by Jim Reddish . . . transferred from Lowell to Avon Park, authority by Jim Reddish . . . transferred from Avon Park (after eight days) to Tampa Work Release Center, authority by Jim Reddish.

Now the questions were coming at Reddish. Who gave you authority to move this inmate around at will? Needless to say, Reddish was in hot water and Hassfurder refused to admit Jerry to the furlough program. Chesser wanted no part of the Dinger and made moves to get him out of the Center.

"What did you do, Jerry?"

"I got on that telephone and called that fat bald-headed prick Reddish. I told him he'd better move me or else!"

"Well, he gave me two choices—back to *The Rock*, or here at D.C.I. I knew you were here, so I said send me to the doc, but what's worse, Chesser sent me here all right, but what a report he wrote on me! I got his cute secretary to give me a peek. The son-of-a-bitch called me a con artist, swindler, hoodlum, gangster, member of organized crime! Christ! Al Capone was a saint compared to me according to Chesser's report!"

"Christ, Jerry! Wait till these rednecked guards see that report! Your only hope is Godwin. At least he knows you from the East Unit."

"Fuck it! I can take anything they can throw. Come on," Jerry said, bounding up from my bed, "I'm hungry. Let's go to the canteen."

DECEMBER 20, 1972
WEDNESDAY

I was working in the law library when the call came through for me to report to the lieutenant's office. Assistant Superintendent Rankin Brown wanted to see me. No doubt this was the answer to my request for a 72-hour furlough.

Jerry was reading *Field and Stream*. He looked up as he saw me getting ready to leave. "Where the fuck are you going, Mo?" he yelled.

"To the Lieutenant's office." I gave the Dinger a rundown on my application for a 72-hour furlough.

"You think the mother-fuckers will give it to you?"

I shrugged my shoulders. " *Quién sabe?*"

"You and the Goddamned spick shit, don't you know Italian? What kind of a Dago are you?"

I didn't bother to answer. It was an old argument between us. As often as I had tried to explain that I needed to know Spanish to help the Cuban and Mexican convicts in prison, it hadn't done any good. "I am Italian," Jerry would say. "Speak Italian!"

I found Rankin Brown waiting for me at the lieutenant's office. He was dressed meticulously as always: maroon slacks, maroon-striped white shirt with a maroon tie.

Brown beckoned me into an empty office. He took the seat behind the desk and cleared his throat.

Here it comes, I thought. A big, fat, "no." The ever present green painted walls gave Brown's face a sickly hue.

The assistant superintendent fiddled with a pencil, twirling it back and forth. Finally he looked up at me.

"Carl, you applied for a 72-hour furlough over the Christmas holiday?"

"Correct."

"Mr. Godwin asked me to tell you that it is impossible, and further to instruct you that you won't be eligible for furloughs for some time. So that . . ."

"Wait a minute, Mr. Brown!" I interrupted. I knew I was agitated, but I couldn't help myself. The denial of the furlough I could stand, but that I wouldn't be eligible for furloughs for some time? That didn't square with the information I had. "Do you know any of the background on the furlough situation?" I asked.

"Well, no. I assumed that you submitted a request just to test the waters."

"No sir! Mr. Godwin spoke with me just prior to my parole interview with Mr. Keller. He assured me that he could see no reason why I wouldn't be paroled. When I replied that I had to see it before I would believe it, he then said if I wasn't paroled he would approve a furlough for me and my family to the Holiday Inn in Lake Placid."

I took a deep breath, trying to contain my temper, trying to speak on an even note. "Mr. Godwin," I continued, "also told me at the time, that Mr. Wainwright would approve a furlough for me. He told Mary the same thing on two separate occasions. Finally, Mr. Wainwright told my lawyers, Madagin and Parker, that if Mr. Godwin wanted me to have a furlough it was fine with him."

Rankin Brown gave me an intense look. "I certainly didn't know about this. I feel I am caught in the middle, and find that most distasteful. I'll talk with Mr. Godwin, and if there is anything further on this, I'll call you out."

I slumped in my chair. "I just don't understand, Mr. Brown. Let me ask you a question, okay?"

"Sure, shoot!"

"If you were a convict and the superintendent told you just what I relayed, what would you do?"

"I would have my bags packed."

"That's exactly what I have done, and now you're telling me, no dice!"

"Well, that's what Mr. Godwin instructed me . . ."

I put up my hand. "Let's not go through that again. Is there anything I can do to help my situation?"

"Nothing, Carl. You have an outstanding record for five and one half years. Nobody could ask a man to have a better record. Your work at the hospital, the way you handle the man, are all exemplary. There is nothing you can add."

"Thank you very much for your time," I said and walked out.

On the way out of the lieutenant's office, I asked and received approval for a phone call to Mary for that night. Something was radically wrong. Somebody was lying. I was miserable. I should have known better than to believe I would get out on furloughs. I walked back to the library, and felt lower than a snake's belly.

The Dinger met me at the library. "What happened?"

"I got turned down," I snapped. By now I was livid with rage.

"Jesus Christ, pal, don't bite my head off!"

"Ah! Shit! Jerry, I'm sorry, but when is this crap going to end?" It took only a few sentences to give Jerry some background.

"What now?" he asked.

"I'll call Mary tonight, and see if she knows anything." Actually I thought the whole procedure was useless.

At mail call that afternoon I found a letter from Parker.

December 20, 1972

Dear Carl:

Jack Madigan is going to call Louie Wainwright tomorrow to see if Louie will okay a 72-hour furlough for Christmas. We'll do everything we can, and I certainly hope it goes through so you can at least spend Christmas at home. Merry Christmas!

Sincerely yours,
Julius F. Parker, Jr.

After reading this letter, I was still in the dark!

I called Mary that night.

"Darling, don't upset yourself," Mary urged. "I will find out what's going on. Perhaps Tallahassee is jittery after your recent turndown on parole."

We had a bad telephone connection, but no matter, just hearing her voice made it worthwhile.

"But, Mary, don't you understand? Somebody is lying! Either Godwin or Wainwright!"

"Not necessarily. It may simply be a play for time. After all, there was some newspaper publicity about your upcoming parole and, if that failed, your release on furloughs. Who knows what pressures may have been placed on Tallahassee by the attorney general's office? We just don't know."

"But Mary . . ."

"Don't worry about it, Sweetie," Mary whispered. "We'll do something about it. We always do."

The rest of the phone call was taken up with Mary's descriptions of Claire, Monica, and Lisa's Christmas activities, the decorations in the house, and the fact that they would all be here to see me, as usual, on Christmas Day.

CHRISTMAS, 1972

The family arrived about 10:00 a.m., including the family poodle, Coco. Mary wore a stunning purple dress, slit up the side, with purple black panty hose. Claire wore an emerald green minidress with matching panty hose. Monica wore black palazzio pants with a beige blouse. Lisa had on a pink-green quilt dress.

Lisa had injured her right foot during the week while riding her bicycle, so she had difficulty walking. I went to the front gate, with permission, and carried her to the visiting park.

What a day! My three daughters tried to talk with me at the same time. Between breaths, Mary injected her two cents.

I tried to keep the conversation away from the parole turn-down. Enough tears had been shed over that to last several lifetimes.

The big joke of the day was that we had no food! That's right, nothing to eat on Christmas Day other than ice cream and soda! Who cared? Did it matter? Not a bit. Being together, that's what counted!

Lisa and Monica had me laughing continuously over their antics. Such clowns! Claire showed me her engagement ring that her boyfriend, Roger, recently placed on her finger. She was bubbling over with wedding plans for the following July.

This would be the second of my daughters to marry. I didn't object to Roger. It was inevitable that she should marry. But it was hard for me to realize that they were grown and growing so far from their father's loving participation.

Visiting was over. I hugged and kissed my children, and held my Mary very close. I didn't want them to leave. After a while, I carried Lisa back to the front gate.

Mary had driven our new car, an Audi, close to the gate. She took Coco out of the car, through the front gate, into the prison. I played with Coco for several minutes. We were happy to be together even if it was simply for a short time Then they had to go.

JANUARY-MARCH, 1973

Mary continued to hammer at Godwin and Madigan and Parker about my furloughs. She and I felt that the commitments had been made but feet were dragging.

Both of us believed it was critical for me to participate in the furlough program. It would be the best way to function in a free society, and gather further support in my quest for parole. Obviously, our personal and family needs would be partially satisfied if I were home weekends. However, the long view was *freedom*. I thought that being "free" weekends, convincing the neighbors that I was a burden to the tax payers as a convict, and most important, that nboody cared that I was out of prison on weekends, would make my situation politically "hot" and force the Parole Commission to parole me the next time around!

It was becoming tiresome and racial tension permeated the prison atmosphere. Fist fights, razor cuttings, stabbings were now a common occurrence. Would it really blow up into a violent bloodbath?

The constant daily yapping, like raunchy alley cats, between black and white convicts had worn down nerves to a volatile trigger point. Jerry was sleeping with a knife and lead pipe under his pillow. He must have appeared to the blacks as Public Enemy Number One because an anonymous letter to the lieutenant's office said that the Dinger would be the first to get it when the riot started!

The catalyst turned out to be an article in the *Miami Herald* published February 18, 1973. It was unfortunate that the article appeared, since what it reported was true.

Harsher Prison Terms for Blacks Confirmed by Martin Dyckman

Tallahassee. Fresh research has confirmed what Florida's black convicts and their keepers have suspected—that they are sentenced more severely and held in prison longer than whites.

With prison so crowded that they are accepting no new inmates, the studies are likely to underscore proposals for sentence review procedures and parole reform.

For equivalent crimes, the black man's sentence is likely to be appreciably longer than the white man's. This is the judge's doing. But the Florida Parole Commission, which could offset the discrimination, isn't doing so . . .

But to Louie Wainwright, director of the Division of Corrections, the results are ominous no matter how unintentional the causes might be.

"It's becoming more evident all the time that black inmates are realizing this," he said of the sentence in duration disparities, "and that's why we are getting the increased reaction from them that they consider themselves political prisoners. The management problem is becoming more difficult all the time."

He was plainly afraid of race riots in his teeming prisons. . . .

The chairman of the Parole Commission, Armond Cross, added fuel to the fire by saying that as many as 3,200 of the prison's population of 10,600 could be paroled, but they won't be released.

The D.C.I. administration moved swiftly. There was a general roundup of "agitators," and some 13 men, both black and white, were sent on to Raiford.

Meanwhile, D.C.I. was bursting at the seams with convicts. The count was as high as 600. But D.C.I. wasn't alone. The whole prison system was packed and violence was a common every day phenomenon in every institution.

The Division of Corrections was helpless, helpless because they didn't have the authority to release prisoners who were deserving to be released, like me. Only the Parole Commission could do that. Chairman Cross made it plain on television, radio, and in newspaper interviews that he couldn't care less.

Tobias Simon, ACLU attorney from Miami, filed a class action suit in Federal Court claiming that incarceration in Florida's prisons was cruel and unusual punishment because of overcrowded conditions, lack of medical care—sound familiar?—and loss of life and limb through violence.

Federal Judge Scott issued an unprecedented ruling ordering reduction of the prison population and improvement in medical care.

Meanwhile, the legislature pointed the finger at the Parole Commission as the major cause of prison overcrowding. Despite the evidence and the admission of the commission that more than 3000 could be paroled immediately, Armond Cross refused. In fact, the Parole Commission released fewer men in 1972 than they had in 1971!

With this in mind, I wrote Parker asking him to urge Wainwright to publicly take up the cause for my parole. I thought the pressure on Cross and the Commission plus Wainwright's private request for my parole and the prison overcrowding, would be a combination of circumstances that had to work toward my relief.

Parker's answer snapped me out of my dreamland:

February 27, 1973

Dear Carl:

I have your letter of February 19. I'm afraid we haven't been able to accomplish much with Louie Wainwright. I'm confident he would not object to your being allowed parole, but he is unwilling to initiate anything or exert any pressure from up here despite our best efforts.

I am writing letters to each of the Parole Commissioners this week suggesting that they could reduce the overcrowded conditions at Florida's prison by at least one by granting your immediate parole on the condition you continue to work at the DeSoto. I dont' think it will do any good, but it certainly can't hurt to try. . . . With best regards I am,

Sincerely yours,
Julius F. Parker, Jr.

Mary and I trying not to look worried during a court recess at my Florida trial. *(April 1967)*

Mary and my mother wait with me at the Florida courthouse. *(April 1967)*

My friend, Dr. Webb, smiles for reporters as he enters the court building. *(April 1967)*

The late Sheriff Ross Boyer and I wait during one court session. *(April 1967)*
UPI Photo

Mary and I smile with optimism while we wait for my Florida trial to begin.
(April 1967)

My family—Mary, Lisa, and Monica and our poodle, Coco—try to pick up the pieces of their everyday lives after my conviction. *(June 1967)*

Mary, Monica and Lisa are forced to spend the Christmas of 1967 without their husband and father.

My lovely wife, Mary, is beaming with joy after my release from prison twelve years later. *(October 1979)*

Mary, as she looks today.

My grown daughter, Lisa, in a recent picture.

My daughter, Monica Coppolino Fuller, with her husband Michael. *(1979)*

PART THREE

Stirrings of Awakening

APRIL, 1973

It was becoming apparent that my furlough chances were improving. I was sent up to the Reception Medical Center in Lake Butler for a full psychiatric and psychological profile. On its findings would rest in part the answer to whether or not I would be released on furloughs.

Naturally, the maneuver was different for me. No other convict had to have two days of testing and interviews by two psychiatrists before being admitted to the furlough program. But then, there was only one "Coppolino."

On April the 3rd, Mary received a letter from Parker saying:

April 3, 1973

Dear Mary:

I talked with Louis Wainwright this afternoon about having Carl transferred to a community correctional center. He said he would much rather have Carl furloughed from his present institution and promised to do whatever he could to start that program with a short furlough in the Lake Placid area.

Assuming the reaction from the press to his initial furlough is not terribly bad, Louie would then try to get Carl into a program of longer and longer furloughs. He is very hesitant about letting Carl go to Sarasota on a furlough, however, and I think all furloughs will have to be taken in an area pretty close to the institution. Louie has asked me to call him back next Monday so he can report on his progress and I'll call you as soon as I have talked to him.

Sincerely yours,

Julius F. Parker, Jr.

This was followed by a letter on May 2:

May 2, 1973

Dr. and Mrs. Carl A. Coppolino:

Progress at last! I apologize for my unavailability the past three weeks, but I have been on the road all over Florida and the Southeast attending hearings and trials. During this time I have been trying to contact Louie Wainwright to see what decision he has made with regard to furloughs. I have just talked to Mr. Wainwright and he advises he has expressed to the superintendent at DeSoto, that you, Carl, should be allowed on the furlough program and the superintendent agrees. Louie told me he expects action to be taken within the next two to three weeks.

The furloughs would initially be limited to Lake Placid, but Louie says he does not foreclose the possibility of furloughs being granted to Sarasota. He has checked with Warren Henderson, Jim Tillman and the sheriff at Lake Placid, none of whom has any objections whatsoever to Carl's being on the furlough program. I am, therefore, hopeful that the furlough program will begin within three weeks and, assuming no violent public reaction, I think that later furloughs may very well be allowed to Sarasota . . .

Julius F. Parker, Jr.

JUNE 23

J.B. Godwin had been transferred to Lake Butler as superintendent and Rankin Brown was now superintendent at the DeSoto Correctional Institution. The classification committee held a meeting at the beginning of the month with Superintendent Brown, and I was one of a group of convicts approved for the furloughs.

The paper work left D.C.I. and went to Hassfurder, as director of the Community Services in Tallahassee (the convicts always felt that this was Hassfurder's reward for the February 1971 riot!). Hassfurder immediately denied D.C.I.'s furlough approval for me, despite Wainwright's assurances to the contrary.

Brown found himself in a quandry; the director of the Division of Corrections indicated to him that I would be approved for the furlough program, yet Hassfurder, an underling, turned down the request and used as a reason, "decision of a higher authority!"

Superintendent Brown solved his problem in the only way possible: he telephoned Mr. Wainwright and related to him what had happened. Wainwright ordered Brown to re-submit the request for my furloughs directly to his attention. This was done. Subsequently I learned that Wainwright hauled Hassfurder onto the carpet over this.

My approval for furloughs came through and I was granted a four-hour furlough for the last weekend of the month. Mr. Brown called me into the lieutenant's office to go over with me the "rules for furloughs." One definite rule applied solely to me: I was prohibited from setting foot in Sarasota County, despite the fact that my home and my wife and children were there!

I filled out my furlough request for four hours and indicated my destination as Arcadia. I had one of two choices—Arcadia and Lake Placid. I chose Arcadia since it was several miles closer.

In a letter to Mary, I asked her to come to pick me up at 1:00 p.m. on Saturday, and to bring a picnic basket with shrimp cocktail, crackers, fresh strawberries and cold champagne! I wanted to feel human again.

Mary arrived that clear, sunny Saturday dressed in a white pants oufit, pearls around her neck, and a wide smile on her beautiful face. She brought me a new pair of slacks and a sports shirt.

I walked out of D.C.I. with my arm around her and headed for the parked yellow Audi. I stopped and looked back for a moment. It was the first time I had been "free" in over six years. Fleetingly the thought came that by 5:00 p.m. I had to walk back into my prison. I ached. This was a torment I hadn't felt before. But I thrust it aside and continued our walk to the car.

Riding down highway 70, I drank in the sights, a red barn, grazing cattle, a windmill slowly turning. Mary drove silently, allowing me to adjust to my new environment. Even the smell of the car seemed strange, but good.

"How far is Arcadia?" I asked, breathing the silence.

"Oh, about nine miles."

It seemed to me we had traveled almost nine miles, but I saw no signs of town.

"Where is it?" I asked.

"Arcadia? Oh, Carl, that's behind us in the opposite direction!"

"What!" I cried, grabbing the arm rest. Mary immediately took her foot off the accelerator.

"What's wrong?" she asked.

I burst out laughing. "Nothing! Nothing! Let's go!"

Mary gave the accelerator a shove to the floor.

Much, much later after shrimp cocktail, fresh strawberries and sharing a split of champagne, we rested in our room at the Holiday Inn.

I've explained what her kisses always did for me. Imagine what the next few hours did for me. You will have to imagine, because I'm not about to tell you. It was sacred time, off the public record—sacred time alone with my wonderful, glorious, incredibly devoted wife.

Lying flat on my back, looking at the ceiling, a cold glass of champagne on my bare chest and Mary curled up beside me, I had to laugh.

"Hmm!" she murmured. "What's so funny?"

I raised my head and sipped some champagne. "Oh! Really nothing, except that after all the tears and struggles we have been through to obtain furloughs, here it's our first four hours together, I am a fugitive!" I started laughing all over again.

Mary rose up and propped herself on her left elbow. A ray from the late afternoon sun peeked through the partially closed blinds and bathed her bare skin with a warm glow.

"What do you mean?" she whispered, a slight apprehension filled her voice.

"Nothing, except that I signed out for Arcadia, and we are in Lake Placid."

"Well, I wanted to stay overnite and visit with you tomorrow and I couldn't see spending that much time in Arcadia."

She lay back and snuggled close to me. Soon she began to giggle and the giggle developed into a roaring laughter. The champagne spilled everywhere, but after a short time neither of us cared.

JULY-AUGUST, 1973

Claire married Roger. Mary and the children said it was a beautiful wedding. Even though I had eight hour furlough time, I decided that I couldn't take a chance and go to the wedding. It was held in an Episcopal church in Sarasota. I couldn't take the chance of discovery in the one place I was never to be: Sarasota.

Two of my daughters now were married, and I had missed both weddings. That left two more at home. Two more weddings that I prayed God I would be a free man to attend when the time came.

Heidi had come up from Costa Rica for visits on several occasions, bringing Esteban, my grandson, with her and of course, Juan, her husband. I had seen them several times on their visits to prison.

My friend, Jerry, had his parents down from Chicago, and they were staying with Mary and the children. In fact, Jerry's parents stayed with Mary for several weeks each winter. My children just adored them. My mother and father had been down during the years of imprisonment and visited with me at the East Unit and at Raiford. They were pleased with my furloughs because they could come down and see me out of prison.

Time moved rapidly as I began to live from one furlough to the next. Since I couldn't go home, Mary and I found ourselves wandering around as nomads. One weekend we would take the children to Highland Hammock Park for a picnic. Another weekend we would stay at a fish camp at Lake Placid and set out lines. By this time I was on 12-hour furloughs, looking forward to 24 hours and finally 48 hours.

Thing were going so well that for the first time Mary and I began to make plans for a future, our future. We went to Punta Gorda and stayed at the Holiday Inn with the thoughts of possibly selling our house in Sarasota and relocating either in that area or in Tampa.

That was a mistake.

On August 21, 1973, a long, detailed newspaper article was released informing the public that I was on furlough. In addition it went on to say that I had taken the last three furloughs in the Punta Gorda area. Newspaper reporters besieged Superintendent Rankin Brown for clarification.

Rankin Brown, in an interview, confirmed my furloughs. "When the new furlough program was instituted," Brown said, "Dr. Coppolino's case and records were reviewed and those, plus his prison performance, made him eligible for the program. Starting in June, Coppolino was given four-hour furloughs, but now they have been expanded to eight hours and twelve hours, and eventually could be forty-eight hours."

Brown continued by saying that Mary picked me up for the furloughs and then came to visit every Sunday during visiting hours. He went on to say that he had known me during most of my six and a half years of imprisonment and described me as a "near perfect prisoner, with not a blemish on his record." Brown said he expected that I would be on full furloughs (48 hours) by late October and might be considered for parole in the future. Brown concluded by saying, "We think it's the best way to get a man back into society and prepare him for life outside."

The newspaper reporters immediately contacted the Parole Commission and asked if I was going to be released in view of the fact that I was already functioning in a free society, albeit for only a few hours.

Ray Howard, a parole commissioner, told The Press that I had been given routine annual parole interviews and would receive another one in November. "We look at the man's record, but we also look for a reasonable likelihood that he won't return to being a criminal convict," Howard said. "The Commission tries to exercise as much leeway as possible in granting parole."

But Cross made his position immediately clear. The chairman said, "A furlough means he is doing well in prison. It doesn't necessarily mean he is a good parole risk."

SEPTEMBER, 1973

By this time the trickle of newspaper articles about my furloughs had become a torrent.

Superintendent Rankin Brown gave another interview which was reported on September the 5th. "As far as conforming," Brown said about me, "I wish I had 599 more like him. He's really applied himself and made an excellent adjustment to prison. He's proven over a period of years to be a good custody risk."

Brown went on to reiterate that I had the run of the prison during the daylight hours and could go wherever I wanted after work. He went on to say that on the weekends I left prison in the company of "relatives."

By this time George Georgieff as a senior assistant attorney general for the State of Florida became alarmed that my favorable press would snowball into a move to free me on parole. His fears were also shared by his surrogate on the Parole Commission, Armond Cross.

On September 12, 1973, Georgieff composed a letter to Chairman Armond Cross and persuaded Attorney General Robert Shevin to sign and release it to The Press. The letter was a vicious collection of lies, told against me and concocted for the purpose of stopping any movement for parole that might be developing.

In the "Shevin letter," as it became labeled for years to come, were listed the following reasons why I should not be paroled: 1. on page one of the letter Shevin points out that "Dr. Coppolino's act in killing his wife was a very deliberate one, executed in such a manner as to evince one of the most depraved minds the jurisprudence of Florida has encountered . . ."; 2. the first paragraph of page two of the letter outlines the great effort and monies expended by the State of Florida in securing my conviction; 3. in the second paragraph on page two, Shevin takes the position that the fact that I had been a model prisoner for six and a half years (which must include the fact that I had been recommended for parole by the prison officials on four separate occasions and that I was free on furloughs weekly) was insufficient basis on which to conclude that I was a proper subject for parole; 4. in the paragraph beginning at the bottom of page two and continuing on page three of his letter, Attorney General Shevin, although conceding that I was acquitted of the New Jersey murder charge, attempted to point out that I was in fact guilty; 5. in the second paragraph of page four, Shevin urges that I should serve a total of 25 years before I would be considered for parole, so I could receive maximum punishment; and 6. Attorney General Shevin ends his letter by urging Cross and the other members of the Commission not to be swayed by the recent news articles.

The response by the news media was devastating. Headlines screamed "Coppolino Parole Opposed by Shevin." Detailed news reports highlighted the fact that Shevin urged Florida Parole and Probation Commission Chairman Armand Cross to reject my application for parole.

The radio in my sleeping quarters in the work release dormitory—I had moved out of the hospital—blared the news on the half hour about Shevin's letter.

Superintendent Rankin Brown called me to the lieutenant's office and told me that the pressure had been placed on Mr. Wainwright "by some members of the Attorney General's office" to have me removed from the furlough program. Brown went on to say that Wainwright refused to do this, but decided to let me go out on furloughs for only 12 hours. I would not be able to move up to 24 hours and then 48 hours for some time.

My attorneys Parker and Madagin were incensed and outraged over

Shevin's letter. Parker called Mary and urged that she and I sue Shevin for slander and libel and whatever else was available and that he, Parker, planned to write a detailed letter to Shevin and Cross.

Mary and I immediately rejected the idea of suing the Attorney General. Our situation was precarious enough without getting involved in a legal battle with Tallahassee. We decided the only thing we could do was sit still and take the flack until this incident blew over, wondering, despite what Superintendent Brown had said, how long we would be together on furloughs.

On September 17, true to his word, Parker wrote Shevin:

September 17, 1973

Personal and Confidential
Honorable Robert L. Shevin, Attorney General
of the State of Florida

RE: Dr. Carl Coppolino

Dear Bob:

I represent Dr. Coppolino in connection with his application for parole. Needless to say, I was very disturbed by reports in the newspapers on September 14, regarding a letter you apparently wrote to Chairman Armond Cross of the Parole Commission.

I have personally been misquoted enough in the papers that I take such reports with a grain of salt and I would, therefore, request that you furnish me a copy of your letter to Mr. Cross.

With best regards, I am

Sincerely yours,

Julius F. Parker, Jr.

Mary and I knew things were bad. I could be taken off furloughs immediately, and the Parole Commission obviously wouldn't parole me in November despite my furloughs; however, neither one of us knew how bad things were until I received a letter from Parker on September 21. In it Parker stated that court action was my only way out. *Parole was impossible.*

While I was trying to digest that piece of bleak news, Armond Cross wrote a letter to Shevin and made it public. Again, The Press ran the headlines: **Coppolino Parole Held Unlikely**. Cross said that he agreed with Attorney General Shevin. "We are aware that some of the more dangerous and professional criminals are likely to become the better inmates," Cross said in his letter to Shevin. "Mr. Brown had no authority to speculate on the matter of parole in Coppolino's case for that is a matter in which this Commission has full discretion and power."

Cross went on to say that the prison officials had commended me for parole as early as December of 1971 and that I was up for parole in November, but that "there is nothing to indicate that parole release is imminent."

I had been turned down for parole even before I was interviewed!

On November the 13th, Parker sent a letter to Armond Cross, refuting point by point the lies in Shevin's letter. Parker concluded his letter by saying "having lived in Tallahassee all my life, I am well aware of the realities of practical politics, and I know full well what the reaction of The Press would be should Dr. Coppolino be paroled. I am also convinced, however, that he is in every way a fit subject for a parole, and I hope that you and the other members of the Commission will have the courage to resist both adverse press reactions and the urgings of the Attorney General and to grant Dr. Coppolino a parole on such terms as you deem proper. He is capable of supporting himself and his family, he is willing to live anywhere in the State of Florida, and his further incarceration can do no service to him nor to the people of the State of Florida who bear the expense of his imprisonment."

Cross' response was swift and to the point:

November 20, 1973

Mr. Julius F. Parker, Jr.
Attorney-at-Law
Tallahassee, Florida

Dear Mr. Parker:

This is in reply to your letter of November the 13th.

The Attorney General's letter to this agency has been made a part of the file and will be only one of the factors considered in this case. The same holds true for your letter of the 13th.

It is our plan to continue to consider this case not less often than annually, our next consideration date being October, 1974.

Very truly yours,
Armond R. Cross, Chairman

However, there was one piece of good news in September. My closest friend, Jerry, the Dinger, went home on parole! How happy were his parents and brothers! And how happy were Mary and the children!

I, of course, was ecstatic! Jerry had served almost nine years on a 90-year sentence; doing more time would not have helped him nor his family. His parents and Mary picked him up on Tuesday, and he spent his first day and night of freedom at my home, sleeping in my bed! Life is nothing if not ironic!

1973 ended on a sad note for me. My father died of cancer in November, and my dream of walking out a free man while he was alive died with him.

JANUARY, 1974

Mary and I continued to live from 12-hour furlough to 12-hour furlough. We kept moving from place to place since I was still prohibited from going home. We kept hoping for an increase in furlough time and a transfer to a work release center closer to home. I had been in prison almost seven years and the outlook was grim.

On January 24, 1974, Parker petitioned Louie L. Wainwright for an extension of my furlough time and a transfer to a work release center, either in Tampa or Lakeland. Wainwright refused.

Meanwhile Mary refused to accept Parker's negative conclusion on my parole possibilities and continued to seek help from any and all directions.

MARCH, 1974

On one of my 12-hour furloughs Mary asked me to call Henry Gonzalez. Henry had been approached by a law firm in Jacksonville. They felt sure they were in a position to secure a parole for me.

I called Henry from the motel room where Mary and I were staying that particular weekend and discussed the matter with him. Gonzalez suggested that Mary fly to Jacksonville and meet with the members of the law firm of Dawson, Galant, Maddox, Sulik, Nichols and Forbes P.A.

Mary did. She met Nichols and Maddox at their Jacksonville firm. After discussing my situation at great length, Nichols indicated to Mary that he and Mr. Maddox felt very positive they could have me paroled.

Nichols asked Mary whether she knew if any of the Parole Commissioners would be favorable.

She answered, "No."

Nichols smiled, picked up the telephone and called Commissioner Ray Howard. After a brief conversation with Howard, Nichols outlined for Mary what was required: Nichols wanted a fee of $60,000 plus expenses for thirty days. I would be released at the end of thirty days or thereabouts.

Mary got up from her chair, and thanked Nichols and Maddox for their time, but stated that what they asked was impossible. We just didn't have that kind of money. $60,000 wasn't a fee. It was a ransom demand!

Nichols looked at Maddox and Nichols asked what could she pay. Mary repied that she was prepared to pay a legitimate, reasonable lawyer's fee of $10,000. When Nichols said that that wasn't satisfactory, Mary flew back to Sarasota.

What was amazing to me was that despite Shevin's letter and the apparent hostility of the Parole Commission, a phone call to Ray Howard plus an agreed-upon fee of $60,000 plus expenses for thirty days would have resulted in my freedom!

Being poor had just cost me five more years in prison!

APRIL, 1974

Claire was now attending University of South Florida and Monica would attend the same college in August of the year. It seemed foolish to keep our house in Sarasota—three bedrooms, three baths—for only two people, Mary and Lisa. In addition, I could never go home on furloughs to Sarasota. Therefore, we put our home up for sale, found a buyer, and set the closing date for June, 1974. Our next question was—where do we live?

With these events in mind, Parker wrote another request to Wainwright asking his assistance in increasing the time of my furloughs and transferring me away from D.C.I.

April 24, 1974

Mr. Louie L. Wainwright
Director
Division of Corrections
Tallahassee, Florida

Dear Louie:

I tried to call you yesterday and again today and was unable to reach you and since I am leaving the country today for ten days, I thought I would write and advise you of my problem.

As you know, Carl Coppolino has been on a twelve-hour furlough program for a number of months now. He should have been on twenty-four or forty-eight hour furloughs by now, but due to understandable pressures, he has been restricted to twelve hours.

Carl's situation has now changed, however, and I hope the change will enable you to allow him to proceed with twenty-four and, hopefully, forty-eight hour furloughs. Carl and Mary have sold their home in Sarasota and that sale will be closed on June 14. Mary and the children are going to move to the Lakeland area. On Carl's behalf I would, therefore, request that he be transferred to the Lakeland Community Correction Center and that as soon as possible he be allowed overnight furloughs. He can then spend the night at home in Lakeland with his wife and family.

Not only has Carl been a model prisoner as far as the furlough program is concerned, but he has just received his fifth recommendation for parole. I don't expect the Parole and Probation Commission to take any action, but I am hopeful you will agree to transfer him to Lakeland allow him to have overnight furloughs with his wife and children. Anything you can do would be greatly appreciated.

With best regards, I am

Sincerely yours,

Julius F. Parker, Jr.

JUNE, 1974

With no response from Wainwright, and a house closing plus moving staring her in the face in just a few days, Mary and I decided that the best place to live would be Tampa. It was a large cosmopolitan town where I could get "lost." Two of our daughters were attending the University of South Florida in Tampa, and there were more opportunities for jobs in Tampa in the field of medical secretary. Mary, by now, had left Sarasota Hospital and was working as an office manager for a local orthodontics surgeon. The opportunities for employment as office manager for a surgeon or general practitioner were promising in Tampa.

With the help of our son-in-law, Roger, Mary moved from Sarasota to an apartment in Tampa. Now she was in Tampa, in an apartment, unemployed, with a husband in prison for more than seven years, and no relief in sight.

By this time the officials in Tallahassee had fired Dr. Jewel Anderson. There was talk that he was not a graduate of a medical school in Mexico, although he might have attended the school without finishing. In any event, he had been released by the division and a new physician came to D.C.I.

During this same period of time, the chief classification officer at D.C.I., Reynolds, kept telling me that I was never going to be paroled, and that my only hope of getting more furlough time was through Wainwright, since Wainwright had issued verbal orders to restrict me to 12 hours.

Mary received a phone call from Parker saying that Wainwright had decided to transfer me and to increase my furlough time to 24 hours. Upon being pressed about where I would go, Parker said Tampa Work Release Center! Further, Parker wanted to file a habeas corpus because he had learned once again from his contacts within the Parole Commission that as long as Cross, Howard, Keller, and Barber were on the Commission I would never be paroled!

The 1974 Florida legislators passed a law increasing the number of commissioners from five to seven and Anabel Mitchell and Charles Scriven were added to the Commission. Now I needed four votes out of seven for parole. Since I knew I already had four negative votes (Cross, Howard, Barker and Keller), no matter what, I was still in serious trouble.

AUGUST, 1974

It was early morning that first week in August when I was awakened by an officer and told to pack. I was being transferred right after the 8:00a.m. count cleared. I pressed him for my destination, but he didn't have that information.

After 8:00 a.m. I said my good-byes to a small circle of convict friends, including my ex-roommate, Ed, who was still working at the hospital with the new prison doctor.

I walked out the prison gates of D.C.I. carrying my personal property (no handcuffs) and got into a State car. The driver and I barreled down highway 70 and made a left-hand turn onto highway 27. I felt sure that I was on my way to the Tampa Work Release Center.

Suddenly the driver made a right-hand turn onto highway 64.

"Hey, Sergeant!" I yelled. "We have to keep going North on 27 to get to Tampa!"

"Doc, you ain't going to Tampa," the officer replied.

"What? What do you mean?"

"You're going to Avon Park."

"You can't be serious, and this is a rotten time for jokes!" I squirmed in the front seat. Sure enough, we were entering the town of Avon Park.

"Take a look at your transfer orders," the sergeant said, pointing to a long white piece of paper clipped to my voluminous record.

One glance said it all. "Carl A. Coppolino, 018591, to Avon Park Correctional Institution." By this time we were entering the prison through the main gate. I remember vividly how much I wanted to come here back in May, 1967, when it was nearer my home, and how the classification officer laughed in my face. Now that we'd sold our house, I was here and didn't want to be. Besides, I wanted to be not in another prison, but in a community work center in Tampa.

The car pulled up in front of a tar-covered building, which was the compound office. I got out and put my belongings down in the sand. The sun was high in the sky and it was hot.

There were three pay telephone booths five feet away from me, all occupied by convicts making calls. Three or four convicts were milling around waiting their turns. One broke from the group and approached me.

"Hey! You must be the doc!" the wrinkled, skinny, rheumy-eyed convict said, holding out a trembling right hand. He wore a black cowboy hat and boots. "My name is Charlie," he volunteered.

I took his hand. "How did you know I was coming?"

Charlie rubbed the back of his gnarled hand across his eyes. I noticed that he was obviously blind in one of them. "The word's been around since yesterday that you were coming. Assistant Superintendent Moody's been in the compound talking to the lieutenant and sergeant." Charlie snorted and blew his nose on a big red bandana. "Real celebrity is coming, that's what Moody said."

I laughed. "Yeah, real celebrity. I'm going on eight years in these places! Some celebrity!"

"You need to call somebody and tell him you're here? You can take my spot if you like."

"What about the compound office?" I asked, jerking my head in that direction.

"Oh! They'll take their time going through your stuff and assigning you a bunk. Things go pretty slow around here."

"Thanks, Charlie, I'll take you up on your offer."

Knowing I needed a dime, Charlie cackled and dug into his pants pocket for the coin. By this time one of the phone booths was empty and a big black convict yelled, "Hey, Charlie, you calling or what?"

"Giving up my spot, Williams, to the doc!"

I entered the phone booth, placed a dime in the slot, and made a collect call, giving the operator my home phone number. I only hoped Mary was there.

The phone rang and rang. Suddenly there was a click. "Hello?" Mary answered.

"This is a collect call from Carl. Will you accept the charges?" the operator asked.

"Yes, I will."

"Sweetie?"

"When did you arrive in Tampa? When can I see you? Are you in the front building on Buffalo Avenue, or in the back building?"

"Hold it! Hold it!" I yelled, grasping the phone tightly in my right hand. The sweat was pouring down my face as the sun's rays beat mercilessly on the telephone booth.

"I am not in Tampa. I'm in Avon Park."

"What are you doing in Avon Park? Parker called me and told me that our move to Tampa was right because he had learned from Wainwright that you would be transferred to the Tampa Work Release Center!"

"What can I tell you, Mary? I read my own transfer orders. It was written out 'Avon Park Correctional Institution.'"

"Something's wrong," Mary said. "It'll take me longer to travel from Tampa to Avon Park to see you than it did from Sarasota to D.C.I. That's no help to me. I'll be spending more time on the road coming to get you and bringing you back. I'm calling Parker."

"Okay. Meanwhile I'll see what I can find out from this end."

Mary called Parker and told him I had been transferred all right, but not to Tampa. When she told Parker I was in the Avon Park Correctional Institution, he asked her, "Where's that?" Parker promised to look into the situation and call her back.

Meanwhile, I had been assigned a bed in barracks #16, and had an interview with the assistant superintendent, Mr. Moody. Superintendent Herbert Kelley was on vacation.

Moody and I mutually agreed that working in the hospital would not be to our best interest and decided that I start work in the library. It was also decided that my furloughs would remain at 12 hours, but once twice a month rather than every week as they had been at D.C.I.! This upset me more than anything else, since I felt I had not made a bit of progress.

That afternoon I began orientating myself to my new surroundings and making friends with a new group of convicts.

There is no question that if you have to serve time for the State of Florida, Avon Park is the place to be. It is a minimum security facility and the only non-prison prison in the system. Everything is slower and low-keyed.

It appeared that doing time would be easier for me. I didn't have to worry about riots or someone's wrapping a pipe around my neck or sticking a knife in my back.

There were no gun towers, no armed guards marching up and down the perimeter of the single fence. The dogs were kept out of sight in a kennel and used strictly for tracking, not attacking. If a convict had to be confined, he was sent to Highlands County Jail. There was no solitary confinement unit at Avon Park.

It was hot, beastly hot. August, I would soon learn, was the hottest month at A.P.C.I. For neighbors I had hogs, love bugs, and a United States bombing range—not to mention about 700 other convicts. I soon agreed that a bunk in the old wooden barracks on this low-lying land, which once belonged to the Federal government and the United States Air Force, was the best in the Florida prison system.

The prison itself occupied more than 500 acres and was placed ten miles east of the city of Avon Park. It was started in the late 1950's and had as its first superintendent the incomparable Louie L. Wainwright.

No matter how nice Avon Park was, it still was a prison. As such, I couldn't escape the regime, routine, and control. Seven times a day the convicts had to be counted in a roll call. The whistle blew, and we responded; no count was longer than four hours apart, and some were as little as one hour apart. The multiple counts were at first maddening to me, but like everything else, slowly fitted into my life style.

I soon saw beyond doubt that Avon Park was the elite of the prison system when I sized up the convicts. There were ex-deputy sheriffs, ex-politicians, ex-county commissioners, ex-policemen, ex-lawyers, and ex-physicians. The place was a compilation of *Who's Who!*

Parker couldn't give Mary an answer as to why I was at Avon Park other than the fact that Wainwright obviously had changed his mind.

It now took longer for us to go home to Tampa on furloughs and back. I found myself traveling 200 miles round trip, and four hours of each 12 hours were spent on the highway.

The prison officials, such as Superintendent Kelley, the furlough coordinator J.C. Prevatt, and my classification officer Mr. Biby, urged Tallahassee to extend my furloughs. In November they received approval from central office to increase my furloughs to 24 hours.

At the same time I decided to leave the library and study electronics. Before it was over, I would spend four more years in the electronic school.

1973

I moved from barracks #16 to another barracks, barracks #4. Barracks #4 at this time was considered "uptown." There was a partition in the middle of the barracks dividing it into two sections of living quarters holding twenty men each. This was a vast improvement over sharing living space with 41 men as was the practice in the other barracks.

In addition, barracks #4 was quiet and clean. The men who worked in the canteen, like Lamar Baker and Russell, lived there. These two men had the tremendous responsibility of stocking the canteen, helping the convicts, and handling over $500,000 a year in business. There are businesses in the "free" world that cannot make the same statement.

I soon made a small circle of friends, with Lamar Baker and Russell heading the list. My daily routine rarely varied except on the weekends, when I would look forward to Mary's picking me up at 3:00 p.m. Saturday to take me home. I would have to be back at A.P.C.I. by 3:00 p.m. Sunday, precisely 24 hours later.

I began using the time I had on furloughs to speak with as many people as I could in Tampa about my situation. Many of the members of our community thought I had been paroled, not that I was still in prison and home only on a weekend furlough!

By this time, Mary and I decided we liked Tampa and should sink some roots. We bought a three-bedroom, two-bath condominium and moved from the apartment. Now I felt I had a home—if only I could get out of prison to enjoy it!

Parker and I went our separate ways and I think with some relief on the part of Parker and Madigan. There was no doubt that my situation was the most frustrating for that prestigous Tallahassee law firm. Confirmed murderers, torture robbers, rapists, and child molesters were paroled out of A.P.C.I. without the benefit of furloughs. Yet I remained in prison. My file in Tallahassee bulged with letter upon letter of recommendation.

Still there was nothing. And the system began to grind me down. I was still very much concerned over my heart. I took my medication religiously, did my walking three miles each day, and tried to avoid the occasional knife fights. Oh yes, we had several murders in Avon Park!

The parole examiner who came to see me for my interview was a man named Rigesby. He was sympathetic, but said that I was a political prisoner and only doing more time would eventually free me—not furloughs, nor recommendations of parole, only time. Still, he felt, I should be reviewed by a Commissioner, not an examiner, and recommended I be seen by a Commissioner in September of 1975. I told him it was a waste of time for him to make such a recommendation. He answered by saying that he had worked for the commission going on 16 years and the commission had never turned down this type of recommendation from him.

Ten days later I received a letter from Ray Howard, now the chairman of the Parole Commission saying that due to the seriousness of my crime I would be re-interviewed in March of 1976! I never saw Rigesby again to ask him why.

It was obvious that no matter what I did, how long I was in the community on furloughs, how many letters were sent to Tallahassee on my behalf, how many lawyers pleaded my case, as long as Cross, Howard, Barker and Keller were on the Commission, I would remain in prison. The Four Horsemen of my own personal Apocalypse!

The Shevin letter seemed to be the greatest stumbling block. Yet I felt that it wasn't Attorney General Robert Shevin personally who was opposed to my release. What led me to believe this was the fact that Superintendent Kelley informed me that Mr. Wainwright had cleared with Attorney General Shevin an increase in my furlough time so that I could be home 36 hours!

Later on I learned that I was the only convict in the Florida prison system who had 36 hour furloughs. That didn't matter. I was thankful to be free for that long a period of time!

Mary started picking me up at 10:00 a.m. on Saturday and bringing me back at 10:00 p.m. Sunday night. By this time, we were taking the children to see the Tampa Rowdies Soccer game, going to the opera, seeing plays, having small dinner parties, and naturally, still trying to get me a parole!

1975 ended on a nice note. One no-go went! One of my "no votes" resigned from the parole commission, Cale Keller.

1976

The holidays came and went. My friend, Jerry, came down from Chicago with his parents and we got together on one of my furloughs. The Dinger looked fantastic! Of course, it was a sad occasion because I was still in prison.

Monica decided that she was old enough to be on her own and wanted to leave college and home. She wanted to enter the business world first with the idea of returning to college later when she had a clearer perspective on what she wanted to do with her life. Besides, she was in love with a boy named Michael Fuller.

Claire was working at Robinson's Department Store and her husband, Roger, was finishing his schooling at the college of engineering at the University of South Florida.

Heidi was still living in Costa Rica with her husband, Juan, and Esteban, my grandson, who was now seven years old!

Life went on at A.P.C.I. Now that I had 36-hour furloughs, I made another push for a transfer to Tampa Work Release Center. I soon found out from Superintendent Kelley that I would remain at A.P.C.I. until I was released on parole. There would be no transfers!

My friend, Lamar Baker, began to receive visits from a beautiful girl named Kathy. He started his push for furloughs. They were granted and Lamar began putting on weight in direct proportion to the time spent on furloughs.

A new "celebrity" arrived at A.P.C.I. Professional sports figure, Rommie Loudd, founder of the Florida Blazers and now a defunct World

Football League team, arrived with a 14-year sentence for delivery of cocaine.

Rommie, a former All-American end in college and a linebacker for the New England patriots, had resigned his position with the Patriots' personnel staff in a bid to be the first black to own a professional team. Instead, here he was with me doing time. Over the next two years, I would learn details about Rommie's case that would lead me to the conclusion that he was innocent, a victim of a political frameup.

Some of my old friends from Raiford were now at A.P.C.I. One of them was Troy Browning, who spent more than 12 years in prison for robbery. Troy was one of the spokesmen during the February 1971 riot, and had received multiple beatings from the guards at Raiford and the East Unit. At one time, Troy was known as one of the best jailhouse lawyers and had spent time in solitary confinement because he tried to help his fellow convicts by filing legal papers in court. Now he found himself at A.P.C.I. with me and I found him much more subdued than he had been five years before. Troy credited his change of attitude to a religious conversion, and to show his sincerity he was working as the chaplain's clerk.

MARCH, 1976

I learned of the death of one of my convict friends from reading the newspaper. Raymond was a used-car salesman who, with his wife, had been convicted of murder under tragic circumstances. By rights, it was an accidental death, but Ray received life for first degree murder and his wife received 20 years for second degree murder. Ray and I spent many, many hours at Avon Park talking, playing cards, and scrounging for food, trying to make the best of a bad situation.

Through a set of fortuitous circumstances, Ray found himself transferred to Tallahassee Work Release Center as a driver. I was so pleased for him since the living conditions there were better. In addition, his chances for parole would be greatly improved.

Ray and I kept in touch once or twice a week by telephone when I was home on furloughs. It was apparent to me that "doing time" was getting to Ray. His wife had been paroled very recently, and he was looking for the same results in his situation.

On many occasions I cautioned Ray not to get his hopes up. He had sufficient experience to realize that nobody knew what Tallahassee and the Parole Commission would do, but Ray felt that through his lawyer, Dexter Douglass, he had made a good presentation for parole. Mary and I talked with him on the telephone for the last time in February.

In that morning's newspaper, I learned the tragic details—Ray had seen a Parole Commissioner at the Center in Tallahassee and had been turned down and given the putoff, "We'll see you again next year."

One morning, about a week later, Ray drove the Work Release inmates to their jobs as was his routine, but this time he didn't return to the Work Release Center. An intensive search discovered the Work Release van in a clump of trees. Inside was Ray, dead. He had attached a hose to the exhaust pipe of the van and threaded it into the cab, turned on the engine, rolled up the windows, and drank in death as his only escape. As a doctor, I was committed to saving lives. As his friend and fellow convict, I really couldn't blame him.

Mary and I were shocked. We felt it more because we liked Ray and because we were under so much pressure ourselves. There wasn't any parole in sight for me either. Would I end up the same way? That desperate? Ultimately beaten?

I wrote to Ray's lawyer to indicate how distressed I was and how bad I felt over Ray's death. The reply to my letter threw me into a deep depression:

March 24, 1976

Dr. Carl A. Coppolino
P.O. Box 1100
Avon Park, Florida 33825

Dear Carl:

I appreciated your letter of March 11, 1976, and like you was terribly distraught about Ray's suicide.

I had talked to him the day before and spent about an hour trying to convince him that he had only suffered a temporary setback and his parole would be forthcoming. I realized at the time I was not getting through to him, but there was nothing I could do about it.

He was a victim of bureaucratic idiocy. He was, likewise, the victim of a prison system that is designed to reward the professional criminal. Ray was one of those people that make me as a lawyer realize that most of my efforts, if they are directed toward obtaining justice, are futile.

I don't intend to let Ray's situation go unnoticed. I am going to find out who intervened to prevent his parole and why.

You might be interested to know that during the last conversation I had with Ray, he told me that one of the people at the prison had told him he had become a Carl Copplino and that no matter how fine a record he had, he would be persecuted just like Carl. This disturbed him very much.

For whatever it is worth, Ray considered you one person who was genuinely interested in his welfare despite all your problems and this speaks very highly of you.

Sincerely yours,

W. Dexter Douglass

Sure it spoke highly of me. It also spoke doom. Now it had entered the jargon. To become a Coppolino was to sink beneath the law at the hands of professional persecutors who considered themselves above it.

My only hope now rested with the Clemency Board, I thought. There was a statute on the law books, Florida Statute 944.30, which read in part that an inmate seving a life sentence after spending ten years with a perfect record could be recommended by the director of the Department of Corrections to the Clemency Board for reduction in sentence, commutation of sentence, or a pardon.

I felt that I had to move in this direction. First, I had to make sure my record reflected that I did not have any discipline reports. Through the offices of the chaplain, this was easily established and verified with the help of Troy Browing:

Office of the Chaplain
June 10, 1976
To Whom It May Concern:

Carl Coppolino's inmate file will reflect that he has not had a disciplinary report filed against him since his incarceration in early May of 1967.

Warren B. Wall
Chaplain

Next, I made a move to have my furloughs raised from 36 hours to 48 hours. This was approved on the local level by classification and R.N. Cooper, the furlough coordinator. However, it was turned down by Mr.

Hassfurder and his special review board.

I couldn't understand this since I thought I had the support of Mr. Wainwright. However, I did remember the difficulty I had with Hassfurder when my furloughs began; he took it upon himself to deny me and was soundly trounced for that maneuver. Perhaps the same set of circumstances existed now; therefore, I decided to write to Wainwright, and ask for his help.

JULY, 1976

While I formulated my plans to make the strongest presentation to the Clemency Board once my ten years were up, after April, 1977, Mary and I took every opportunity on furloughs to strengthen our own ties and those with our children.

We began to go fishing. Heidi and our grandson were up from Costa Rica visiting, and we took them to the Tampa Rowdies Soccer game. One weekend, Mary and I went fishing at Lake Panasoffkee, spent the night in a friendly trailer, rushed home, picked up Lisa, Heidi, and Esteban, and went out to Tampa Stadium to watch the Rowdies play against Pele. Then we raced back home to drop off the children, have some supper, get back in the car for the drive to A.P.C.I. I had to be back in prison by 10:00p.m. Sunday night!

The Parole Commission's strengths was brought back up with the appointment of Maurice Crockett. At best, I felt that Mr. Crockett would be neutral toward me. But I still felt my freedom rested with the Clemency Board.

Meanwhile, my friend, Lamar Baker, received his parole! I was so delighted to see him leave. Mary was happy because she particularly liked Lamar.

Lamar and I sweated the next two weeks, as time seemed to stop for him. He said, "I won't believe it until I am on the other side of the main gate, driving down highway 27." With that I could readily sympathize.

Lamar's day came and went and I was still stranded in prison.

But disaster was about to strike!

At approximately 10:00 a.m. I was called to the furlough office by Pat Casey, the new furlough coordinator. I knew that it had to be confirmation of my approval for my 48-hour furlough. It wasn't. It was disaster! The furlough program at all prisons was suspended indefinitely. There would be no more furloughs until further notice.

Mary and I had often talked about this possibility. My freedom hung on such a slender thread! Now the thread was broken. My last furlough as a matter of fact turned out to be July 17 to July 18, 1976. As I write this book, in February of 1980, the furlough program is still not reinstated in the main prisons.

I went to the telephone and called Mary at her job. She was now working as an office manager for a general practitioner. She took my news philosophically. "It was good while it lasted. Remember, Carl, when Judge Silvertooth sentenced you to life, he didn't say anything about furloughs. So, I consider that it was an extra, a gift."

"What the hell are we going to do?" I asked Mary.

"The way I see it, the Division stopped the furloughs. We haven't any control over that, so I don't see what we can do. I think we should start another push for parole."

SEPTEMBER

Lamar Baker came back to visit Russell and me. He was now established in Tampa and thought that my best chance for clemency or parole was to organize and move the community to support such a request. He promised to do all he could.

Meanwhile, Claire and Roger had a child, a baby girl named Rachel. Mary and I now had two grandchildren. I felt time passing me by.

Lamar and Mary's campaign of rallying local support for clemency or parole began to move. Tom and Carmen Benoit offered their help. The Benoits were very active in Tampa. Carmen Benoit worked for the Metropolitan Bank and began drumming up support for me through her family ties, the Spoto family.

Tom was an independent contractor and took every occasion he could find to speak with his tradesmen, his customers, and his building suppliers in his attempt to generate public support for my release.

1977

Monica is married! Monica had been hinting to her mother and me that she and Michael planned to get married. It happened on January 15. It was the third wedding that I missed. This left Lisa as the only child still at home. Lisa, wait for me, my heart pleaded. I felt even greater the urgency to get out of my hell hole.

Help came from an unexpected quarter. Bob Miller, who was the convict clerk for the West Unit psychologist, Winkie, back in 1967, came to visit me. He had been out of prison five years and was working for Townley Engineering as a district salesman. At present he was involved in church affairs, learned I was at A.P.C.I., and had contacted the chaplain to see me.

It had been almost eight years since I had seen Bob, but he hadn't changed. He was tall and huskily built with an outgoing and very warm personality. We renewed our ties of friendship, and Bob promised to contact Mary and the people he knew in Orlando who would be interested in supporting my application for clemency or parole.

Within two weeks, Bob's promise was made good.

James H. Bryan, a chaplain and the director of the Florida Chaplain Service—an organization involved with prisons and jails—came to Avon Park to speak with me. After our in-depth interview Bryan went to Tallahassee on my behalf and spoke with officials in Governor Askew's office, the Parole Commission, and Louie L. Wainwright. In addition, he submitted the following document to Governor Askew and Chairman Scriven of the Parole Commission:

The Honorable Reuben O.D. Askew
Governor of Florida
Tallahassee, Florida 32304

Dear Governor:

I have submitted a parole plan for Carl A. Coppolino to the Parole Board. After being informed that he may come before the Clemency Board before he goes back before the Parole Board, I thought it would be helpful if I sent a copy of his parole plan for the Clemency Board's evaluation.

Respectfully,

James A. Bryan, Chaplain

The letter on parole plan that Chaplain Bryan referred to was one that he set forth with Chairman Charles Scriven of the Parole Commission. In this detailed plan among other points Chaplain Bryan emphasized the following:

> *"Consideration:* Carl has no previous convictions. He developed and kept a positive attitude. He qualifies for the Clemency Board which means he has not even had a reprimand and no discipline reports for ten years. He has been involved in an education program: Ecology; Art Appreciation; Music Appreciation; all with an A average being involved in an occupational training. He received a vocational certificate in electronics. Since he would not be practicing medicine, he felt he could use his knowledge to do medical electronics sales. He has been involved in his newly trained field. He has a full time job teaching and repairing electronic equipment at A.P.C.I. He has been active in the Chapel Program when asked; the chaplain felt he would do well outside and is ready for release. He has assisted other inmates, dealing with their problems, some being sent to him by officials at the institution. He has been given "outstanding" in his progress reports on attitude, school work, and his work record. He has had letters sent on his behalf to the Parole Board from two sheriffs, one from the arresting county, physicians, Division of Corrections employees, his chaplain, businessmen (some with job offers) and respected citizens from the community. He has had an extensive psychiatric evaluation prior to being accepted for the furlough program. He has had approximately 125 furloughs to go home with his family over a three year period with a perfect record on each leave before the furlough program was ended for all inmates.
>
> Rehabilitation is primarily a change of attitude and Carl definitely projects a favorable attitude toward work and others and has learned to accept himself and his future. As I understand it, parole is based on: the offender's adjustment to the rules and regulations of the institution (ten years with a clean record shows he has done that); the probability that he will not commit a criminal act again (those who have offered him employment and letters of recommendation which include a job offer from the Department of Offended Rehabilitation show many feel he is ready for release); and acceptance by the community. Considering the fact that his wife and children are awaiting him, that letters have been received from those he visted with during the 125 furloughs, along with his attitude and achievements since incarcerated, I sincerely present this parole plan for your thoughtful consideration.
>
> Respectfully,
>
> James H. Bryan, Chaplain

Mary and I decided I needed legal representation for my petition for clemency before Governor Askew, despite the fact that Wainwright would automatically recommend me according to Statute 944.30.

We decided upon a local lawyer in Tampa, Robert T. Hughes. Hughes was an ex-policeman from New York who had lived in Florida for many years. He attended law school in Florida and had studied under a man who was now sitting on the Florida Supreme Court, Justice James Adkins. Most important for Mary and me, Hughes was honest and dependable. We were sick and tired of the wheeler dealer lawyers. Finally, he was Lamar's friend and attorney, and as far as I was concerned, that was a high recommendation.

On February 9, Mary had an appointment with Hughes and decided that we should ask him to join our team. When Mary visited with me on the following Sunday and discussed Hughes' ideas, I felt we had made a good choice.

One of the first things Hughes did was to call the General Counsel for the Division of Corrections, Raymond Gearey, to find out what would be the procedure for Wainwright's recommendations for clemency for me under Statute 944.30. The only other known case involved Pitts and Lee. My situation was entirely different.

Hughes started my battle.

Mr. Raymond Gearey
Attorney at Law
Tallahassee, Florida

Dear Raymond:

I appreciated very much your talking with me on the telephone the other day concerning Dr. Carl Coppolino. I have read over Florida's Statute 944.30 several more times after we discussed it, and still have not come to any conclusion as to who does the recommendation and to whom the recommendation is given for a reasonable commutation of sentence. I hope that by the time you receive this letter, you can furnish me with the above information.

As I advised you, we are not looking for any publicity; as a matter of fact, we wish we could file papers on behalf of Dr. Coppolino under the name of "Joe Doe" or some other name. We do not want to cause a controversy.

I believe that Dr. Coppolino's record while in prison for the last ten years has been exemplary. He has had no reports written against him, and I think you will find (and I believe you told me) that all his recommendations have been favorable. Dr. Coppolino would like an early release like anyone who is in prison, and to start a new life upon his release. He has not sat around while in prison but has improved his mind greatly by taking all courses which were available to him. I think he would be a very low-risk parolee, especially in view of the fact that he has had furloughs in the past and has never breached his trust to the state of Florida.

I think we both can agree that he has been a model prisoner . . .

I, of course, will cooperate in every respect with the Department of Corrections in order to provide any and all information that it may need for the filing of petition and hearing that may occur as a result of it. If you need any witnesses, evidence matter, or character witnesses, we will be more than happy to provide you with a list of the same. I will also be glad to prepare any affidavits which you may need from Mrs. Coppolino or her children.

Most cordially,

Robert T. Hughes

In the meantime I had my yearly interview by a parole examiner. I received a "no recommendations." When I asked the parole examiner, Mr. Jenkins, about the possibility of action by the Clemency Board on my behalf, he laughed. He told me that I still needed the recommendation of the Parole Commission before any clemency action could be taken! I pressed him about the mechanism that was utilized, and Jenkins admitted that he didn't know. He wasn't alone. Hughes learned from Geary that nobody in Tallahassee took Statute 944.30 seriously, despite the fact that it had been on the books for years! Furthermore, nobody ever heard of a convict's trying to get relief under 944.30! Now I understood the reason for Jenkin's laughter. Hughes had his work cut out for him. However, he did find out that Wainwright planned to submit my name to the Clemency Board by May the first.

Bob Miller came back and told me that Chaplain Jim Bryan spent March 2, 3, and 4 in Tallahassee. Bryan had spoken to an official in the Governor's office, a cabinet official, and of course to Mr. Wainwright, urging support for clemency or parole for me.

Bob indicated that there were two young lawyers from Orlando named Dick Bates and Marvin Rooks who were deeply concerned individuals and wanted to do all they could to help me, short of acting as my attorneys.

On March 15, Bates and Rooks came to A.P.C.I. to see me. We were to visit in the chaplain's office. While they waited for me to join them, Troy

Browning and Rommie Loudd made sure that the lawyers knew all about me, my record, my years in prison, and my innocence.

After meeting with me for almost three hours, Bates and Rooks decided that "enough is enough." I must be freed, not only based on my record in prison, but, most importantly, based on my innocence. Bates decided that he would make what contacts he could, and Rooks would act as back-up.

On March 22, Bates wrote to Attorney General Shevin. In his letter Bates stressed my upcoming petition for pardon and urged favorable action for three reasons:

> In addition to the foregoing, I believe that it would be worthwhile to consider the following factors in regard to Dr. Coppolino's petition: he has spent ten years confined based upon his second degree murder conviction, which I am advised is more than the average amount of time served for such a conviction; he has a perfect record and has been recommended for parole by prison officials on at least six separate occasions; until security was recently tightened, Dr. Coppolino spent approximately three years on weekend furloughs with his family in Tampa, and there were never any complaints or concerns expressed with respect thereto.
>
> I appreciate your consideration of this letter and will look forward to hearing about the outcome of Dr. Coppolino's upcoming appearance before you and the cabinet.
>
> Yours very truly,
>
> H. Richard Bates

Bates sent basically the same letter to Governor Askew and a member of Askew's cabinet, William D. Gunter, Insurance Commissioner.

The response Bates received from Tallahassee was different from the response he expected. Alice Ragsdale, the Governor's Clemency Coordinator, called Dick Bates in an attempt to dissuade him from continuing to help me! It upset him so much that he decided to write another letter to the Governor:

> April 18, 1976
>
> Honorable Reuben O.D. Askew
> Governor of State of Florida
> Tallahassee, Florida
>
> Dear Governor Askew:
>
> In my letter dated March 2, 1977, I requested your consideration of certain factors bearing upon Dr. Coppolino's petition to be filed on

section 944.30 of the Florida Statutes, which petition, it is my impression, will be filed on or about April 28, 1977. This past Saturday, I spent most of the day visiting with Dr. Coppolino and other inmates at the Avon Park Correctional Institution, and I would simply like to reaffirm the foregoing letter and express to you my willingness to be made available to you and the cabinet on Dr. Coppolino's behalf, if there is any area in which I might be helpful to him based upon my knowledge of this case. In that regard, I would be happy to travel to Tallahassee to confer with you and any other members of the cabinet as an interested citizen and not as an attorney.

In fact, it might be of some interest to you to be apprised of the fact that I received a telephone call from a Mrs. Ragsdale from the Attorney General's office. I had sent a letter similar in content to both Attorney General Robert Shevin and Insurance Commissioner Bill Gunther on behalf of Dr. Coppolino. Mrs. Ragsdale indicated to me that there was nothing presently pending under section 944.30 on behalf of Dr. Coppolino, which I would assume is correct since the petition will presumably not be filed for another ten days. However, based upon my conversation with Mrs. Ragsdale, I got the distinct impression that any further efforts on my part relative to the anticipated petition were futile in light of the fact that I was advised that the cabinet was very unlikely to give any serious consideration to Dr. Coppolino's petition because of the fact that the Parole Commission is deemed to be most knowledgeable in all such matters. I was told that probably the only way I could be of any assistance to Dr. Coppolino is to write to the Parole Commission.

I trust that my efforts in corresponding with you will not be futile since it is my humble opinion that in light of Dr. Coppolino's record, the Parole Commission has abused their discretion, probably because of the notoriety of his case, in not granting him parole prior to this date.

Thank you for your consideration of this appeal on Dr. Coppolino's behalf, and again, if I can be of service to you and the Cabinet in your consideration of this matter, I trust that your office will be in contact with me.

Yours very truly,

H. Richard Bates

The more Dick Bates thought about the Ragsdale call, the more incensed he became. He decided as a concerned citizen to write to Lieutenant Governor Jim Williams, and enclose copies of the two letters to Governor Askew.

PART FOUR

Early Morning Sunlight

Mary received a phone call from our friend Jeanne King, a free-lance newspaper reporter and the wife of Earl King, Assistant Editor of the *New York Daily News*. Jeanne had covered both my New Jersey trial and my Florida trial. After my conviction in Florida, Mary and I felt that aside from the family and my attorneys, Jeanne King was the only other person who believed I was innocent.

Jeanne had an interesting story to tell. A physician's wife, Nenita Favor, had died in a New York hospital under mysterious circumstances. The New York medical examiner's office had performed an autopsy on the late Mrs. Favor 48 hours after her death. Her husband, Dr. Arsenio Favor, was suspected by the New York Medical Examiner's Office of having murdered her using an injection of succinylcholine.

Jeanne went on to say that she had telephoned the New York Medical Examiner, Dr. Michael Baden, and while waiting for Dr. Baden to speak with her, Jeanne heard the Medical Examiner's conversation with an unknown party on the other telephone line. Dr. Baden was telling his other caller that it would be impossible to find any traces of succinylocholine in Mrs. Favor's body since she had been dead for 48 hours prior to autopsy. Dr. Baden ordered that Mrs. Favor's tissues be sent to three other laboratories in an attempt to see if they could detect the succinylcholine in her tissues. He doubted it because Mrs. Favor had been dead for 48 ours before the autopsy. Jeanne King was stunned. She thought, Carl's wife was dead, embalmed and buried for four months and this same Medical Examiner's Office through Umberger and the then Medical Examiner, Dr. Helpern, testified in Carl's trial that they found succinylcholine in Carmela's body using a test Umberger had developed!

Jeanne said that once Dr. Baden spoke with her on the telephone she screamed, "There is a man in prison in Florida for the past ten years, namely Dr. Carl Coppolino, because of the testimony out of your office about a test made on a body buried for four months! Now I heard you say that you can't test for succinycholine because Mrs. Favor had been dead for 48 hours before the autopsy! What the hell's going on?"

Mary asked Jeanne about Dr. Baden's reply. "Only that he would talk with me about it later," Jeanne answered.

I called Jeanne King about her conversation with Baden and she said she would keep on digging. Perhaps she would go to see Dr. Umberger, who was now retired. There was talk, she said, that the New York Medical Examiner's Office would call in Umberger to work on Mrs. Favor's tissues.

I informed Jeanne about the push for clemency that was presently before Governor Askew; she promised me that she would do all she could and secure what affidavits she could to be presented to the Governor.

Neither of us knew that this was the opening shot of the battle that would ultimately condemn the falsified evidence and perjured testimony by the State of Florida witnesses at my trial—evidence that eventually led to my conviction—and the concealment by a State of Florida witness of evidence after my conviction that would have freed me in 1968, since it showed that I was innocent.

APRIL—MAY

The national newspapers carried the story of Dr. Favor and made the comparison between the Favor and Coppolino cases. In addition, Umberger was called out of retirement to use the test he supposedly developed in my case to determine if any succinylcholine was present in Mrs. Favor.

Mary and I were worried, not only about the possible spill-over onto our efforts to free me through the Clemency Board, but, under the circumstances, a gnawing suspicion that Dr. Favor was going to be framed, just like me. How else could you explain the meaning of the conversation overhead by Jeanne King? There was nothing we could do now but wait to see what Jeanne turned up. I wasn't too hopeful in view of the fact that the *New York Daily News* was already hinting at Dr. Favor's arrest!

On April the 7th I spoke with Jeanne and she told me that the New York Medical Examiner's Office had sent Mrs. Favor's tissues to the three laboratory centers and they could find nothing, since Mrs. Favor had been dead for 48 hours before autopsy!

On April the 8th the newspaper reported that Dr. Favor had been arrested for the murder of his wife, Nenita, by an injection of succinyl-choline. Umberger would have to stand alone, since Milton Helpern died on April 22.

Later in the month, Mary called Jeanned King and learned that the State of New York decided not to use Dr. Umberger and his so-called test in their continued investigation of the accused Dr. Favor! Jeanne had not been able to nail any information in affidavit form. All she had was hearsay, rumors that said that Umberger's tests were useless and that the New York Medical Examiner's office would not consider them in the Dr. Favor murder investigation. But nothing official. Nothing the courts would recognize.

Dr. Michael Baden, the New York Medical Examiner, was one of the new breed of forensic scientists. He was honest and dedicated to truth and his principles. Later, his integrity would cost him his job and ruin a promising career.

On April the 18th Hughes, in the company of Representative Lee Moffit of Tampa, met with Judge James Adkins and Louie L. Wainwright.

Moffit, as the senior Legislator for Hillsborough County, had thoroughly investigated my situation, and found the circumstances unusual: I had spent more time in prison for a second degree murder conviction than anybody else with no previous record; my prison record plus the more than three years spent in the communities spoke for itself, and I should have been released long ago; and the Parole Commission was blaming the legislature for crowding the prisons because of enacting laws requiring judges to pass mandatory sentences for different crimes. Some members of the legislature were blaming the Parole Commission, had not paroled those men deserving of parole, and the representatives and senators had used my case as an illustration.

Hughes had asked Wainwright about the possibilities of transferring me closer to home, by placing me in a Tampa Work Release Center. Again, Wainwright resisted. All he would do was move me to another prison closer to Tampa. I turned down his offer. I had the good will of the officials at A.P.C.I. and was not prepared to become adjusted to a new prison.

On Thursday, April 28, I completed my tenth year and learned from the chief classification officer of A.P.C.I., Mr. Ballantine, that my name was on the list submitted by Wainwright to the Clemency Board coordinator, Alice Ragsdale, for presentation to Governor Askew and the Cabinet.

Hughes started to collate a drive for names on petitions from as many counties as possible. Eventually he was able to submit to Ragsdale and the Governor, signed petitions from Orange, Osceola, Hillsborough, and Pinellas counties urging the pardon board to take favorable action on my petition.

Hughes had spoken with Ragsdale while he was in Tallahassee. She told him essentially the same thing she told Bates by telephone: that the petition was only a formality, that nobody paid any attention to 944.30, and that my only hope was release by the Parole Commission. It was a *Catch 22* situation—if I *had been* released by the Parole Commission, there would be no need to petition the Clemency Board on the bassis of 944.30! To be told that 944.30 was only a formality and that my release had to come through the Parole Commission made the circle complete. No exit.

Since he was there, Hughes decided to speak with Ray Howard. Howard told him flatly that he would never vote for my parole. While Bob Hughes was meeting Wainwright, Ragsdale, and Howard on the 19th and 20th of April, I had a surprise visitor, James Russ.

It was more than ten years since I had seen Jimmy. We almost didn't recognize each other; he had a full-faced beard and I was much thinner than he remembered.

We spent two hours together in the classification conference room, and used most of that time catching up on what happened to our respective families. Soon we were down to the reason for Jimmy's visit.

He had come with an offer to help, not as an attorney, but as a friend. Jimmy confirmed that it was an open secret in Tallahassee that Georgieff had vigorously opposed my release these many years. I explained to Jimmy my plan to work through the Clemency Board via 944.30.

Jimmy was skeptical over my ultimate release by the Pardon Board. However, he would work with Hughes and contact those people he knew that might be able to have some positive input into the Clemency Board. He felt that the points already stressed by Hughes, along with Mary's and the children's devotion to me, would weigh heavily in my favor.

I told Russ about Bates' efforts via letters to Gunter, Shevin, Askew and Williams. Jimmy offered to follow up with Gunter and to poke around in Tallahassee.

Lastly I brought up the Dr. Favor situation, particularly the conversation overheard by Jeanne King. Russ said it meant nothing unless it could be documented. The idea that Umberger and Helpern phonied the test results was nothing new to us; however, proving it was a different matter. Jimmy promised to write me and let me know what he found out.

Lamar Baker came to see me. He brought a cake and fresh oysters. We went out to the pistol range and Russell joined us. It was a beautiful Saturday, the first time I had been outside the fence since furloughs were suspended.

Lamar told me that the LaRussa brothers, attorneys in Tampa, were slated to become campaign managers for Attorney General Shevin for Hillsborough County. Shevin was the strongest contender for the Governor's race scheduled for the following year. However, everybody suspected the candidate list would be long prior to primaries. Lamar said he would talk with Rudy LaRussa and bring to his attention the amount of support I had through letters, telegrams, and petitions.

Carmen Benoit was related to the LaRussa brothers. She mentioned to Mary that she would do all she could to make sure that Rudy and Jimmy LaRussa would bring the facts in front of Shevin. Tom, Carmen's husband, joined her and the Spoto-Benoit families began to work vigorously in one last push for my release.

In the meantime, some of the black leaders in Tampa such as Big John Stephens, owner of a famous Bar-B-Que restaurant in Tampa, had organized petition drives among their supporters in the hopes of persuading Tallahassee and the Pardon Board to act favorably upon my clemency petition. Bigh John Stephens brought one of my petitions to a ministers' convention in Jacksonville where about 25 ministers signed, plus 35 other people, representing 25,000 votes.

In addition, Lamar Baker was back to see me on May 21. He brought some food for me and informed me that he had talked with the LaRussa brothers about my support. Rudy LaRussa said they were sure Shevin would be interested in the votes supporting me.

I received several letters from Russ. He had nothing solid to report, but was still poking around.

Meanwhile, Bob Hughes went back to Tallahassee to see the chairman of the Parole Commission, Charles Scriven, and came away with nothing.

JUNE

Bob Hughes found out from Alice Ragsdale that the Governor's office was flooded with letters, telegrams, and petitions in support of my release. She went on to say that the Executive Office had never before seen such across-the-board support for the release of an inmate, support that obviously was not organized, but spontaneous. However, Ragsdale went on to say that she still felt it would be up to the Parole Commission to act, that 944.30 and the petition for clemency were only a formality.

Dick Bates was keeping up his campaign with Governor Askew. On June 21, he wrote Governor Askew:

> "You will recall that I wrote to you on behalf of Carl Coppolino by letters dated March 22, 1977, April 18, 1977, and April 27, 1977. I have been advised that no decision has been made as of this date concerning Dr. Coppolino's petition, so I would like to take this opportunity to reconfirm my total support for his release in the immediate future.
>
> . . . as you continue to consider his petition, and I am certainly aware of the fact that it is no small matter for you to essentially overrule the past decisions of the Parole Commission . . .

Jimmy Russ came back to see me on June 24. He confirmed the amount of my support recorded in the Governor's Office and indicated that the Attorney General's office was keeping a careful eye on what was happening. His advice to me was to continue doing what we were doing, namely flooding the Governor's office and the Parole Commission with letters, telegrams, mailgrams, and petitions documenting the support I had for my immediate release.

The Tampa Tribune ran an article by Rick Barry with my picture in their June 25th issue. The tone of the article was that I had been repeatedly turned down for parole despite serving such an excessive amount of time on second degree, being a model prisoner, and having been home on furloughs for three years.

JULY

There was tension in the air at A.P.C.I., and talk of another riot. The guards were nervous. I called Mary and told her, as a safety precaution, to skip the Fourth of July weekend even though I knew my advice would be ignored. I was right. She arrived on Sunday with a new hairdo and a new dress. She looked absolutely beautiful!

The tension at the prison was due to over-crowded conditions. Everywhere I looked, there were endlessly long lines at the mess hall, laundry, and canteen.

Incidents of violence were escalating—first fights and convicts being attacked by other convicts with weapons were becoming a daily occurrence.

On June the first, the United States Fifth Circuit Court of Appeals in New Orleans upheld U.S. District Judge Charles R. Scott's ruling in May of 1975 that the over-crowded conditions in Florida's prison violated the inmates' constitutional rights. The inmate count was 5000 higher than the designed capacity for the prison system.

During the first four months of 1976, there were 290 separate reports that some prisoner hit another prisoner or guard. By the end of April of 1977, the number of such attacks stood at 345. And these were only the ones reported. Many incidents that I witnessed were never seen by the guards and, therefore, not reported. There was constant danger everywhere.

Things had become so bad at the East Unit—now called Florida State Prison—that almost 60 percent of that prison's population was "locked-down." "Locked-down" meant that the convicts were kept in their cells 24 hours a day!

The horror stories reminiscent of 1971 came filtering down to me. Through my underground pipeline I heard about the beatings of convicts by guards. For instance on March 15, 1976, four guards escorted convict Amos Sloan into "S" wing at Florida State Prison to "counsel" him for his abusive language.

The initial counseling offered to the hand-cuffed Sloan was a blow that knocked him to the floor, and what followed was a savagely unmerciful beating.

In addition, I kept hearing about beatings at River Junction Correctional Institutions in Gadsden County, but it was hard for me to verify these because of distance and poor communications.

AUGUST, 1977

My friend, Troy Browning, had been paroled and was speaking in front of church groups about the injustice of my imprisonment. He called Mary and told her how he had explained to anybody that would listen, that I was innocent and being held a political prisoner. Browning said that many people told him they were going to send telegrams to Governor Askew urging my release.

Bob Hughes went back to Tallahassee to go through my jacket at the Parole Commission. While he was there, he conferred with Justice James Adkins because Adkins had an official position with Governor Askew's Criminal Justice Commission. Adkins confirmed to Hughes that my case was explosive, and that the support I had did help, but he had no idea whether I would receive any relief. Dick Bates talked with Lieutenant Governor Williams by telephone urging the Lieutenant Governor to use his input to Governor Askew to explain my situation and to urge the Governor to move on the petition for clemency. Lieutenant Governor Williams promised Bates that he would talk with the Governor. Dick followed up his call with a letter to Lieutenant Governor Williams:

Honorable J. H. Jim Williams
Lieutenant Governor
The Capital State of Florida
Tallahassee, Florida

Dear Lieutenant Governor Williams:

The purpose of this letter is simply to confirm our telephone conversation this morning concerning Dr. Carl A. Coppolino.

I certainly understand Governor Askew's deep concern for the men presently on death row and the fact that his attention has no doubt been diverted solely to that particular problem. However, as I indicated to you, I would very much appreciate your advising him of our telephone conversation and the fact that I would be most appreciative of some word concerning the petition for clemency that has been filed on behalf of Dr. Coppolino.

As I indicated to you, I would consider it a privilege to travel to Tallahassee for the purpose of meeting with you and/or the Governor concerning this particular matter even if our time together would be limited to fifteen minutes or less. Let me assure you that my interest in Dr. Coppolino is purely as a citizen and lay person, and not as attorney.

Thank you again for returning my telephone call and your consideration of this particular matter.

Yours very truly,

H. Richard Bates

I had my six-month progress report at the classification office on August 31. My classification officer, Mr. Cloud, read me a letter that was in my file from Mr. Wainwright. The letter directed the classification team to recommend me for clemency action by the pardon board! Cloud said that the best they could do at this level was to recommend me for parole, which they did. Now I needed to wait for the parole examiner to come back to see me sometime in October.

My friend, Jerry, now from Chicago, had been on the telephone to Mary and suggested to her and me that I think about a parole to Chicago. Perhaps that might help sway the Parole Commission to release me. Mary and I told Jerry we would consider it.

Lisa didn't care for her high school; therefore, we decided that she could use some in-depth teaching and sent her off to private school at Howey-in-the-Hills. This left Mary alone at home and able to spend more time circulating petitions.

Hughes had informed Mary that he was now convinced that there would be no action taken by the clemency board, and that Alice Ragsdale was right, the petition was strictly a formality.

OCTOBER

My many friends throughout the country kept the pressure on the Parole Commission and the Governor's office while I waited to see the parole examiner.

By now I detected a sense of futility in Hughes, Bates, Russ and others. Only Mary refused to give up. My friends, Bob Miller and Troy Browning, were busy, but frustrated. A sense of doom washed over me.

OCTOBER 7

My twelfth wedding anniversary arrived and I was still in prison. I felt down, depressed. I tried to think of the pluses in my life: Mary and Lisa loved me and kept coming to visit; Monica and her husband, Michael, were frequent visitors; Claire and her husband, Roger, were very busy but stayed in touch. Heidi and Juan had been up from Costa Rica and visited with me although they were back there now. My mother had been down to Florida from Brooklyn and had stayed with Mary at our condominium. I thought about the many friends and supporters I had that I had never met, and I felt blessed.

The *New York Daily News* reported in its October 7 issue that District Attorney Michael Davidson asked the court for a two-month continuance in the Dr. Favor case. Mary and I suspected that Dr. Michael Baden realized he had no adequate testing procedures to detect succinylcholine.

OCTOBER 20, 1977

I was interviewed by the parole examiner, Wesson, at 3:30 p.m. He informed me that Wainwright had formally requested the pardon board to act on my behalf according to 944.30. However, the Parole Commission had vigorously opposed my release in my recommendations to the Governor.

In view of the Commissioner's action, Wesson put me off another year. He did say that it was mandatory for the Parole Commission to take a vote since I had been formally recommended for parole by the Division of Corrections.

I left the interview discouraged and defeated. Apparently, those on the outside who were frustrated and who felt the situation was hopeless, namely Hughes, Bates, and Russ, were right.

It was almost 5:00 p.m. before I could reach Jim Russ by telephone. I told him the bad news. Russ said that there had been changes on the Parole Commission of which I was not aware; J. Hopps Barker had retired and Jack Blanton had been appointed to his place. That made two gone, two to go.

Russ had an idea. There was an attorney by the name of Carlton in Tallahassee, and he had been Chief Justice of the Florida Supreme Court. Jimmy thought that if anybody could get the Commission to see my side before the vote, it would be Carlton. Russ would call Carlton and get back with me.

While I awaited Jimmy's call, I reached Mary at home and told her the bad news. Mary took it without comment, saying she would be there on Saturday, and we would discuss what we would do now, if anything.

Russ called back and said Carlton would be at the Parole Commission on Monday the 24th and that he would take my case only if Carlton thought he could be successful. It was a fair offer and I accepted.

OCTOBER 22, 1977
SATURDAY

Mary visited. It was a black day for both of us. All the work, all the effort, all the speaking engagements, letters, petitions, trips to Tallahassee, lawyers, paid and unpaid, more than ten years in prison, and all for *nothing!*

My heart was acting up again, no doubt from the pressure. Mary was short and impatient with me, reflecting her inner turmoil.

She said that Russ had not called her, but she did expect to hear something after Carlton saw the Parole Commissioners on Monday. Neither of us held out any hope for the future. We were exhausted.

Lisa wrote me a letter; she was crushed over my parole turn-down. The other children were as expressive. The whole family was in mourning.

NOVEMBER

I wrote Dick Bates about my bad news. He was very upset and wrote a letter to Lieutenant Governor Williams that was clear and to the point:

November 4, 1977

Honorable J. H. Jim Williams
Lieutenant Governor
The Capitol
Tallahassee, Florida

Dear Lieutenant Governor Williams:

You may recall that I discussed with you briefly by telephone the status of Dr. Carl A. Coppolino with particular reference to the fact that by law he is entitled to consideration for executive clemency by Governor Askew. Since I have never been in criminal law, I must confess that my degree of confusion relative to the deposition of Dr. Coppolino's case is probably attributable to my ignorance in regard to such matters. However, I am considerably disappointed and somewhat frustrated by the apparent attitude of the Parole Commission concerning his case.

I have recently learned that Dr. Coppolino was interviewed in recent weeks by Mr. Wesson of the Parole Commission, and notwithstanding the recommendations of such prison officials as Mr. Louis Wainwright that Dr. Coppolino be paroled and the tremendous public support that has been expressed for him, Mr. Wesson indicated that he would not recommend his parole at this time.

I am frankly amazed that after spending over ten years with a perfect record in the Florida penal system and providing every conceivable evidence of being ready, willing, and able to make a substantial contribution to our society, this man continues to be rebuffed in his desire to gain his freedom. I am again writing to you for the simple purpose of expressing my whole-hearted support for the release of Dr. Coppolino, either on

parole or by some form of pre-release work program and would respectfully request that you take whatever steps are appropriate to check
into the present status of this matter with a view toward effecting
Dr. Coppolino's release through proper channels. I certainly would
appreciate anything that you can do in this regard.

Yours very truly,

H. Richard Bates

He received an immediate response:

Dear Mr. Bates:

This acknowledges receipt of your recent letter on behalf of Dr. Carl A.
Coppolino. I have referred a copy of your letter to Ms. Eleanor Mitchell,
Assistant General Counsel, who advises Governor Askew in matters
regarding executive clemency. As you are no doubt aware, the Parole
Commission is an autonomous body and has sole statutory authority
and jurisdiction regarding parole. Any action on my part beyond bringing your letter to the attention of the chairman, which I am pleased to do,
would be considered inappropriate.

I have forwarded a copy of your correspondence to Mr. Charles Scriven,
Chairman of the Commission, for his review and consideration. Thank
you for your letter and with kind regards, I am

Sincerely,

Lieutenant Governor Jim Williams

Several days later, Bates received an answer from Eleanor Mitchell,
Assistant General Counsel to Governor Askew, which left a crack in the
door, but I wasn't impressed. In fact, I had almost given up hope.

November 22, 1977

South Orange Avenue
Orlando, Florida

Dear Mr. Bates:

Your November 4, 1977, letter to Lieutenant Governor Williams concerning the case of Carl Coppolino has been referred to me.

At this time, I am only able to report to you that all cases of persons who have served ten years without disciplinary reports including that of Dr. Coppolino, are being reviewed. We do expect that the review of these cases will be completed in the near future, at which time Governor Askew, through the clemency coordinator, Mrs. Alice Ragsdale, will announce the results.

Thank you for your continuing interest.

Sincerely,

Eleanor Mitchell
Assistant General Counsel

NOVEMBER 13
SUNDAY

Mary visited with me. She was very depressed. Neither one of us had heard from Russ and could only assume that Carlton was unsuccessful in his attempts to have the Parole Commission vote favorably.

Mary wasn't feeling well. She had developed ulcer sores in her mouth, and I was having increasingly difficult episodes of angina pectoris.

NOVEMBER 20
SUNDAY

My friend, Lamar Baker, visited me. He was upset over the turn of events, and he didn't like the way I looked. We tried to come up with a plan of action, but found nothing.

DECEMBER, 1977

Dr. Arsenio Favor was indicted for murder on December 8. The *New York Daily News* ran a large article on December 9 crediting Dr. Umberger with a solution to the problem of detection of succinlycholine.

However, through Jeanne King, Mary and I were aware that the New York City Medical Examiner had rejected any work Umberger could possibly have done.

Again, Mary and I felt that Dr. Favor was being fitted for a "frame." Perhaps we could help Dr. Favor. Mary decided, after speaking with me, to get in touch with Mr. Cutler, Dr. Favor's lawyer, and offer to him the transcript of my trial.

Jim Russ talked with Eleanor Mitchell by telephone. She told Russ that my case was still on Governor Askew's desk. She indicated that nobody knew what the Governor would do. There was still no word from Carlton.

Hughes called Alice Ragsdale. Mrs. Ragsdale said that my file had been on Governor Askew's desk for more than six weeks. She indicated that she would try to get the Governor to make a decision one way or the other.

CHRISTMAS DAY

Christmas Day was a somber occasion for all of us. I had earrings made out of bone for Mary and pendant pins for Monica and Lisa, plus a pipe pick for Michael. All the items were made of bone.

Monica and Michael decided to take jobs in the Dominican Republic, working for Michael's father, Warren Fuller. They were leaving the country for the Dominican Republic after Christmas.

We looked toward 1978 with little hope. Unfortunately, I still had no idea how bad things were. I was soon to find out.

The holidays were over, thank God. I had the flu and felt utterly debilitated. My heart was still acting up, but I tried not to let it bother me.

I found myself on the telephone to Mary two and three times a day. She was in despair, and I was in a deep depression. She had a new job as office manager for an orthopedic surgeon. This helped her take her mind off our unrelievedly tormenting situation.

Russ wrote me a letter on January 4, 1978. It was bleak to say the least:

January 4, 1978

Dr. Carl Coppolino
Avon Park, Florida

Dear Carl:

This letter will serve as a follow up to my last telephone discussion with you.

As regards to the Governor's commutation, this apparently hit a dead end. I have heard nothing from the Governor's office and my only information is the press article referring the Governor's authority to act generally in this area and the failure to find mention of your name.

As regards to the Parole Board, I have made several phone calls to the office of Sam Spector (Carlton's associate) without reaching him or having my calls returned. I can only assume that he has nothing relevant to report to me. I am of the present opinion that it serves no good purpose at this particular time to pursue either Spector or Carlton for assistance . . .

In closing, I can only say that my best wishes and prayers are with you and that patience and perseverance are desired virtues.

Sincerely,

James S. Russ

On the following day, Mary received a letter from Robert Hughes, which drove a spike into my heart:

Mrs. Mary W. Coppolino
Tampa, Florida

Dear Mary:

I heard from Mrs. Alice Ragsdale in Tallahassee today concerning the Governor of Florida's review of all inmates that have been in prison for a period of ten years and have not given any problems. Alice Ragsdale read a letter to me from Governor Askew sent to Chairman Scrivin of the Florida Parole Board in which he states that, pursuant to Florida Statutes 944.30, he has decided not to exercise executive clemency in any of the cases that he had before him. That would include Carl's case also. I am at this time at a loss to tell you what further action we can take other than to try to keep the pressure on the Parole Commission.

I had hoped for a better response from the Governor's office or at least some pressure from the Governor on the Parole Commission to act on Carl's behalf, but apparently after reading Carl's file and going through everything, his "moral convictions" would not let him see fit to ask the Parole Commission for an early release.

Most cordially,

Robert T. Hughes

Difficult as it seemed, Mary and I had to regroup. If we faltered now, all was lost.

Lamar and his wife, Kathy, came to visit me on Saturday, January 21. I learned how disappointed were my supporters in Tampa. Reports had come in from my friends who had mounted their petition campaigns in my support. Bates was beside himself with frustration. My friend, Jerry, felt helpless. I received mail from people all over the country who had learned by word-of-mouth about my plight. Carmen and Tom Benoit were outraged over the treatment I had received. Carmen, through the Spoto family, made sure that her relatives Rudy and Jimmy LaRussa were made aware that she and Tom were extremely displeased over my treatment.

FEBRUARY 9, 1978
BLACK TUESDAY

I was called into the classification office by Chief Classification Officer Ballantine. He was very agitated, and I sat next to his desk. Ballantine had worked with the Division of Corrections for a number of years. When I first arrived at A.P.C.I., he was the furlough coordinator. From that position, he moved up as classification officer, and now was chief classification officer with a group of men under him. Because of his position, he had to be in constant communication with Central Office in Tallahassee, and with the Parole Commission.

What he had to tell me turned my legs into jelly. Ballantine didn't drag it out—I would not leave prison. There was strong pressure being exerted through a judge (Schaub?) and the Attorney General's office (Georgieff?) to ensure that I'd never be released. No matter what I did or my supporters tried to do, it would be useless.

I walked out of his office and back to my barracks in a daze. Later on I learned from my fellow convicts that I sat on my bed staring into space for the better part of an hour. I saw nothing, and heard nothing.

Images drifted in and out of my mind—Lisa as a baby, Monica playing her oboe, Claire desperately putting on her makeup before her date arrived, Heidi cooing to the birds, Mary and I watching the sunset as the warm gulf breezes swept our faces and our hair.

Now nothing. I was doomed to a living death—the numbing, boring, crowded, stench-laden hate, the violence-filled daily existence of prison. My emotional and psychological collapse was almost, but not quite, total.

Painfully I struggled off my bunk and made my way to the telephone. My first call was to Mary. She said that Ballantine's news had always been part of our reality, and we agreed that it was a kick in the teeth.

I called Lamar Baker at his place of business in Tampa Bay Center and gave him the grim news. He was shocked, stunned. He said there was little that could be done. This was an election year, and Shevin was running for Governor. He added that I had quite a bit of support in Tampa, but my supporters were frustrated and had their own problems. He offered to go back again to the LaRussa brothers for whatever that might do. He agreed with me that the situation, unfortunately, looked hopeless.

Bob Miller came with his wife, Jayne, to see and comfort me. Bob had been on the phone with Mary trying to see what could be done.

Troy Browning was out on parole, and he called Mary, outraged over what had transpired with my case.

About this time a "funny thing" happened—an illustration of the fact that nobody knows what the future will bring.

As mentioned previously, the newspapers in the Punta Gorda area had learned that I was on furloughs, had called Superintendent Rankin Brown and had written a series of articles which finally resulted in Attorney General Robert Shevin's letter to Armond Cross and the slowing down of my furloughs.

Mary and I had been spotted at the Holiday Inn in Punta Gorda by a man named Howard Harnum who was at that time on the Punta Gorda police department and in plain clothes. Harnum had called the newspapers after he observed Mary and me checking into the Holiday Inn. I learned about this from Harnum himself. He was now a convict (prisoner #060811) with me at A.P.C.I. What a strange turn of fate!

FEBRUARY 19
SUNDAY

Mary arrived for her Sunday visit. She was depressed and distant. She told me that, besides what Ballantine had revealed, she had felt for some time now that I would never be released from prison. It wasn't right, it wasn't fair. I was convicted of a crime that never happened, and all this was beside the point. What Ballantine said made the picture complete as far as she was concerned—I would die in prison.

MARCH

The pressure was affecting the family in many ways. There was a disturbance at Howey and Lisa didn't want to stay there. Mary discussed the situation with me, and brought Lisa back home. After much struggle, Mary placed her at Tampa Preparatory School. However, Lisa was not happy there, and stayed only until the end of that school year. Monica and Michael were unhappy in the Dominican Republic and planned to come home. Mary was sick on and off for the next 30 days with mouth ulcers, stomach upsets, and flu-like symptoms. I wasn't in any better shape. I had the flu again, and found that my weight had dropped below 150 lbs.

APRIL

Governor Askew ordered the Florida Department of Criminal Law Enforcement to investigate Parole Commissioner Armond Cross! The charges that were lodged against Cross were serious: he was accused of conducting 30 parole revocation hearings in two hours; of having a drinking problem; and of submitting an inaccurate parole revocation report on William E. Baker. The United States Fifth Circuit Court of Appeals in New Orleans ordered Baker's immediate release. In its order the Court said that Cross had violated Baker's right to Due Process throughout the hearing, including the nine numerous appeals to have an attorney present. Cross, according to the Court, also refused Baker the opportunity to question his accusers despite the colorable claim that he had not committed the offense upon which revocation proceedings were based. The bulk of the charges against Cross stemmed from an investigation of the Parole Commission by the House of Representatives Committee on Corrections, Parole, and Probation. The chairman of this committee was Representative Don Hazelton.

Hazelton had submitted his report to Governor Askew and had urged the Governor to take action. The title of the committee's report was "The Oversight Report." In addition, Representative Hazelton sent out a newsletter which summarized in detail his findings about the Parole Commission and Armond Cross in particular.

APRIL

Mr. Ballantine informed me that my name would again be submitted at the end of the month for Clemency Board consideration. Neither he nor I thought there would be any positive results.

Mary received a call from Murray Cutler, Dr. Favor's attorney, with a follow-up letter. Mr. Cutler was grateful for our offer of the copy of our transcript and planned to have his associate, Mr. Tom Cavanaugh, come to Florida to see her. Cavanaugh was a retired New York Chief of Detectives, who was also an attorney. Cavanaugh had a son named Brian, who subsequently became Assistant State Attorney for Broward County and would be accompanying his father. Destiny was about to take charge of my life.

On April 26, 1978, I had a meeting with Tom Cavanaugh and his son, Brian. We met in the same conference room at the classification building in which I had previously met with Russ.

Tom Cavanaugh was a strapping gentleman, 6'3" tall, with a pale Irish complexion. He carried himself with easy dignity. His son, Brian, was about the same height with the same coloring and large, intense blue eyes.

After preliminary social conversation, I discovered that Tom's wife, Isabelle, was practicing medicine at Methodist Hospital in Brooklyn. It turned out that she was the same Isabelle who practiced obstetrics and gynecology when I was practicing medicine at Methodist! I remembered Isabelle very, very well because she had always been so kind to me.

Tom and Brian related to me that Isabelle knew Carmela and me when

Carmela was an intern, and had maintained throughout the years that I could not have killed anybody.

"Carl," Tom began, opening his black briefcase. The late afternoon sun struggled to pierce the grime covered windows of the conference room. We were seated around a highly polished mahogany table. The overhead lamp light bounced off the wood and gave Brian and Tom's face a yellowish cast. No doubt, I didn't look any better.

I was curious as to the reason for this personal visit. Cutler wanted my transcripts and whatever else we had. Cavanaugh was scheduled to look them over and take what was needed.

"Carl," Tom repeated. "I have two documents I would like you to read and give me your impressions on."

The first document had on its frontspiece: "Investigation into the Death of Nenita Favor, before a quorum of the Fourth April, 1977, Grand Jury. Presented by: Michael Davidson, Esq., Assistant District Attorney, Deborah Kramer, Grand Jury Reporter.

The New York State Grand Jury report ran from page 382 to 413, and concerned the sworn testimony of Dr. Umberger. The Assistant District Attorney Davidson had been questioning Umberger about his tests concerning of succinylcholine.

Umberger had testified under oath in the Grand Jury proceeding that he still had not developed a test for detecting the presence of succinylcholine in the human body! Dr. Umberger said that he needed time to formulate a test, to develop methodology to detect succinylcholine in the human body!

The second document had a frontspiece that was similar to the first. It contained the sworn testimony of the medical examiner who succeeded Dr. Helpern, Dominick J. DiMaio, M.D. His testimony covered pages 417 to 438.

Dr. DeMaio testified under oath at this Grand Jury proceeding that there was no known method of detecting the presence of succinylcholine in the human body in the United States!

I looked first at Tom, then at Brian. "I knew it! I knew it!" I shouted. "This is fantastic!"

I went on to tell the Cavanaughs of the hints dropped by the late Sheriff Ross Boyer and F. Lee Bailey and of Jim Russ' suspicions that there were no tests and that the evidence given by Umberger and Helpern was phony.

"What happens now?" I asked Tom.

"We are scheduled to go to trial with Dr. Favor next month," Tom said. "The present Medical Examiner is Dr. Michael Baden and I will have some hard questions to ask of him. Perhaps there are more documents that can shed further light on your situation."

"Doctor," Brian interrupted, pointing to Umberger and DiMaio's sworn Grand Jury testimony, "these documents conclusively prove that at the very least you didn't have a fair trial. The State of Florida's witnesses perjured themselves for whatever reason." Brian smiled, "Also it vindicates my mother's faith in your innocence."

I related to the Cavanaughs the telephone conversation Jeanne King overheard Dr. Baden make. Tom said, "It'll be hard, but maybe I'll be able to ask him about that on cross-examination."

We ended our meeting with the Cavanaughs promising to keep digging because they felt that whatever help was given me had to help Tom's client, Dr. Favor.

APRIL 30
SUNDAY

Mary visited with Lisa. Mary had her hair cut short and had on a new green dress. Lisa had on a pair of slacks and had brought her algebra homework so that I could help her go over some of the more difficult problems.

Mary appeared in good spirits, for the first time in months. She agreed that the Umberger-DiMaio sworn testimony had to help, somehow, somewhere. She said that Tom had promised to get us some copies.

MAY

I received a letter from Brian Cavanaugh written on May 12, promising to help:

May 12, 1978

Carl Coppolino, M.D.
Avon Park, Florida

Dear Carl:

My father asked me to acknowledge on his behalf his receipt of your kind letter. We will definitely get all of the material you requested to you, as well as any additional pertinent matter we encounter.

Dr. Favor's trial has started; the judge would not allow anymore contin-
uances. Perhaps, however, as you pointed out, this will work to our
advantage, as the prosecution will not now have the luxury of extra time
in which to develop, or even manufacture, their case.

The state apparently is not going to show the presence of succinic acid,
but will rest on the inference based on negative postmortem reports that
succinylcholine was the only cause of death. This is a weird stretching of
the imagination, but according to my father, the medical examiners of
New York and Nassau Counties, as well as the Chief Pathologist at
Brooksdale Hospital, are going to so testify.

Dad is going to try to use some reverse psychology by injecting Umberger's testing procedures into the controversy. If they denigrate the
validity of Umberger's test, perhaps it will have a beneficial reflection on
your case. We shall keep you informed as to the status.

My mother sends her best to you and wants you to know that you are
continually in her prayers.

If there is any other possible thing that we could do for you, please don't
hesitate to ask.

Truly yours,

Brian T. Cavanagh

On May 20, Tom Cavanaugh called Mary and informed her that the New
York State District Attorney's Office had called Dr. Francis Foldes as a
State witness in the Dr. Favor case. Foldes testified that there were no
tests to find succinylcholine.

This information was mind-boggling! One sovereign jurisdiction (New
York) used my defense in another sovereign jurisdiction (Florida) to
prove the prosecutor's point that there were not tests. By inference, that
was my point—namely that Umberger and Helpern were liars!

Mary called Jeanne King to bring her up to date. In addition, Mary
called Henry Gonzalez and asked his opinion about these new developments.

Gonzalez cautioned that we should not be hasty. The Umberger-
DiMaio testimony sounded promising, he stated, but he emphasized that
we should wait for the final outcome of the Dr. Favor case before going
public with our information.

I called Jim Russ about the sworn Grand Jury testimony and followed
up my conversation by sending him copies. Jimmy was keenly interested
and wanted to digest them first-hand.

JUNE

My old friend Dominic, from 3T in Raiford, was back in the system and with me in A.P.C.I.

Dominic had a dream, a belief that prison change would come by uniting middle class America in the struggle to make meaningful changes in Florida's prison system. It was an idealistic vision, but certainly one that had merit.

On June 12, Dominic received a non-profit corporate seal from Secretary of State Bruce Smathers, and Citizens United For a Free Society was born (C.U.F.F.S.). He had formed the corporation in A.P.C.I. Dominic decided to publish a newsletter despite the fact that he was a convict. He called it "From the Inside and Outside."

Another one of our friends, Dick, was back in the system. Dominic was able to convince Dick's wife, Patty, to open a Florida office for C.U.F.F.S.

The first issue of Dominic's newsletter came out and created a stir in the prison system:

During the past eleven years that I have been confined in the Florida Penal System, I have seen some of the most atrocious injustices and acts of cruelty ever contrived committed against many by the system, perhaps not purposefully, but certainly as a result of the misconception of our government's insistence upon maintaining a laissez-faire attitude toward the autocratic authority of the Penal System.

Over the years, I have observed how the system turns young kids into murderers, sociopaths, and sexual deviants and how families of prisoners are mistreated and ignored, unless they have plenty of money to hire lawyers and/or are influential enough to have their loved ones transferred to an easy place where a quick parole can be more easily obtained. All of us in the joint know how the "system works" for the esoteric few, don't we? We also know how most prisoners work all day long in furniture factories, tag plants, roads, tobacco factories, etc. unrewarded for their work, but are, on the other hand, harshly punished and harrassed for lack of it.

While the empires of the pharaohs in control of the system increase one hundred fold, victims of crimes go uncompensated and uncared for. Hate is planted in all of us and then the hate is subtly directed and used against us in the name of justice. As a result, crime marches on and society loses. Prison construction increases, more harsh laws are enacted, more accountants, lawyers, and judges are employed by government, more people are arrested and imprisoned for longer periods for more insignificant reasons. Slowly . . . rights are eroded and made ineffective. Taxes increase astronomically, but crime does not decrease. Instead it is intensified and fear is predominate; all we have to do is look around us to realize the extent of this truth.

My health began to deteriorate more rapidly now. Weight loss and sleepless nights were taking their toll. My lungs were filled with fluid and my episodes of cardiac asthma had returned. I realized that my body was reacting to the severe stress I was under.

On one hand, I had the definite information from Ballantine that I would not leave prison, that there was no hope. On the other hand, I had sworn documented testimony out of Umberger's mouth that he obviously perjured himself at my trial. I had testimony from Helpern's successor as the New York Medical Examiner and speaking for the New York Medical Examiner Office that there were no known tests to detect succinlycholine in the human body.

I had this information, yet I was helpless to make it work for me. How could I forge a key to the front gate out of these papers?

Meanwhile, I found myself calling Mary at all hours of the night, frightened over my health. She was always encouraging and supportive. I don't know how she did it.

I called Russ and informed him of what Ballantine had told me, namely that I was back on the list for possible clemency action by Governor Askew. Russ said that the best he could offer would be to call Eleanor Mitchell, Assistant General Counsel to Governor Askew, and see what the feeling was in the Executive Office. Russ agreed with my negative view of the clemency outcome.

Jimmy wrote me a letter on June 27 confirming our view:

June 27, 1978

Dr. Carl Coppolino
Avon Park, Florida

Dear Carl:

This letter will serve the dual purpose of confirming the contents of our telephone conversation of this date and to report to you my subsequent conversation with Eleanor Mitchell. Concerning the potentiality for a favorable clemency consideration by the Governor, she advises that, in her opinion, it is zero. It would serve no purpose to detail the reasons in this letter other than to say that they do not personally relate to you or your case, but are rather a matter of policy on the part of the Governor.

In her opinion, your situation before the Parole Commission has improved substantially by virtue of the recent legislation which requires the Parole Commission to adopt guidelines similar to those used by the United States Parole Commission . . .

Ms. Mitchell also spoke highly of the new Commission Chairman, Mr. Crockett, as a fair-minded person who believes in the concept of rehabilitation as well as being aware of just how the Federal Parole Guidelines have been applied during the last several years. She authorized me to use her name in any dealings I might have with Mr. Crockett on your behalf.

In a nut-shell, the "new" Florida Parole Commission now appears to be your best bet . . .

Sincerely,

James M. Russ

To complicate matters further, the jury in the Dr. Favor case could not reach a verdict. The result was a hung jury. Russ advised that there be no publicity over the Umberger-DeMaio testimony since there had been no finality at Favor's trial.

Death still stalked the men at A.P.C.I. and had as its helpmate the lack of medical care at the prison.

Inmate Donald Kossman was a cheerful lawyer in his fifties. One morning Donald complained to me about chest pain and nausea. I urged him to see the prison doctor. On Thursday, June 22, Kossman went to sick call. The medical technician on duty sent him back to the barracks with some aspirin.

That Thursday night Donald had severe chest pains and again was nauseous. On Friday, June 23, Kossman again saw the medical technician. He was prescribed *cold pills*. Later that morning, one of the prison doctors became concerned and transferred Kossman to a local hospital.

Donald Kossman was pronounced dead at the hospital about 1:00 p.m. Friday afternoon.

Things were bad at A.P.C.I., very bad. A typical day's activities included the following:
July 1, 1978
Midnight: Count
2:00 a.m.: Count
4:00 a.m.: Count
6:00 a.m.: Count
6:45 a.m.: . . . The whistle screamed . . . no matter where you were in

dreams, the reality of prison in Florida's A.P.C.I. "Country Club" hit you. The shriek of the whistle stopped your longing and put you into the here and now.

Donald Kossman was dead, the sentence passed and no reprieve. He didn't have to die. For some reason I thought of him. He had been dead about a week. The "medical technicians" had told him he had the flu and gas pains when he complained of chest pains the week before. They gave him ascorbic acid pills and antihistimine tablets. A couple of days later Donald died from a myocardial infarction. He had had a history of heart attacks. Poor guy, he was waiting to go out on work release. He never had a chance to make it. He was only 54 years old.

7:00 a.m.: Breakfast was served to you after you'd been standing a seeming eternity in line. Paint was peeling inside the chow hall. Puddles were on the floor. Last night's dinner remained on four or five tables.

Breakfast was fried eggs, grits, biscuits, margarine, coffee and milk. The coffee tasted like warm Kool-Aid; the milk was sour, and it curdled in the coffee. Biscuits were cold. The eggs were cold. At least the grits were just hot enough to melt a pat of margarine.

Don Kossman had never missed a meal. One could always count on seeing him in the chow hall. He wasn't really liked, so he usually sat alone. Why was I thinking about Don?

7:20 a.m.: Washed my hands. Bathrooms were all full. 750 men to use 50 sinks (unless some were broken) 40 toilets (one-half were usually out of order, but if the urge was paramount, people used them anyhow until they were overloaded, overflooded, or jammed), and 40 urinals. The stench was unbelievable! Toilets were overflowing, and a couple of guys had diarrhea. I didn't wash my hands. I wiped them on my pants and went to sit in front of the barracks.

7:30 a.m.: I sat out front drinking my fifteen-cent cup of canteen coffee and waited. Tony sucked his teeth. Ballard sat there saying nothing. The hacks were on the P.A. system.

"White, Barracks #7, report to the compound office immediately." I wondered why the wanted him. Ballard said a snitch just came out of the office. White was in trouble.

8:00 a.m.: White came out of the compound office, putting stuff back in his pockets and tucking in his shirt. Strip search.

8:15 a.m.: Count. Today was visiting day. I would not have a visitor. Some of the luckier guys would, though.

Dominic had a visit. He wanted me to write something for his newsletter or bulletin, but I didn't know whether I would do it. Dominic was still high on his Citizens United For Free Society Incorporated (C.U.F.F.S.). But what good could one guy do against the awesome power of the State?

Dominic didn't say much, but from a few words with him, I knew he had a good heart. He had been in ten years or more; maybe it was getting to him.

8:19 a.m.: Count clears. I went to urinate. God! It was already full. I went over to another latrine. It was full too. I waited.

I didn't know if the State planned this or not. The lack of bathrooms, or bathroom space, or whatever, reduced us to a childlike stage where it was a major chore to perform a necessary biological function. I wished I had known about this when I was studying for my degree. Imagine being able to reduce 750 human beings to infancy. Freud said that pleasure was release from pain. Hell, I realized now what a pleasure it would be to use a normal bathroom again.

12:00 noon: Count. I lay on my bed reading about ways to run a profitable chicken farm. God! What a reduction to absurdity.

12:20 p.m.: Count cleared. It always took longer on visiting days. I went to stand in line. All the guys were letting their "home boys" buck the line. It outraged me because I didn't do that. Maybe it made them feel like men.

12:40 p.m.: I got in the chow hall door. I got to the trays and looked through for a clean one. Then I looked for a clean cup. Then, a clean fork and spoon. Flies were all over the bread. Two State hot dogs, beans, greens, and mustard. I didn't drink the iced tea, which had no ice, because I was terrified of tooth decay. I knew guys who had been waiting for years for dental treatment. I drank a cup of water instead.

3:00 p.m.: Visitors left. Dope was out on the compound, probably brought in by the guards. The guards brought it in on visiting days to shift the blame from themselves to the visitors. Two sissies came by trying to earn enough to get "high."

Don and I had once hashed over the prison system. He thought it was a realistic, although harsh, punishment for actual transgressions. Don was in for cashing a couple of bad checks. He felt the only thing to do was to live through it and not get caught in a jam serious enough to bring you back. I held that it was a totally outrageous system of, and for, idiots. Plenty of these men deserved to be here forever. My idea was that a person had to hold onto the essentials of decency, of humanity, regardless of all the adverse circumstances, and that one must just forget the experience when released. Don said that to forget this and not seek to change it was beastial. Who knows? He's dead. I'm alive. Was he right? Could I really do anything?

3:45 p.m.: . . . Court cleared. Dinner. One slice of bologna, one slice of salami, potato salad, greens, leftovers—I never really figured out what they were—and beans. The bologna was tinged with green.

4:45 p.m.: . . . Fight. It was either over dope, money, or a sissy. I stayed away, not wanting any hacks to see me.

Don once said I was a survivor. He said I was strong enough to survive the damage to mind and body. Who knows? Was there a way to draw the public into this?

I remembered once, a guy Don owed slapped him and said he would take it out in sex if Don didn't pay up. Don paid. Is it wrong to speak ill of the dead? Am I, or is it the truth?

5:00 p.m.: I went to sit in the library. The usual crew was in there trying to find the magic of a law book. Law books were stolen out of the library, probably by people who couldn't read.

7:30 p.m.: I went to get a *Tab* out of the vending machine. It shocked me. A bunch of guys were waiting there, waiting to see me jump. I didn't and this puzzled them. After all, by now I knew the machine would shock me.

8:05 p.m.: Count cleared. I went to sit outside and think. Ordinarily Don would be out playing gin rummy now. I wondered about him. I saw his transcripts from Northwestern. Doctorate, with excellent grades, the early years. Why him, in prison? Why me?

9:00 p.m.: I went to take a shower. Two sissies in there. I told them to go somewhere else. They did, with a lot of grumbling and cussing. I cut myself shaving. The water overflowed in the toilets. The place was, as usual, flooded.

10:00 p.m.: Count.

10:05 p.m.: Count cleared. Lights out. I lay in bed thinking about Mary.

12:00 midnight, July 2, 1978: Count.

2:00 a.m.: Count.

4:00 a.m.: Count.

6:00 a.m.: Count.

6:45 a.m.: The whistle screamed, dragging me from where I wanted to be into where I was.

WEEKEND OF JULY 8

Mary and Lisa came to see me. Lisa wanted to talk with me about retailing and marketing as a career choice. She would be attending King High School in the fall and at present was working at Robinson's Department Store and loved it.

Mary was frustrated since nobody was able to generate any positive movement either from the Governor's office or the Parole Commission. Bob Miller and Lamar Baker had been in touch. Lamar couldn't get the LaRussa brothers to move Shevin, despite my documented support, and Bob Miller's efforts using the reams of petitions, mailgrams, and telegrams echoed hollow.

We tried not to talk about my health and the lack of care, but it was staring me in the face. My weight was back down to 150 pounds, and I was constantly fatigued. My face became "skulled" in appearnce.

The incidents of neglect at the medical clinic were compounding. One black convict by the name of Snow had broken his right wrist playing football on Saturday the eighth. The medical technician on duty ordered ice packs, then heat. The injury was finally x-rayed on the eleventh and a cast applied on the twelfth!

JULY 15

Bob Hughes was still pressing Tallahassee. He planned to speak with Justice Adkins again, but he did not feel confident anything would come out of his meeting.

AUGUST

The classification committee recommended me for parole again. I should be interviewed by a parole examiner sometime this month. Sure, I thought, something has to break this time!

AUGUST 8
WEDNESDAY

Mr. Ballantine called to tell me that the Parole Commission had called and instructed him to add my name to the August parole interview list. I was encouraged, but refused to get my hopes up.

AUGUST 25

Dick—the jewel thief from Miami and my friend—and I were sched-uled today to see Mr. Sullivan, the parole examiner.

Dick went in first. He came out 45 minutes later with a dark look on his face. "Nothing," he said. "See you again next year."

I walked into the office. Mr. Cloud, my classification officer, sat to one side. A beefy-faced, rotund individual smoking a pipe sat behind the wooden desk. The desk lamp gave his eyes a jaundice look.

"Sit down, Coppolino," his voice rumbled.

I sat down across from Sullivan and watched as he fiddled with his pipe. The silence drew out like a piece of taffy in the winter time. I remained calm. This wasn't a new experience for me, and I didn't expect anything. Hadn't Ballantine informed me that the Commission wouldn't ever let me go?

Sullivan began going over my case. He said that despite the many years I had spent in prison, the years on furloughs, I still had a ghoulish image with the Parole Commission. In addition, despite the numerous recom-mendations for parole, he would not go along with the recommendation.

Then Sullivan said a strange thing. "I understand you have some information regarding the drug test in your trial. Can you fill me in about that?"

"Yes, I can." I outlined for Sullivan the discrepancy in Umberger's sworn testimony and DiMaio's flat statements, the fact that the Second District Court of Appeals wrote that in their opinion my conviction rested solely upon the testimony of Halpern and Umberger.

Sullivan jotted some notes on a sheet of paper. Then he looked up, "I would do all I can to document this, Coppolino. Your case is going to be voted on in two to three weeks. The Commission will vote either to go along with my year set-off or to take different action. Quite frankly, you don't have a chance for parole at this time. However, I urge you to place·in front of the Commission any information that can be of mitigating na-ture."

After I left the interview, I called Mary to tell her the bad news, which had been expected. However, we had some hope—the Grand Jury testi-mony of Umberger and DiMaio.

Next, I called James Russ and explained to him what Sullivan had said about the "new evidence." Russ thought it was simply a stall, an excuse for the Commission to do nothing. But Jimmy agreed with me that presented promptly, it might be beneficial sometime in the future.

On August 28, Russ wrote me a letter saying that he had an appointment with Maurice Crockett, chairman of the Parole Commission, at 11:00 a.m. on September 5. He went on to say, "I shall prepare a written analysis of the evidence pictured in your case as compared against the recent case from the New York City area. I shall deliver this analysis to Mr. Crockett at this conference."

Sullivan had not left the prison immediately after my interview. He stayed on for another week, interviewing other convicts for parole. During this week, Mr. Ballantine and my classification officer, Mr. Cloud, pressed Sullivan about the reason why I was turned down. After all, Sullivan had recommended parole for convicts who had served six, seven, or eight years on their life sentences for second degree murder. Coppolino had served 11 years looking for 12, and Sullivan had offered no hope.

Sullivan made it plain that he would never put his name on a recommendation for my release. Furthermore, he said that my release was opposed by the Attorney General's office (Georgieff?) and Judge Schaub!

When Ballantine informed me of what he had learned, plus what he already heard from Tallahasee about me, I went into a severe depression. All seemed absolutely lost.

Commissioner Armond Cross had been cleared of all charges levied against him by the "overlook" and Representative Don Hazelton. He was again active on the Commission and a powerful force against me.

AUGUST 30

My friend, Rommie Loudd, was seen by Sullivan and recommended for parole! This was great news and climaxed Loudd's struggle for freedom.

Rommie had not been alone in his struggle. His strongest fighter was Representative Arnett Girardeau, Democrat from Jacksonville. Dr. Girardeau, a dentist, was a member of the committee on Parole and Probation, the same committee that had Representative Don Hazelton as its chairman. Dr. Girardeau had taken an interest in Rommie's situation and began to investigage the mysterious circumstances surrounding Loudd's arrest and conviction.

Dr. Girardeau's investigation unearthed reams of documents that threw the Loudd's arrest and conviction into serious question. There was information suggesting the manufacturing of the evidence and perjured testimony.

Mary and I were very close to Rommie, his wife Bettye, and their two children. It had long been apparent to us that the Loudds were also trapped as political prisoners, just like us.

The newspapers suspected that there was something wrong with the Rommie Loudd conviction and periodically came into A.P.C.I. to interview Rommie.

Rommie was a "born-again Christian" and in light of his faith never pointed a finger at those he felt had caused his unjust conviction and imprisonment. Like me, he had been stripped of position, power, and money. Yet he smiled because he had found peace with God.

Representative Girardeau championed Rommie's cause with the officials in Tallahassee, and now Rommie had a recommendation for parole and he and I would be voted upon on the same day.

SEPTEMBER

Tom Cavanaugh called Mary and wanted to come down and speak to the Parole Commission on my behalf. James Russ was hostile to the idea since he felt he would be in better shape to present the Umberger-DiMaio material if he could do it quietly. The critical fact was that Dr. Favor had not had his second trial and, therefore, the material in our hands had not been presented in court.

In addition, I kept hearing Henry Gonzalez's advice, "Wait for the results of the Favor trial before going public." Henry had been with us since practically the first day. His advice had always been sound. I knew if Cavanaugh spoke in front of the Commission, The Press would soon be active, and I wasn't sure that Russ wasn't right when he urged me to be quiet for now.

Mary decided that it would be best if she went to Tallahassee to speak in my behalf. With this in mind, Mary wrote to Mr. Crockett on the fifth of September for permission to attend the hearing, and to speak in front of the Commission.

Mr. Crockett's response was prompt and cordial. He would see her as soon as she arrived in Tallahassee. In addition, he informed Mary that my case would be voted on September 21.

SEPTEMBER 5

Jim Russ spent the day in Tallahassee. First, he had a detailed meeting with Chairman Maurice Crockett. Crockett quickly told Jimmy that he was not a voting member of the Commission, but would vote if there was a three-to-three tie. Crockett was familiar with all the negatives in my case. As the hour-long conference continued, Russ felt that Mr. Crockett was responsive to his petition upon my behalf and that his response was based upon the duration of my confinement, my perfect prison record, and my extraordinary family fidelity and support.

Russ had prepared a detailed brief, which was the written analysis of the new medical evidence that had been unearthed by Tom Cavanaugh. In addition to the brief, Russ left a letter for Mr. Crockett that demonstrated our position point-by-point. This four-page letter had as its emphasis the following paragraphs:

Approximately one year ago, Dr. Umberger testified in a New York State Grand Jury homicide investigation as an expert witness concerning the identification of succinylcholine in the human body. At this Grand Jury proceeding which occurred more than eleven years after Dr. Helpern first advanced his professional opinion at the Coppolino preliminary hearing, Dr. Umberger testified under oath essentially that as of September, 1977, he had not perfected a technique for identifying the presence of succinylcholine in the human body . . .

Dr. Helpern, having retired as the chief medical examiner for New York City in 1974, was succeeded by his long-time assistant, Dominick J. DiMaio, M.D., who also testified at the New York Grand Jury investigation in the fall of 1977. Also relying upon the research by Dr. Umberger concerning the presence of succinylcholine in the human body, Chief Medical Examiner DiMaio unequivocally contradicted the professional conclusion advanced by Dr. Helpern in the Coppolino case. Dr. DiMaio flatly stated under oath that there was no method of detecting the presence of succinylcholine in the human body any place in the United States.

Chairman Crockett was most impressed with Russ' presentation, especially the new evidence. He promised Jimmy that each member of the Commission would have the detailed brief available to them prior to my vote on September 21.

Dr. John Feegel was at this time assistant medical examiner for Atlanta, Georgia. In addition, he was professor of pathology at Emory University. Since John had tried to help me in the past, I wanted his independent appraisal of the Umberger-DiMaio testimony.

Mary spoke with John at his office in Atlanta. Feegel was excited about this recent turn of events. He advised that we go slowly in hopes that other information might be pried loose through the Dr. Favor trial. Feegel told Mary that my biggest problem was the opposition by Georgieff. This, of course, was nothing new.

SEPTEMBER 14

Monica, Lisa, and Mary took an early plane for Tallahassee. Their first appointment was for 10:00 a.m. with Ray Howard. Mary didn't expect anything from Howard. He had made his opposition to my release quite plain right after the aborted efforts of the Jacksonville law firm in March, 1974. Howard was emphatic in his refusal even to consider my record, my furloughs, and the new evidence. His refusal extended to the point where he indicated that he probably could *never* vote for my release, no matter what the facts were.

Their next appointment was with Charles Scrivin. Scrivin made it plain that he did not know my case and had never opened my file; yet he had been chairman of the Parole Commission for the previous two years all through the petitions, the visits by lawyers, and the push at Governor Askew's clemency board!

It was too much. Mary broke down sobbing with bitter frustration. Monica and Lisa soon followed suit. Never had they seen their mother so upset. Listening to Scrivin and seeing their mother' grief made them almost unconsolable.

They left Scrivin's office weeping pitifully.

Mary and the children's next appointment was with Armond Cross. He never showed up, thank God. They had had enough misery.

Finally the day was over, with Mary and the children visiting with Chairman Crockett. Crockett made them feel comfortable and was very sympathetic to our plight. He urged that Mary speak with Annabel Mitchell and Jack Blanton. Mary made appointments with the secretaries of Blanton, Mitchell, Russell, and Cross for Monday, September 18.

The family left and flew home, exhausted.

On September 18, Mary returned alone to Tallahassee. Her first appointment was with Annabel Mitchell. Mrs. Mitchell was extremely positive in her attitude and felt I had served more than enough time. She indicated that she would do all she could on September 21, but cautioned Mary that I had an uphill fight. Next, Mary saw Armond Cross. He was cordial, but noncommittal. Mary concluded that Cross was still a powerful force against me, despite his recent excoriation by The Press and the House of Representatives Committee on Corrections, Parole, and Probation. (He had been cleared of all charges).

Jack Blanton was like Annabel, very positive in his attitude, but wouldn't commit himself at that time.

Roy Russell told Mary that he was extremely familiar with my case—think about how many people had spoken to him about me throughout the years—however, he thought that he would not be sitting on my panel when my case came up for a vote.

While Mary was speaking with Chairman Crockett, she asked the chairman his feelings concerning Rommie Loudd. Crockett said that the Commission was deeply impressed with the documentation Representative Girardeau had unearthed during his investigation. Chairman Crockett indicated that Loudd's record in prison plus the information given to the Commission through Representative Girardeau would probably lead the Commission to go along with Sullivan's recommendation for parole for Rommie.

SEPTEMBER 21

Mary flew to Tallahassee early that Thursday morning. While she waited for the voting to begin, the UPI reporter recognized her, and soon there were television cameramen present in the hearing room.

When my case was called, Mary rose to her feet and spoke to the first panel of commissioners, Howard, Mitchell, Scrivin, and Blanton. Mary's plea was straight and simple—"Help put my family back together. We're willing to do whatever you require. We're willing to cooperate. We've been with you a long time." She did not mention the new evidence. She felt, and I agreed, that the setting was inappropriate.

I needed four votes. The panel split two by two. This necessitated a convening of the second panel of two commissioners, Cross and Russell. At this point the proceeding petered out. The afternoon panel in an informal talk agreed to continue my case for another year. It was obvious that I didn't have four solid votes for parole.

Immediately after finishing with my plea, the Commission voted on Rommie Loudd's case. Loudd quickly received four votes confirming

Sullivan's recommendation for immediate parole.

I was up at 5:00 a.m. on the twenty-first. I tried not to think about what faced Mary at Tallahassee. I tried not to think of all the negatives, the "death sentence" reported to me by Ballantine. I tried not to think about Russ' brief presentation. Would the Commission listen? Would it matter at all? I tried not to think about whether he had done enough. How many more letters, petitions, telegrams, mailgrams, visits to the Commission by lawyers, visits to the Governor's office by lawyers, clemency board petitions, recommendations for parole, or dead, mind-numbing years in prison would be enough?

I skipped my meals. I walked up and down the road in the hot sun. The instructor at the electronic school where I worked gave me the day off. He knew the pressure I was under.

My friends Dominick, Dick, and Rommie helped me with my vigil. I had made arrangements with the chaplain's office for Mary's call to come directly from Tallahassee as soon as she heard. Mary informed Rommie's wife, Bettye, that she would be in Tallahassee and would call her when Rommie's case was voted upon.

Noon came. No word. 1:00 p.m. came. No word. By 4:00 p.m. I was a nervous wreck. At 4:30 p.m. the phone rang at the Chapel. Chaplain Wall answered it.

Mary said to tell Rommie to pack his bags, he had been paroled. Then she asked the chaplain if she might speak with me. Chaplain Wall handed me the telephone.

"Hello, Carl?" Mary's voice came from a distance. I could hear commotion in the background. Before I could say anything, she said, "I am at the airport, and they are calling my flight."

"What happened?" I whispered in exhaustion.

"They turned you down. But I think we have our foot in the door." Mary went on to say, "They didn't expect Jimmy Russ, the new evidence, your documented support, and then me. I believe they had it in their minds to turn you down, no matter what. But we have some people now willing to listen. It will take time," she said. Then she closed, "Look, I have to go. I will see you next weekend. Call me at home."

I put down the phone and informed Chaplain Wall of what had happened. In my sorrow, I was still overjoyed with Rommie's release. He needed to be home with his family.

I left for the barracks to rest, but it wasn't in the cards. The radio was broadcasting the news about my turn-down. Later on that evening I watched television news and saw and heard Mary make her fruitless presentation to the Parole Commission.

My supporters were crushed once again. Jimmy wrote Mary and me a letter on September 22.

September 22, 1978

Dr. and Mrs. Carl Coppolino
P.O. Box 1100
Avon Park, Florida

Dear Carl and Mary:

I am writing to console you in your disappointment.

Without knowledge beyond what I read in the newspaper, I can only say that this is a setback, but not a defeat. I am at your service to do whatever you think necessary for the next year.

When I was in the deep dark pit, I found strength in the thought ". . . Thy will be done."

Best wishes,

Jim

Letters of condolences poured in from others—Bob Miller, Bob Hughes, Troy Browning, Tom Cavanaugh, and Lamar Baker. Carmen and Tom Benoit spoke with every one of their friends in Tampa, expressing their anger and frustration over my continued imprisonment.

On September 23, Bob Miller went to Tallahassee on another matter and spoke with Annabel Mitchell. Mrs. Mitchell told him that she was very encouraged by the rest of the Commissioners' attitude toward me. She felt that, in time, there would be a positive move to release me.

Miller was beside himself. "In time? How much time?" and reminded Mrs. Mitchell that a man can stay in prison so long that he is no longer of any use to himself, his family, and society.

Mrs. Mitchell whole-heartedly agreed and added that she liked Mary very much and that she was very sympathetic to my family.

OCTOBER, 1978

Tom Cavanaugh was in constant contact with Mary. It was his opinion that I would die in prison. This sounded like Ballantine! *Unless* we were to go public with the Umberger-DiMaio testimony, I agreed. But how? Dr. Favor's trial had been postponed again, and I felt I needed more information!

In desperation, Mary called Bettye Loudd to ask her for Representative Girardeau's phone number. Since he had been so successful in getting the facts in front of the Commission concerning Rommie, perhaps he would help us.

OCTOBER 12

An extraordinary meeting took place at my home that Thursday, October 12. Tom Cavanaugh had flown in from New York to talk with Mary about his discoveries concerning Umberger and DiMaio. Representative Arnett Girardeau called Mary and asked that she meet with him. Mary invited Arnett to our home so that he could question Cavanaugh.

Their meeting lasted from 4:00 in the afternoon to 10:00 that evening. Dr. Girardeau read the Umberger-DiMaio testimony and knew from his own scientific training that my conviction for murder was faulty.

Next, Dr. Girardeau, with Cavanaugh, went over the brief prepared by James Russ, and which had been submitted to the chairman of the Parole Commission, Maurice Crockett. After reading Dr. Helpern and Dr. Umberger's testimony from my trial, Representative Girardeau knew there was something radically wrong.

The first discrepancy that struck Dr. Girardeau's eye was the so-called puncture wound described by Helpern as an injection site. Helpern described it as ending in the fat tissue just under the skin. Yet Dr. Girardeau knew that it would be impossible for succinlycholine to have acted if deposited in fat tissue. He knew as a dentist that succinylcholine had to be deposited into deep muscle in order to be effective.

In addition, Dr. Girardeau knew that any injection of succinylcholine was always accompanied by an inflammatory reaction. This area of inflammation would be there for anybody to see and find no matter how long the body had been dead. There was no inflammation reaction visible in Carmela's so-called puncture wound!

Dr. Girardeau concluded that night at my home that my deceased wife, Carmela, could not have been killed by an injection of succinlycholine for many reasons. The so-called puncture wound ended at the fat layer under the skin and not in the muscle. There was no inflammatory process at the "site." Umberger had testified in Naples in 1967 that he had perfected a test to detect the breakdown products of succinylcholine—however, ten years later in 1977, he testified in New York City that he had no test and needed time to develop one. After careful questioning of Lisa and Mary, strictly from the point of view of human nature, Dr. Girardeau concluded that no child could love her father for so long and under such trying conditions and be as supportive as Lisa and the other children if I had the instincts of a fiendish killer. In addition, Dr. Girardeau, knowing human nature, could not believe Mary would have given 12 years of her life, emotional energy, and money to be so supportive of a man with the traits of a cold-blooded killer.

The evening ended with Representative Arnett Girardeau and Tom Cavanaugh working together to find out more. The first person they wanted to talk with was Dr. John Feegel.

OCTOBER 24

Tom Cavanaugh called Mary. He said that he had been in contact with Dr. John Feegel and thought it best to use an investigative firm, John Mandel, to see if there was more evidence that could be pried loose.

Mary kept Jim Russ informed about the situation.

Dr. Ed Webb, my dearest friend and a fellow anesthesiologist, had been alerted by Mary and me on the new developments. Dr. Webb had testified, reluctantly, for the prosecution at both the New Jersey trial and Florida trial. After my conviction he remained in contact with me and Mary and the children. Ed was convinced of my innocence, not only on a personal basis, having known me for so many years, but also on a scientific basis.

Not only was Dr. Webb an anesthesiologist, but he worked for E. R. Squibb, one of the manufacturers of succinlycholine, and was well aware of its pharmachological action. Dr. Webb knew that unless succinlycholine was administered by deep muscle injection, there would be no drug effect. In addition, he was well aware of the fact that it was necessary to have an inflammatory reaction at the injection site when succinlycholine was administered. Dr. Webb knew that there was no inflammatory reaction at the so-called injection site of Carmela's body.

In addition, Dr. Webb had been called in by the State of Florida to speak with Dr. Milton Helpern. He had heard Dr. Helpern maintain unequivocally before my trial that it was impossible to detect the breakdown products of succinlycholine in Carmela's body. How must Dr. Webb have felt listening to Umberger and Helpern testify at my trial? How must he have felt after I was convicted, and how must he have felt when, after the trial, he told F. Lee Bailey about Helpern's remarks only to have Bailey ignore this crucial piece of information. Why did F. Lee Bailey ignore this information?

NOVEMBER 10

Dr. Webb met with Tom Cavanaugh and gave him the same crucial information he had given Bailey.

NOVEMBER 19

Troy Browning came down from Kentucky. He and Tom Cavanaugh met and Troy began calling newspaper friends to inform them of the new evidence.

I had learned that I was on the clemency board list, again, for possible action by Governor Askew. In view of this and the interest now generated by the Umberger-DiMaio testimony, I asked Jim Russ to speak with Justice Adkins. Justice Adkins was already familiar with my case from Bob Hughes, and the Justice was still the liaison officer for Governor Askew and the criminal justice system. It seemed appropriate to bring Justice Adkins up to date on the latest developments so that he could in turn apprise Governor Askew.

NOVEMBER 29

Jim Russ had his meeting with Justice Adkins. The Justice was well familiar, as I suspected, with my situation and was very sympathetic.

Russ brought Adkins up-to-date, but stressed the inordinate length of my time in prison, the three years on furloughs, and the lengthy on-going support of Mary and the children. Adkins agreed that the Governor should be apprised of these facts, and he picked up the telephone. His call to Governor Askew went through immediately. Justice Adkins related the facts to the Governor and urged Askew to take a hard look at my case. Justice Adkins urged that I receive some sort of relief.

Russ walked away from this meeting pleased that something positive seemed likely to come out of it.

DECEMBER 5

Mary called Representative Arnett Girardeau and informed him of Jim Russ' meeting with Justice Adkins, and the Justice's conversation with Governor Askew. Representative Girardeau was very pleased. He had already started his own investigation and felt he would have something concrete in a week or two.

DECEMBER 9
SATURDAY

I was awakened at about midnight by a correctional officer. He told me there was an urgent phone call for me. I jumped out of bed, found my way through the darkened barracks out the screen door, and stumbled into the public telephone booth.

"Hello, Dr. Coppolino?" A strange female voice was on the other end of the receiver.

"Yes," I croaked. My mouth was dry from sleep.

"This is Frances Williams of the Gannett Newspaper Ft. Myers News Press. What are your comments on the news that broke today about the fact that the medical evidence in your trial may have been falsified?"

I was instantly awake. "What? I don't know what you're talking about!" I gushed, excitedly.

"The Ft. Lauderdale News broke a front page story on new evidence uncovered concerning your case. It is now on the wire. The Associated Press will undoubtedly pick it up. Don't you know anything about it?"

"No, I sure don't," I said. "I don't know a thing about any newspaper story."

"Would you like me to read it to you?"

"No thanks." I was struggling to become fully awake.

"Could I come out to the prison and interview you? This is a big story, Dr. Coppolino."

"No. Not now. I'll call you. Thank you for the information."

I left the phone booth and walked to the outside latrine. There I met my friend Roy.

"You look like you've seen a ghost, Carl!" he rasped, coughing on a cigarette.

"Roy, they found out that I am innocent!"

"What the hell are you talking about?" Roy burst out, sitting down on the bench in the latrine. He suffered from advanced pulmonary emphysema but still smoked three packs of cigarettes every day.

I told Roy about the phone call I'd received from Frances Williams.

He shook his head in disbelief. "Doc, you must have been dreaming. There are no miracles. And this isn't Christmas. Therefore, Santa Claus hasn't visited."

DECEMBER 10
SUNDAY

I called Mary at 6:30 a.m. She knew about the *Ft. Lauderdale News* article because Tom Cavanaugh had called her, all excited. In addition, Representative Girardeau knew all about it.

Tom Cavanaugh arrived at the prison that night grinning from ear to ear. We met at the control room.

"Here," he said, "read it."

The title of the newspaper article read: **THE COPPOLINO TRIAL: WAS EVIDENCE IGNORED?** by Marion Hale.

> The fabric of evidence which put Dr. Carl Coppolino in jail twelve years ago for the murder of his wife may be coming rapidly undone. Coppolino was convicted in his sensational trial in Naples on falsified medical evidence, according to doctors who conducted tests for the prosecution. Two toxicologists who worked on the case told *The News* this week that the test results were altered to support the State's case. Coppolino was convicted of second degree murder and sentenced to life in prison.
>
> The attention of the nation was riveted on the trial which was marked by broken love triangles, a scorned mistress who claimed Coppolino hyp-

notized her, the courtroom charisma of defense lawyer F. Lee Bailey and, most importantly, highly technical medical evidence.

According to the appellant court that later upheld Coppolino's conviction, he was found guilty "almost solely" on medical evidence, evidence toxicologists now say was altered. Twelve years later, two toxicologists, Dr. Franco Fiorese and Richard Coumbis, charged that Umberger misrepresented their findings on the witness stand. The two doctors worked independently on the case—Coumbis under Umberger in New York and Fiorese from the state toxicology laboratory he headed in Illinois.

Umberger, whose testimony the appellant courts say convicted Coppolino, had asked Fiorese to conduct the tests because Fiorese had done considerable work with succinic acid. Coumbis con-ducted tests in the New York Medical Examiners' office under Umberger's direction.

When he completed the study, Dr. Fiorese submitted a report finding normal levels of the acid in Carmela Coppolino's brain, but Umberger and Helpern, now both dead, ignored the report.

Yesterday Dr. Coumbis, now chief toxicologist for the State of New Jersey, said the test conducted by him and other chemists in Umberger's laboratory showed the acid level in her brain "was definitely within the normal ranges."

Both Fiorese and Coumbis watched with the nation, as Umberger, they say, altered the test results—resulting in the conviction of Dr. Carl Coppolino. Outraged, Coumbis and two colleagues at the laboratory, Dr. James March and Dr. Joseph Calise, talked with defense attorney F. Lee Bailey, who was defending Coppolino in the Naples court room, but Bailey, who was unavailable for comment yesterday, didn't call them as witnesses. The three toxicologists later resigned in protest of Umberger's testimony.

Dr. Coumbis said he wasn't sure why Bailey didn't ask him to testify, but guessed the lawyer thought he could win the case without his testimony. . . .

During an emotional interview, Dr. Fiorese, who is now affiliated with a Joliet, Illinois, hospital said he was prepared to confront Dr. Umberger and Dr. Helpern, leaders in the field of toxicology. He said he was prepared to accuse them of ignoring solid scientific evidence to win fame that would come with testifying in a trial that made front page headlines across the nation. Not only were Umberger and Helpern noted doctors, but they were also Dr. Fiorese's friends. He had studied under them when he worked in Umberger's laboratory in the Medical Examiner's office headed by Helpern.

But, as Fiorese said last week, "To me friendship is one thing and toxicology is something else."

Dr. Coumbis justified his admitted twelve years' silence in a way that reflected his academic background. He pointed to Umberger's acknowledgment from the witness stand that he would not publish his findings. To Coumbis' way of thinking, "if it's good enough to put someone in jail, it's good enough to publish." In Coumbis' opinion, therefore, the jury must have realized that when Umberger acknowledged he would not publish his findings in an academic journal, his statements must lack credibility. But, according to the Second District Court of Appeals, Coppolino's conviction rested "almost solely" on Umberger's evidence.

Coumbis said, "The scientific evidence was not there. I felt quite bad about it." Coumbis had lost touch with the two colleagues who resigned with him. When last he talked with them, Dr. March was teaching at a medical school on Long Island and Dr. Calise was working for a pharamaceutical company in California.

When the doctors, Coumbis, Calise, and March, openly criticized Umberger for his testimony at the Coppolino trial, Helpern, their boss, publicly insulted them. The three men resigned rather than work for Helpern and Umberger, who they belived had falsified test results for the sake of front page news.

Dr. Fiorese and Dr. Coumbis accused Dr. Umberger of misrepre-senting their research, but they weren't the only scientists who looked at the trial skeptically. Five other toxicologists contacted by *The News* said Umberger's theory, that high levels of succinic acid in the brain indicated the presence of the paralyzing drug, was faulty.

While the doctors pondered the scientific implications, Coppo-lino's second wife, Mary, fought for his release. In her eyes, he was innocent. Her efforts to free her husband had resulted in an investigation by state Representative Arnett Girardeau, Democrat from Jacksonville and Chairman of the House Corrections Parole and Probation Committee.

Dr. Girardeau said he would look into the case after reading what he claimed were "inconsistencies" in Umberger's testimony in the Coppolino case and his remarks twelve years later to the New York Grand Jury. Dr. Girardeau said he wanted to investigate further before deciding whether to use his influence as chairman of the House Committee to try to free Dr. Coppolino.

Mary Coppolino's belief in her husband's innocence had also resulted in Supreme Court Justice James Adkins discussing the case with Governor Reubin Askew.

Shakily, I handed the newspaper clipping back to Tom. It took twelve years for the truth to come out! There must be more information available, I reasoned. Cavanaugh agreed with me and promised to find it.

The big question remained, *what did F. Lee Bailey know?* Newspaper articles appeared in all the Florida press and most of The Press, nation-wide, were asking the same question. Efforts were made by the media to question Bailey, but Lee refused to accept any telephone calls.

Judge Schaub refused to comment, explaining that since he was a Judge, it wouldn't be appropriate.

William Strode, however, was vociferous in his defense of the State's conviction. However, when pressed about Dr. Fiorese's report to the State's expert witness, submitted in October, 1968, and which conclusively proved my innocence, Strode acknowledged that he hadn't known of the report. Strode admitted that without Umberger and Helpern's testimony, Florida would have had no case. "Dr. Coppolino would have been granted a directed verdict of acquittal."

DECEMBER 11

Meanwhile, Bob Hughes began another effort to force Governor Askew to act. The timing was right. The newspapers were filled with stories seriously questioning my guilt and Governor Askew was leaving office in January. The petitions, letters, and mailgrams were in my file on his desk.

Dr. John Feegel conferred with Bob Hughes. My supporters in Osceola, Orange, Pinellas, and Hillsborough Counties were asking Hughes what else could be done on my behalf.

Governor Askew held his last clemency board in December, but did not act on my petition.

DECEMBER 12
TUESDAY

I began to speak with reporters and give interviews. It was the first time in 12 years. Before this, I had nothing to say. Now I had solid facts upon which to repeat my statements of innocence.

My first interview was with Marion Hale of the *Ft. Lauderdale News.* This was quickly followed by an interview with Frances Williams of the *Ft. Myers News Press.*

Another toxicologist came forward, Dr. James March, and the *Ft. Lauderdale News* was hard-hitting in its article:

Tuesday, December 12, 1978—The headlines read: **TWO READY TO TESTIFY COPPOLINO DATA ALTERED.**

Another toxicologist, Dr. James E. March, told *The News*:

. . . that Umberger's conclusions were based on "atrocious" testing methods. March, who worked with Umberger in the New York Medical Examiner's Office at the time, is now a research scientist at The University of New York Medical School at Stony Brook.

Although he did not work on the test, March said he was well aware of the testing procedures used in the case. He also said he was willing to testify if the case were ever reopened. March said watching Umberger testify about the testing methods was "a devastating experience." He called Coppolino's conviction and jail sentence "monstrous."

March and Coumbis, who also worked in the New York Medical Examiner's Office at the time, and a third co-worker, Dr. Joseph Calise, discussed their charges with the defense attorney, F. Lee Bailey. They said they came to Naples during the sensational trial and offered to take the witness stand. But Columbis said Bailey told them, "Don't worry about it. There is no need."

Bailey's reported assurance came after Umberger testified he did not plan to publish his findings in a scientific journal. Coumbis and March said that scientific evidence not good enough to be published was not good enough to convict a suspect.

"The jury did not understand that," March said.

The three men, Coumbis, March, and Calise, resigned after the trial. After they volunteered to testify, their boss and medical examiner, Dr. Milton Helpern, publicly insulted them. March said they filed a five hundred million dollar slander suit against Helpern which was settled out of court without a trial. Bailey had refused to discuss the case with the news.

Again The Press kept hammering at the essential question—Why didn't F. Lee Bailey make available to the Naples jury the devastating testimony of the three doctors?

DECEMBER 17

Mary and Lisa visited. Yesterday was Lisa's sixteenth birthday. As she beamed at me, she said, "This newspaper publicity is the best birthday present, Daddy. It will bring you home to us."

Mary had spoken with Frances Williams and had learned that the *Ft. Myers News Press* supported my immediate release. In addition, Miss Williams said that she had personally spoke with Dr. Fiorese and had published her conversations.

Dr. Fiorese said, "I did not complete my tests until after Coppolino's trial. At that time I considered my findings conclusive—Carmela Coppolino had *less* than a normal amount of succinic acid in her brain and liver and there was nothing to even remotely suggest she had been injected with any drug."

"I took my findings to Helpern and Umberger and they were displeased. They ignored them. Coppolino should not have been imprisoned and he would not have been if Umberger had not misrepresented himself."

DECEMBER 24
SUNDAY

The Sunday edition of *The New York Daily News* dropped a bombshell. In a two-page story, Cavanaugh screamed that I was innocent. Representative Arnett Girardeau said, "Apparently the expert testimony given at the trial was not expert. I suspected the jury was overwhelmed by the reputations of these experts. Now it seems as if there is something very wrong."

However, the biggest uproar was caused by Dr. Rappolt of San Francisco. Dr. Rappolt was executive editor of *The Journal of Clinical Toxicology*.

"Umberger's testimony was preposterous," the report said. "It stank to high heaven. Every toxicologist knows there is no normal level of succinic acid. I remember that we followed the evidence and toxicologists were shaking their heads and asking, 'How could he say that?' There were several editorials in medical journals afterward addressing the question, but there was nothing more we could do."

"Why would Umberger commit perjury?" *The News* asked.

"He was under the influence of Helpern," Dr. Fiorese said. "He wanted to keep his job and to do that he had to do what Helpern wanted."

New York Attorney Henry Rothblatt told *The News*, "I will tell you that I was amazed at the courage of the men who quit (Drs. March, Coumbis and Calise). They were prepared to hurt their own careers because they believed in the truth."

Dr. James March told *The Daily News*, "I can only speak for myself, but I certainly left the medical examiner's office because of the Coppolino case."

Drs. March, Coumbis, and Calise were all available to F. Lee Bailey. Why didn't he use them?

The New York Daily News pursued this question. Again other newspapers began tracking Bailey in order to have the same question answered. Bailey found himself confronted with that question no matter where he went, but he refused to answer.

Theories flew, but the most plausible was reported in The Press. That theory was that Bailey had supreme confidence that he would win the case in Naples and, therefore, felt he had no need of the toxicologist's testimony.

Don Moore's *The Islander* asked Tom Cavanaugh about Bailey. Cavanaugh told *The Islander* that the three toxicologists had gone to Bailey and told him that Umberger and Helpern had lied under oath. Cavanaugh said that apparently Bailey didn't think their testimony made any difference!

The Islander asked Cavanaugh what reason Helpern and Umberger would have to falsify their testimony on the Coppolino case. It seems there was a personal vendetta between Bailey and Helpern. Bailey made him look like a monkey during an earlier murder case in New Jersey, where Coppolino was accused of murdering the husband of a former girl friend.

"I've known Dr. Helpern for years," said Tom Cavanaugh. "He was an egomaniac and he did not like what Bailey had done to him on the witness stand in New Jersey. Helpern told Bailey, 'I'll get even with you if it's the last thing I do.'"

As Cavanaugh saw it, he told *The Islander*, Helpern's reason for lying during the Coppolino trial was to cause F. Lee Bailey to lose the case.

JANUARY, 1979

Mary had gone to Ft. Lauderdale to meet with famed Florida criminal attorney, J. Leonard Fleet. Fleet had been recommended to us by Tom Cavanaugh. Mary and I didn't see the point of having a Florida attorney or any other attorney for that matter, but Tom Cavanaugh had insisted.

Mary had dinner at the home of Leonard and his wife, Ellen. Fleet felt he could be useful. However, Mary would not make any decision. It was up to me. Fleet planned to fly up to A.P.C.I. and speak to me later on that week.

I asked John Feegel to come to see me. John was an attorney and although he could not handle my situation alone because of his other responsibilities, he could give me the benefit of his wisdom. Feegel responded and planned to see me on the fourteenth.

JANUARY 6

J. Leonard Fleet was a tall, handsome man with sandy hair and blue eyes. He had been deaf since childhood and "heard" by reading lips. He had a sophisticated piece of electronic equipment that he used as a hearing aid, but most of the time he relied on his ability to lip read.

Fleet was very persuasive in his presentation. He felt that he could be of use by virtue of his contacts in Tallahassee and his personal relationship with former Attorney General Robert Shevin.

I had explained to Leonard that the Shevin letter was written, I presumed, by Georgieff, and I told him of all the various attempts Georgieff had made, and successfully, to keep me in prison. I was very honest and told Leonard that I had had my bellyfull with lawyers and that I didn't like them.

He laughed, and then made me a proposition I couldn't turn down. Fleet would not charge me a fee nor charge me expenses unless we filed in court, then I was to bear only the court cost. In return, he felt the exposure in the media, plus being part of the team that was responsible for my release, was payment enough.

We shook hands on it.

JANUARY 11

Don Moore's *Islander* interviewed Doctors Coumbis and Fiorese. Don Moore learned about Helpern's secret request that Fiorese confirm his bogus findings.

The Illinois toxicologist told Don Moore that Dr. Helpern was very concerned about the information he had presented in the original Coppolino trial. What was bothering Helpern was the possibility that Bailey might ask for a re-trial and that as a result, the validity of his original findings would come under fire and might be thrown out. Consequently, the nationally known New York City medical examiner contacted Dr. Fiorese secretly after I went to prison and asked him to run a complete test for toxic substances on Carmela's brain and liver. He did.

"After doing these experiments I concluded it was difficult to establish the guilt of Dr. Coppolino," Dr. Fiorese told Don Moore. He explained that he not only tested for toxic substances in Carmela's brain and liver but also performed a bacteriological analysis on the organs to find out if she had been killed with a bacteria of some kind. This test proved negative.

To further substantiate his findings, Dr. Fiorese told Don Moore that he had the United States Department of Public Health's laboratory in Atlanta check some of his findings and the remainder of his tests were reviewed by other experts in the field. They all concluded that there was no indication that Mrs. Coppolino had been murdered with succinlycholine.

Dr. Fiorese explained to Don Moore that Dr. Helpern didn't want to accept these findings. We discussed them at length with several of his helpers. Even so, Fiorese provided Helpern with an eight-page report outlining exactly what he had done and what his conclusions were.

Dr. Fiorese now let go with the latest startling piece of information. He told Don Moore, in Moore's newspaper *The Islander*, that at this point in time F. Lee Bailey had learned indirectly that Dr. Fiorese was making further tests on Carmela's organs. Fiorese went on to say that Bailey had written to him asking for his findings. "Unfortunately, I could not get involved in giving my opinion in that way because it was unethical," Dr. Fiorese said. He further explained that when he was asked by Dr. Helpern to make tests on Carmela's organs, it was with the understanding that the results would be given to no one but Helpern; however, Dr. Fiorese pointed out to Don Moore that Bailey could have obtained the information through court action. The doctor blamed Bailey for this oversight. "Bailey wasn't too smart about it," Fiorese told *The Islander*.

If Bailey had taken this action, I might have been a free man ten years before. At least that was what Dr. Fiorese apparently believed.

Dr. Fiorese's revelation, that F. Lee Bailey did not follow up in his request for the evidence that showed I was innocent, sent reporters searching for an answer from the famed criminal attorney.

Dr. Fiorese's eight-page report conclusively showing I was innocent was submitted to Dr. Helpern in October, 1968. It was suppressed by this State of Florida witness. Bailey learned about Fiorese's report. Why hadn't he made a diligent effort to secure the information? Wasn't it a fact that if Bailey had made this report public, I would not have had to spend eleven more years in prison?

The Press haunted Bailey's office, but never received an answer to this pressing question.

JANUARY 14

John Feegel arrived. It was late at night and John had a slight problem getting in to see me. I had been called and asked by the control room if I wanted to see someone named Dr. John Feegel. I could understand the institution's skittishness over new things and people. Since the publicity had broken about the Umberger-Helpern perjured testimony, A.P.C.I. had been inundated with phone calls and visits by the media. I had given about 20 interviews, either through the telephone or in person.

There didn't seem to be any change in John since the last time we had met. Perhaps his beard had become a little grayer. John and I got down to the heart of the matter, which was, what would be the fastest way for me to get out of prison? As Feegel saw it, Representative Arnett Girardeau was the key. He felt that Dr. Girardeau's personal investigation would bring forth the documentation necessary for the Parole Commission to act.

After parole, it was Feegel's opinion that I should not seek a new trial, but apply for an unconditional pardon. Feegel said he thought that Attorney General Jim Smith would be agreeable to a pardon since this would give the State of Florida what they wanted, "Coppolino versus State," an undisturbed case law on the books, and would give me what I wanted, the conviction wiped clean from my record.

I agreed to think about his ideas and explained to John that Leonard Fleet would be chief counsel in order to handle the many paper details, but that I wanted him, John Feegel, to handle the toxicologists. Dr. Fiorese knew John and respected him. In addition, John could speak with the same language as Doctors March, Coumbis, and Calise. Finally, I wanted John to guide Representative Girardeau in his independent investigations.

JANUARY 18

Don Moore of *The Islander* questioned Representative Girardeau. The chairman of the House of Representatives committee on Corrections, Parole and Probation told Mr. Moore, "There is enough doubt in my mind that a man who was tried for second degree murder has spent twelve years in the penitentiary on material that is suspect. He deserves an opportunity to be paroled because of his exemplary character while in the penal system. My gut reaction is that I am going to recommend that Coppolino be paroled. It's only in very rare cases that we review findings like this. *It has to be a case of severe injustice,"* Representative Girardeau stressed.

JANUARY 21
SUNDAY

The pressure kept building up. Rick Barry, senior reporter of *The Tampa Tribune,* came to interview me. His article was published in Sunday, January 21, on the front page.

Mr. Barry gave a balanced picture of my situation. His questioning of the ex-prosecutor, William Strode, had Strode concede that "without their evidence (Umberger-Helpern) we (the State of Florida) could never have gotten past a directed verdict of acquittal."

Rick Barry's investigation led him to Bailey's office. Bailey's receptionist answered his queries with a terse "Mr. Bailey is not making any comments on that case."

JANUARY 23

The morning newspapers screamed their headlines:

LAWMAKER DOUBTS TRIAL EVIDENCE, MAY SEEK RELEASE FOR COPPOLINO
Representative Arnett Girardeau said he might seek the release of Dr. Coppolino based on information that indicates the former Sarasota physician may have been sent to prison on inaccurate evidence."

I had known that this news would be released to the media by Dr. Girardeau because he had come to see me on the nineteenth.

At about 7:00 p.m. Dr. Girardeau arrived at the control room. We met in the lieutenant's office. It was our first meeting.

Arnett was a quiet man, of medium height, and in his late forties. He grasped my right hand tightly.

"Hello, Doctor!"

I grinned. "Hello, lifesaver!"

He laughed. I could feel an aura of strength and purpose radiating from this man. He was precise and meticulous in his movements. There was no doubt in my mind that Dr. Girardeau was the type of man who would only take a position after he had all the facts and that he would not alter his stance once he was convinced that his course of action was correct.

"Dr. Coppolino," he began.

"Call me Carl, please."

"Carl, I have received the Umberger-DiMaio material, and have taken advantage of Cavanaugh's experience as a former detective. I have spoken personally with Doctors Coumbis and Fiorese. I plan to talk with Dr. Rappolt in San Francisco, Dr. March in New York, and Dr. Feegel in Atlanta, whom I understand is your attorney and a medical examiner. Correct?"

"Correct."

The overhead lamp made Dr. Girardeau's skin look blacker than it was. He was comfortably dressed in a blue suit and had loosened his tie. On the desk between us rested a tape recorder and a brief case bulging with documents.

Dr. Girardeau pointed to the documents. "Carl, these are primary sources, not hearsay, not newspaper clippings." He cleared his throat. "My investigation so far has led me to the conclusion that your trial was horribly handled. Why didn't Bailey use the information March, Coumbis, and Calise gave him? Why didn't he follow up on Dr. Fiorese's report after your conviction?"

I explained to Dr. Girardeau that J. Leonard Fleet was deeply concerned over the failure of Bailey to use March, Coumbis, and Calise. "Fleet thinks that this might weaken my efforts for a new trial," I said. "My efforts for a new trial, therefore, would rest basically on Dr. Fiorese's work since it showed I was innocent and was suppressed by the State while I was on appeal and before the Second District Court of Appeals ruled in November, 1968."

Dr. Girardeau agreed. "Bailey botched your trial—there is no doubt about that. Do you have any more information for me?"

"Yes, Dr. Girardeau. Leonard Fleet called Bob Shevin. Did you know he has an office in Miami?"

"Yes."

"Fleet asked Shevin about Georgieff. Shevin admitted that the letter he signed in September, 1973, was written by George Georgieff. Shevin said Georgieff was committed to do all he could to prevent my release from prison and that it was something personal with the man."

Girardeau was staring into space. Finally, he spoke, "You know I am familiar with the Pitts-Lee case. There have been suggestions from various quarters that Georgieff took it upon himself to keep those two men in prison. Therefore, what Fleet found out, which confirmed your suspicions, is not surprising."

It was 9:00 o'clock in the evening. As Arnett closed his briefcase, he said, "The Chairman of the Parole Commission, Maurice Crockett, is very interested in my investigation." He added that the rest of the Commissioners wanted to be informed of my progress, which he certainly planned to do. "I will be back to see you. I don't want to give you false hopes, but it does look promising for you, Carl."

We shook hands. I knew I had found a friend.

JANUARY 30

Dr. Girardeau was busy. I received the following letter from John Feegel:

January 29, 1979

Carl A. Coppolino, M.D.
Avon Park, Florida

Dear Carl:

I talked by phone with Representative Arnett Girardeau at his office in Jacksonville per your request in your most recent letter. He is quite supportive to your cause and requested from me a letter expressing whatever professional opinions I care to express, including personal conjecture. He is forwarding to me his copies of what he feels are pertinent parts of the original trial transcript relative to Dr. Umberger's, and perhaps Helpern's, testimony. I will take note of this information and get him a letter from the Atlanta Medical Examiner's office within the next few days. He then intends to bring this information to the attention of the chairman of the Parole Commission and feels that my position as medical examiner and associate professor of pathology will carry some weight in the expression of these opinions.

I hope this will all be successful for you so that you can carry on the second half of this fight as a paroled prisoner rather than from your comfortable quarters as a guest of the state. Besides, as a taxpayer, I am sick of supporting you at Avon Park, so I'd like to see you get the hell out of there.

Best regards,

John R. Feegel, M.D. J.D.

FEBRUARY

The children were excited. Monica and her husband and Lisa sensed that things were going to happen. I was working at the prison nursery now, and had access to the orchid house. A.P.C.I. had 2000 orchids and they were all different varieties.

Each Sunday I would present Mary and the children with a rose or an orchid. It was hard not to make plans, not to think about the future. However, we were gun shy because we had been disappointed so many times in the past.

Nevertheless, we made plans. I had been studying commodities and had developed a trading technique that seemed to be successful, no matter what kind of market. It was my hope to be able to form a corporation and trade commodities profitably. In addition, my friend Lamar Baker and I had plans for a book. We thought about forming our own publishing company and starting with my book as the first piece of business.

Mary had been alone for so many years, she just reveled in the thoughts of having me home. Lisa, although she had seen me in prison and at home on furloughs, looked forward to having a full-time "daddy."

Monica, although married, joined with Michael in the hopes that we could be a family whole and intact again. Meanwhile, my supporters were flooding the new Governor Robert Graham with telegrams and mailgrams.

My friend Dominic had left on parole in December. He was now president of C.U.F.F.S. and in his official capacity sent Graham the following mailgram:

> When evidence has been obtained that has shown perjured testimony and fabricated evidence in the case of Dr. Carl Coppolino who has spent twelve years in prison, why has he not been released? Is this what is meant by justice in the criminal justice system?
>
> C.U.F.F.S.

Patty, my friend Dick's wife, was working for C.U.F.F.S. and started another drive for names on a petition and with mailgrams directed to Governor Graham. Their petition read:

February 18, 1979

Dear Governor Graham:

You are now leader of a state that used to be famous for sunshine, beaches, water sports, and other tourist-related activities; we are nationally known as the state which condoned such injustices as the Pitts-Lee affair and most recently, the Carl Coppolino case. Although the facts of this case have been reported in every paper in Florida, you and the Parole Commission have managed to completely disregard it. Does the Commission think that by admitting that a mistake has been made, it will diminish them in any way to take steps to rectify it? Will it remove the mantle of infallibility they mistakenly believe they acquire with the job? Is there one person on the Commission with the courage to speak up for justice?

No one can give Carl and Mary Coppolino and their children the twelve years they have lost. There is no magic formula which will enable Carl to experience the joy of seeing his children growing up. Nothing can remove the pain and loneliness they have suffered, but you and the Commission have the power to stop compounding the injustice they have endured.

FEBRUARY 15

I had a progress report and received another recommendation for parole. I called Fleet and told him about it. Leonard informed me that he had made contact with Bill Gunther, Insurance Commissioner and Cabinet Officer. Gunther informed Fleet that he was sending his liaison officer to the Parole Commissioner in my behalf. Fleet felt encouraged over this. He thought the Shevin letter had been neutralized by exposing the fact that it had been written by Georgieff (although signed by Shevin) and that the evidence was solid and proved that I had been framed.

One very important fact troubled Leonard Fleet. Bailey had an opportunity at my trial to use the information presented to him by Doctors March, Coumbis, and Calise, but had not. Fleet felt this clouded our possible petition for a new trial. Leonard thought the State would fight under the rule of law that the defense had access to this information in April, 1967, and had failed to use it.

When I questioned Leonard about the Dr. Fiorese report as the basis for a new trial, Leonard was positive, but still didn't like the idea that the State would have the opportunity to muddy the water. He said that Bailey's actions bordered on legal malpractice. Leonard said he was planning to write to Bailey. I told him that Lee would ignore his letter.

Marion Hale of *The Ft. Lauderdale News* and Frances Williams of the *Ft. Myers News-Press* had been in Tallahassee. They reported that the mood of Tallahassee was positive at the Parole Commission.

I called Jeanne King. She said that the New York City medical examiner's office was concerned over the turn of events in my case because they planned to be prosecution witnesses in the Dr. Favor case that was finally coming to trial in May.

A strategy meeting was held in New York City on February 28. Fleet, Doctors Feegel, March, Coumbis, Girardeau, Webb, and Tom Cavanaugh, and John Mandel attended.

Dr. Girardeau learned from Columbis and March that they had told Bailey they were prepared to testify at my trial, that Umberger and Helpern were wrong, and had falsified the evidence.

This prompted Fleet to intensify his attempts to contact F. Lee Bailey:

March 1, 1979

F. Lee Bailey
1 Center Plaza
Boston, Massachusetts

Dear Mr. Bailey:

As you are probably aware, I am representing Dr. Coppolino in his attempts to obtain his freedom from his present incarceration in the Florida Department of Corrections.

I have obtained from Mrs. Coppolino a copy of the transcript from the Collier County trial. The issue that I know I will have to confront in any evidentiary hearing in reference to newly discovered evidence is the question of why the testimony of Dr. James March, Dr. Richard Coumbis and Dr. Calise was not utilized. I would appreciate any assistance which you might be able to give Dr. Coppolino in reference to the decision not to present the above named toxicologists.

If you have the opportunity to do so, I would appreciate your calling me
at my office, collect, person-to-person.

Your courtesy and cooperation are appreciated.

Cordially,

J. Leonard Fleet

F. Lee Bailey never answered that letter.

MARCH 9 to 11

Another strategy meeting was held at the DeLido in Miami Beach. This
session was attended by Ed Webb, Girardeau, Fiorese, March, Feegel,
Tom Cavanaugh, John Mandel, J. Leonard Fleet and Mary. In addition,
Marion Hale of the *Ft. Lauderdale News* and Frances Williams of the *Ft.
Myers News-Press* were invited to attend. They did.

Dr. John Feegel reported at this strategy session that he had attended a
forensic scientist convention the previous week in Atlanta and had asked
the toxicologists there for help in proving that Carmela didn't die from an
overdose of succinlycholine. Dr. Feegel said that at least six toxicologists
believed that Dr. Helpern testified contrary to what was true. John said
that this was the most charitable analysis they could make. They didn't
have it in their hearts to actually use the words *false* and *perjurious*
testimony. John continued by saying that the scientist thought my sensational trial had put their profession in a bad light and were now willing to
help, since Helpern had died.

A survey by the *Ft. Lauderdale News* of almost a dozen leading scientists
across the nation showed that they all believed it was impossible to
determine if someone had been killed by succinlycholine. The inference
was obvious: Umberger and Helpern had fabricated the evidence and
given perjured testimony in my case.

The bombshell at this strategy meeting was dropped by Dr. Franco
Fiorese. He reported that after discovering Carmela had died of a natural
death, Helpern asked him to falsify the results of his tests "to finish off
Dr. Coppolino."

Dr. Fiorese told Frances Williams of the *Ft. Myers News-Press*, "I refused to cooperate. Helpern and Umberger wanted me to assist them in their assassination of Coppolino and I could not do such a thing."

"Helpern and Umberger turned their backs on me. Coppolino was the victim of Helpern's consuming hate for F. Lee Bailey. Coppolino's guilt or innocence was never the issue."

The nation had just begun to digest the startling information given by Dr. Franco Fiorese—when the next dramatic piece of evidence was revealed. Dr. James March, one of the original toxicologists who risked his career and came to my trial in Naples to speak with Bailey, was now head of the Long Island Research Institute at Stony Brooks University Medical School. At this strategy session, Dr. March told Frances Williams of the *Ft. Myers News-Press*, "I was in charge of the laboratories (New York City Medical Examiner's Laboratory) on July 27, 1967. Helpern issued a press release which said in part that seven months of painstaking intensive work by chemists in the Medical Examiner's office had conclusively established that Carmela Coppolino died after a fatal injection of succinlycholine.

I was in charge of the laboratory and I was aware of no test. There were no entries in the laboratory log of any test performed by anyone in the laboratory. If there were tests performed in the office on the brain and liver and other organs belonging to Carmela Coppolino, who the hell did them?" March asked. "Where was the data? Where were the log entries? I say there was no work; Helpern and Umberger perjured themselves; they lied to get at Bailey.

"People keep asking me why I waited so long to tell all of this," March continued. "I have been trying to tell someone for twelve years."

Then Dr. James March gave the most crucial piece of information. "We (March, Coumbis, Calise) told Mr. Bailey what I am now saying, but Bailey seemed content that he would win the case without too much trouble and certainly without our help so we returned to New York."

March said that he, Calise, and Coumbis were suspended for one year with pay the day they returned to work. "Helpern was mad," March said. "He couldn't fire us so he suspended us for one year with full pay. Can you imagine that? Until this day, there is no documentation as to why we were suspended. Of course, the three of us knew."

Dr. March said it all in three words—"Coppolino was framed!"

I spoke with Fleet right after this meeting. He said he had interviewed Dr. Fiorese for more than seven hours. Fleet said that Helpern had kept Fiorese's reports secret. It wasn't known yet, he continued, whether Dr. Helpern ever told the Florida prosecutors about Fiorese's report.

Representative Girardeau closely questioned Dr. Fiorese, Dr. Webb, Dr. March, Dr. Feegel, Tom Cavanaugh, and John Mandel. Arnett collected signed statements from all of them and planned to present them to the chairman of the Parole Commission, Maurice Crockett.

The statements were very specific, and collectively came to the same conclusion—Umberger and Helpern falsified the autopsy results on Carmela's body and then perjured themselves. I was framed.

Dr. John Feegel's statement to Representative Arnett Girardeau read in part:

> It is my conclusion that the original testimony offered at the trial of Carl Coppolino by Dr. Milton Helpern, the chief medical examiner for the city of New York, and Dr. Charles J. Umberger, chief toxicologist for the medical examiner's office of the city of New York, was in error and not substantiated by scientific finding available at the time of the testimony. Various scientific information and documents reviewed by me have led me to the conclusion within reasonable medical probability that abnormal levels of succinlycholine were *not* proved to be present in the body of the victim, Dr. Carmela Coppolino, as testified to by witnesses for the state at that trial. The autopsy report for Carmela Coppolino does not indicate any specific cause of death sufficient to substantiate the charges upon which Carl Coppolino was convicted at that time.

Dr. Franco Fiorese gave Representative Girardeau a copy of his eight-page report, the report that would have freed me if it had not been suppressed by Dr. Helpern.

The conclusion of Dr. Fiorese's report on his examination of Carmela's tissues reads in part, "The brain and liver levels of succinlycholine acid in Carmela Coppolino are consistent with those normally occurring in embalmed and non-embalmed tissues. The condition of the organs, the type of specimens submitted, and information and data accumulated precludes any conclusion that Carmela Coppolino was a victim of a lethal dose of succinlycholine."

Dr. Fiorese's statement to Dr. Girardeau was quite clear:

> Based on these determinations and other research performed by me, it is my professional conclusion that the testimony offered by Dr. Milton Helpern and Dr. Charles Umberger at the trial of Florida versus Coppolino April, 1967, was and is still unsubstantiated by scientific knowledge and that such testimony was false and without positive value.

Dr. James March said in his statement in part:

> "It is my conclusion that the scientific proof offered in the trial of *Florida verus Coppolino* by Dr. Milton Helpern and Dr. C.J. Umberger was false."

Dr. Ed Webb related to Representative Girardeau the details of the meeting he attended at the New York Medical Examiner's office at the end of 1965. Present at the meeting were Dr. Helpern, two police detectives, and Webb himself (representing E.R. Squibb, a manufacturer of succinlycholine). The purpose of the meeting was an investigation into Carmela's death by succinlycholine.

At the conclusion of the meeting Dr. Webb reported that Dr. Helpern had stated, "Gentlemen, you don't have a hope of bringing a conviction in this case."

Dr. Webb went on to say, "During the Florida trial, not in the courtroom, I remember asking one of the medical witnesses why the toxicology report read that succinlycholine had been found, when to the best of my knowledge it could not have been so positively reported . . ."

Dr. Webb finished his statement to Representative Girardeau with, "Consequently, whatever caused Carmela's death, I have never felt that succinlycholine played a part in it."

Tom Cavanaugh gave a two-page statment to Representative Girardeau based upon his investigation and experience as a New York City Police Department detective for 30 years. The last paragraph reads, ". . . . the attached statements of eminent members of the scientific community negating Dr. Umberger's findings in the Dr. Coppolino matter militate toward the conclusion that Dr. Coppolino was not guilty of the crime charged."

John C. Mandel, as head of the John C. Mandel Security Bureau, Incorporated, investigated my trial and conviction. In his statement to Representative Girardeau, John Mandel made the following points:

> 1. Eminent toxicologists employed at the medical examiner's office of New York City were aghast at the manner in which the toxicological examinations were conducted in the Coppolino case at said office. They alleged the selection of particular individuals, some of whom were among the least qualified in the unit, the secret testing, all reported at night to Dr. Charles J. Umberger, and the conclusions were all in violation of accepted scientific reasoning.

2. Dr. Franco Fiorese, then chief toxicologist for the state of Illinois, conducted tests on the tissue from the body of Carmela Coppolino, pursuant to a request to perform same made by the Medical Examiner of New York City. Dr. Fiorese's examinations proceeded over a period of fourteen months and were totally consistent with accepted scientific philosophy. The results proved that not only had the deceased, Carmela Coppolino, not died from the drug, succinlycholine cholide, which had been allegedly used, but that no other toxin was present. These tests were performed subsequent to the conviction of Carl Coppolino, but never revealed to the defense because Dr. Fiorese had been directed by his superiors in the state of Illinois to disclose his results only to the Chief Medical Examiner of New York City.

3. Efforts were made to have Dr. Fiorese falsify his results to make them cosistent with the fallacious testimony presented at the trial.

The investigation conducted by my organization leads me to the conclusion that Dr. Coppolino was a victim of a monumental miscarriage of justice.

The Press learned about my February progress report with a recommendation for parole. The paper work had reached Tallahassee right after the DiLido Hotel strategy meeting.

Al Lee, public relations director for the Department of Corrections, told the Press, "The classification team at Avon Park Correctional Institution has recommended parole consideration for Coppolino. Such recommendations are not ordinary. He must be a pretty outstanding individual in terms of adjustment and rehabilitation."

Frances Williams of the *Ft. Myers News-Press* learned from her source within the department in Tallahassee that I could be interviewed for parole in two weeks and that Representative Arnett Girardeau was spearheading the thrust to release me stating that he felt I was the victim of falsified medical testimony.

MARCH 13

Dr. James March, Tom Cavanaugh, and John Mandel arrived at A.P.C.I. in the morning. We met at the lieutenant's office in the control room.

Mandel was a heavy-set, jovial man with a twinkle in his eye. He began telling me "cop stories" and about some of the fixes in which he and Cavanaugh had found themselves while working together as detectives. In Mandel's opinion, the reason I was convicted rested upon three facts: falsification of the autopsy results by Helpern and Umberger and their subsequent perjured testimony; the failure of Bailey to use the material given him by Dr. March, Dr. Coumbis and Dr. Calise; and, the suppression of Fiorese's report by Halpern.

Dr. March was a delightful man, tall and distinguished, with a British accent. Jim quickly and in an animated manner related to me what happened in Naples in 1967. March and Coumbis had come down to Naples at their own expense. March had kept detailed notes of what had and had not gone to the New York City medical examiner's office. He had brought this document with him in an attempt to give F. Lee Bailey the truth. He was ignored.

"You wouldn't have been convicted if Bailey had listened to me and put me on the witness stand," March said vehemently.

Just at this time the officer in charge of the control room said that Mr. Wesson, the parole examiner, had arrived to interview me. My visitors left to go into town to find their lunch. I went to the classification office.

My meeting with Wesson was brief. Because of the change in the law, the Parole Commission was not required to interview convicts within 30 days of receipt of a recommendation for parole by the Department of Corrections. Wesson was curt and seemed to take great delight in telling me my interview was cancelled, and that my yearly interview date of August, 1979, would stand.

I tried not to display my displeasure and disgust. The newspapers, radio, and television had been filled for months with reports that I had been convicted on falsified perjured testimony by the State witnesses. Yet I could not receive a chance for release because of a bureaucratic foul-up!

When Mandel, Cavanaugh and March returned, they were anxious to hear the outcome of my parole interview. I told them. Now there were four people upset, but there wasn't anything we could do. Tallahassee was in control.

Later that week on Friday, March 23, I received a telephone call from Representative Arnett Girardeau. The phone call came to my classification officer, Mr. Cloud.
office.

"Hello, Doctor!" Representative Girardeau's soft cultured voice came clearly over the wire.

"Hello, sir."

"I called because I know you are concerned over the cancellation of your parole interview by Mr. Wesson. There is nothing to be worried about. The law had been changed, and for some unknown reason your case was the first to be processed under the new legislation.

"I have received the signed statements from Doctors Feegel, March,

Webb, and Fiorese," Representative Girardeau said. "In addition, I have statements from Cavanaugh and Mandel. The chairman of the Parole Commission is extremely interested in these documents.

"Finally, Carl, I have a letter from Dr. Rappolt, the editor of *The Journal of Clinical Toxicology.* His letter backs up his public statements.

"Had you learned about Commissioner Cross?" Representative Girardeau was referring to Cross' sudden death by a heart attack. I had heard it over the radio on Monday the nineteenth. Despite my best intentions, I couldn't help thinking about my own serious heart condition and about how sick I was several years ago. I had spoken with Cross about it at my interview in November, 1971, and he was completely unsympathetic. It is ironic, I thought, that his heart should kill him, while my bad heart continued to keep me alive.

"Yes, Dr. Girardeau, I heard."

"There will be a new parole commissioner appointed to bring the strength of the Commission back to seven members. I believe by the time you are interviewed in August, the Commission will feel it is prepared to take whatever action it deems proper.

"I will be down to see you soon, Carl. You have been patient these twelve years. Be patient for a little while longer."

"Yes, sir. Thank you for calling me, Dr. Girardeau, and for taking the time to keep me informed. You have relieved my anxiety."

"See you probably in June. Good-bye, Carl."

Beth Blechman of WFLA TV, channel 8 (NBC), came into A.P.C.I. to film and interview me. Leonard flew up to meet with us. Ms. Blechman decided to do a semi-documentary on my case, dividing it into three themes: Frame-up; Cover-up; Conspiracy to keep me in prison.

The program was aired in two segments on the six o'clock news, and generated a massive response. Tallahassee heard it and listened. The first segment at six o'clock Monday, April 2, opened with these words: "The State of Florida has an innocent man in prison, Dr. Carl Coppolino . . ."

Ms. Blechman recited three points: Dr. Umberger's Grand Jury testimony, Dr. Fiorese's report, and the suppression of the report by Dr. Helpern.

APRIL

I received a detailed letter from Tom Cavanaugh concerning the trial of Dr. Favor. Dr. Michael Baden, as acting New York City medical examiner, testified against Favor for the State of New York. Cavanaugh wrote ". . . .although Rappaport (Dr. Favor's Chief Counsel) did not want to go too deeply into the Coppolino trial testimony, I prevailed upon him to ask 'What is acute classic toxicity?' Helpern made this terminology famous at your trial. He (Baden) hemmed and hawed and finally admitted that it meant nothing to him. We can use that sworn testimony to our advantage."

This piece of information was critical. Helper had stressed in his testimony that Carmela had died of an injection of succinlycholine. And in Helpern's opinion, it was a case of "acute classic toxicity," which was a false statement. Dr. Michael Baden was an assistant to Dr. Helpern at the time of my trial and was aware of what Dr. Helpern had done to me. Later Dr. Baden would be fired by the Mayor of New York City, Mr Koch, because Baden allegedly refused to falsify medical evidence for the New York City District Attorney!

Cavanaugh went on in his letter to describe the conduct of Dr. Vincent Mazzia. Dr. Mazzia was a well-known anesthesiologist who testified for the State of Florida and against me in my trial.

Cavanaugh wrote about Mazzia, "Dr. Vincent Mazzia proved to be the malpractice prostitute I believed him to be."

Mazzia talked with Dr. Favor's lawyer, Ed Rappaport, and was sure that the evidence known would not convict Dr. Favor. However, Mazzia wanted to talk with Favor as Cavanaugh put it in his letter, "but wanted to talk to Archie (Favor) first to make sure that he believed in his innocence. Mazzia, Ed Rappaport and Archie conferred for six hours at the conclusion of which he said he would testify. Now for the shocker!

"Mazzia said his normal fee would be twenty thousand dollars, but in view of the fact that Archie . . . being only a resident, his fee would be between five thousand and ten thousand with five thousand dollars up front before he would take the stand. His wife was also adamant. Because we were spending money out of our own pockets, we sent Mazzia and his wife back to Colorado. I wonder what has happened to the milk of human kindness and common decency."

MAY

Dr. Favor was acquitted! Marion Hale of the *Ft. Lauderdale News* wrote the headline and the story:

SURGEON'S ACQUITTAL IN NEW YORK BUOYS COPPOLINO BID

The acquittal of a New York City doctor charged with killing his wife with a powerful muscle relaxant may help Dr. Carl Coppolino, who has been held in a Florida prison for twelve years on a similar charge, win his freedom.

Both Coppolino, convicted after a sensational trial in Naples, and Dr. Favor, the New York surgeon, had been charged with murdering their wives with succinlycholine choride, a potent drug generally used during surgery.

The Favor case, believed to be the second such case in the country, ended Saturday in New York with the jury acquitting him after an eight-week trial.

J. Leonard Fleet, an attorney representing Coppolino, said he plans to tell the Florida Parole and Probation Commission the verdict in the Favor case in hopes the Commissioners will reconsider releasing Coppolino. Tom Cavanaugh, a retired New York police detective who has worked on both cases, said the Favor verdict "is a definite plus for Coppolino."

Cavanaugh said he believed the turning point in the Favor case was the testimony of Dr. Franco Fiorese, chief toxicologist at Silver Cross Hospital in Joliet, Illinois. During the Favor trial, Fiorese testified that the level of succinic acid found in Nenita Favor's body was not high enough to prove she had died from the drug. He based his testimony on the test he conducted for the Coppolino case.

Cavanaugh said the verdict verified Fiorese's test of the drug.

Coppolino's second wife, Mary, said yesterday that her husband, who was being held at the State prison in Avon Park near Sebring, was "very pleased" about the verdict in the Favor case.

JUNE — JULY, 1979

Representative Girardeau and Chairman of the Parole Commission Maurice Crockett arrived at A.P.C.I. on June 8, unannounced. I was rushed to the control room at about one o'clock. Dr. Girardeau wanted to see me, and we met again at the lieutenant's office.

Arnett's face was lined with fatigue. Months later he told me that I looked drawn and haggard, a picture of exhaustion. We must have made quite a ghoulish pair together!

Our meeting was short. Representative Girardeau said he had shown all of the Parole Commissioners but one, Ray Howard, the results of his independent investigation, along with the signed statements from Doctors Webb, March, Feegel, Rappolt, Mr. Cavanaugh, and Mandel.

"However, Carl, I have something serious to relate to you," Dr. Girardeau continued. "George Georgieff has asked in writing for permission to appear in front of the Parole Commission and argue against your release!"

I closed my eyes. We were sitting side by side on the plastic-covered couch in the lieutenant's office. The metal cabinets, official bulletin board, and other sundry items of prison's "officialdom" weighed down upon me.

"Why does that man fight me so much? Why has he made my life and, by extension, my family's life so miserable? And now," my voice began to rise in despair, "with clear-cut evidence that I was framed, Georgieff still opposes my release!"

"I know how you feel, Carl, and I think the situation will take care of itself."

"Dr. Girardeau, when will I be interviewed?"

"I don't really know. Certainly not later than August, perhaps before." Representative Girardeau rose to his feet and extended his right hand. "The next time I see you, it will be at my home."

I grinned. As I stood beside Arnett, I thought how strange life was! Before this legislator came into my life, I really had no hope of leaving prison. Now with his help, I could be spending Christmas at home, free, the first in 14 years.

Later that afternoon, I met briefly with Chairman Crockett at the prison library. Maurice Crockett was a large black man with a kind expression on his face. His voice and mannerisms were soft and gentle.

Mr. Crockett wanted to speak with me about Mary. He was extremely impressed by her and wanted me to convey his best wishes to her. He thought that the Parole Commission was now prepared to act upon my parole. However, I had to be interviewed by the examiner and that could be any time between then and August.

We shook hands and said our good-byes.

After meeting with Dr. Girardeau and Mr. Crockett, I felt, for the first time, that I was definitely headed for home.

I received from Cavanaugh a letter written the eighth of June. He had spoken with Dr. Michael Baden, knowing that Baden had knowledge of what Dr. Helpern had done to me. Cavanaugh described his encounter with Dr. Baden: "We had our first meeting informally with Dr. Michael Baden. I expected a fencing match and was not surprised. At least we established the ground rules, which were, briefly—that we did not want to hurt anyone, but we just sought publication of the truth, which we already knew; that his office was going to be scrutinized; that no one had testified before from that office and could only be injured if he lied or withheld information; that he, Baden, would have to take a position somewhere along the line, a position already revealed in the Dr. Favor trial when he testified under Cross that acute classic toxicity meant nothing to him; that, in substance, he could be revealed as a great pathologist furthering justice."

On the fourteenth of June, Dr. March wrote me more details about the Baden meeting: "I brought Coumbis to one of our meetings. He is a close friend of Mike Baden. Coumbis met with Dr. Baden Wednesday and, as expected, Baden said he would cooperate, that he wouldn't "hide" anything. He also said that whatever public records were still available, he would produce. As I said, on the surface he seems cooperative, but he sitll is the Chief Medical Examiner for the City of New York, and he is going to protect his ass. He told Coumbis he wasn't going 'to stick his neck out.' He also discussed with Coumbis the possibilities of law suits . . ."

Even though the news from March's letter was gratifying, since I instinctively felt Michael Baden had to know what Helpern had done to me, it wasn't until I reached the last page of Dr. March's letter that I became stunned.

Dr. March had described how he kept meticulous notes about what was and what wasn't done by the toxicologists under Umberger. Now he alluded to a tragedy that occurred to one of the toxicologists who had worked on my case—the pressure of what was done to me in Naples that April, 1967, had put this man in a mental institution!

Let Dr. March tell it in his own words: "I can't wait until the newspaper accounts appear and the articles read 'New York City Medical Examiner toxicoloigst worked *secretly, at night, kept no records, gave oral reports.* This is explosive stuff that no one has ever heard about or will hear about unless this case is tried in The Press. I would love to see in the paper the episode where Steve Andryoskaus, one of the leading toxicologists in the case, was summoned to Naples in 1967; he never testified, returned to New York on the same plane with Coumbis and me and wound up in the psychiatric ward of Bellevue a day or so later. He was a honest man, but had no guts. He was also promoted two times while he worked on the case. He knew plenty and kept his cowardly mouth shut."

I was very upset about Dr. Andryoskaus. I could imagine the torments he went through after seeing what happened to me. Yet at the same time,

I thought of the misery Mary and the children had suffered these 12 long years because I had been unjustly convicted.

I received a letter from Cavanaugh written June 15. Tom confirmed what Dr. March wrote me: "We heard from Baden. He told Coumbis that he will not take sides at this time. He will cooperate in any way possible with records, and will hide nothing. This is encouraging because it implies that he is hoping that we can come up with damaging evidence against Hepern. I think he will prove to be an ally."

Dr. John Feegel appeared on the *John Eastman TV Show* and spoke about Dr. Favor's trial and acquittal and its relationship to me. He stressed the fact that the Favor acquittal had forced the New York examiner's office to be stuck with a proposition for which they had no proper ruling.

AUGUST, 1979

I called Mary early on Saturday, August 4. Representative Girardeau had called her the previous Tuesday and said he planned to appear in front of the Parole Commission on my behalf. Arnett said that with the appointment of Dr. Greadington, who took Cross' seat, the Commission was back to full strength. Most important was the fact that the Commissioners were very curious as to why Georgieff as assistant Attorney General would go to such extraordinary lengths to actively oppose my parole.

Mary went on to say that she would be at A.P.C.I. on Tuesday with Tom Cavanaugh.

AUGUST0 7

Tom Cavanaugh, his brother Joe, his son Jimmy, and Mary, arrived at 1:00 p.m. and stayed until 5:00 p.m. We discussed strategy.

I voiced my opinion that I wanted Dr. John Feegel at my parole hearing in Tallahassee and that I wanted one of three people to speak—Mary,

Leonard Fleet, or Dr. Feegel. We all agreed that it would depend on Chairman Crockett, since he was the one who would grant the permission.

Tom had some startling information—he had spoken with a toxicologist named Stoholoski. Dr. Stoholoski had worked with Dr. Helpern for a number of years and hinted to Tom that Helpern had fabricated the medical evidence in other cases besides mine! The one other case Stoholoski mentioned specifically was the Alice Crimmins case.

Months later, Cavanaugh was even more precise in a letter to me dated December 31, 1979. Tom Cavanaugh charged in his letter that Helpern distorted the evidence and perjured himself in four cases, and that "this could have been done by expounding on the four cases we know about (there are probably many more) that Helpern, through perjurious and distorted reporting methods, used to further his philosophy that the end justified the means."

AUGUST 28,1979
TUESDAY

Mr. Samuel Cooper, parole examiner, called me to the classification office. When I arrived, I found Chief Classification Officer Cornell and Mr. Cooper were present.

Mr. Cooper was very pleasant and straightforward, in contrast with some other parole examiners I had been exposed to! He kept asking me if I had any questions and ended by saying he was going to recommend to the Parole Commission that I be released immediately.

I thanked Mr. Cooper, saying that his words were music to my ears and that I was sure my family would be overjoyed to hear the news.

I called Mary at 10:00 a.m. at her office. She and the orthopedic surgeon for whom she works were very, very happy to hear the recommendation that Mr. Cooper was going to submit to the Parole Commissioners in Tallahassee. Next I called my Lisa and gave her the news from Mr. Cooper and asked her to inform Monica.

Finally, I called my friend, Lamar Baker. He was as excited as I. Lamar had worked long and hard through petitions, lawyers, and businessmen in organizing support for my release. In addition, he did all he could to help Mary and the children whenever they needed help. Now I had to wait out the time for the vote in Tallahassee. That was the crucial test.

Mary wrote a letter to Chairman Crockett and asked for permission to speak in my behalf; Leonard Fleet did the same, as my attorney. Mr. Crockett turned Mary down and gave Fleet permission to address the Commission.

Mr. Crockett informed The Press that a hearing examiner had recommended that I be paroled next month after serving 12 years of a life sentence for murder of my first wife. The chairman went on to say that the full Commission would vote on the case the following Wednesday, and that Representative Arnett Girardeau had been informed about the meeting and would be permitted to speak on my behalf if he wished to do so. Chairman Crockett was very specific in his point that the Commission would not consider my claim of innocence. "We don't retry the case," he said. "We take what the court has done and consider whether the prisoner has been rehabilitated and can be restored to society with no danger to himself or to others."

Chairman Crockett told Frances Williams of the *Ft. Myers News-Press*, "We've got reporters and television people coming from all over the country for Coppolino's parole hearing. Looks like we're going to have a full house, so we've scheduled Coppolino for 8:00 Wednesday morning."

SEPTEMBER, 1979

The vote on my parole was scheduled for Wednesday, September 26. Representative Girardeau had requested that Mary ask Doctors Webb, Feegel and Fiorese and also Tom Cavanaugh and John Mandel to be present at the hearing. Leonard Fleet had been granted permission to speak in my behalf by the chairman of the Parole Commission and would arrive in Tallahassee the night before.

Marion Hale of the *Ft. Lauderdale News* and Frances Williams of the *Ft. Myers News-Press* had spoken with Georgieff and said that the assitant attorney general definitely would appear and speak in front of the Commission prior to my vote.

On Tuesday, September 25, Attorney General Jim Smith informed the media that his office would *not* oppose the recommendation made to release me on parole as long as my attorneys didn't bring out, officially, the new evidence. "If they want to base his release on his behavior and rehabilitation, that's okay with us," said Smith's spokesman, Don North.

Mary met with Dr. Girardeau, Leonard Fleet, Tom Cavanaugh, John Mandel and Doctors Feegel, Webb, and Fiorese, Tuesday night at the Brown Derby in Tallahassee for dinner. It was the last strategy meeting prior to the 8:00 a.m. vote in the morning.

During dinner it was decided that Fleet would address the Commission first, and if Georgieff spoke in opposition to my parole as he had indicated to the media that he would, then Representative Girardeau would speak.

The entourage left the Brown Derby and went back to the Holiday Inn where the strategy brain-session continued until 3:00 a.m. Mary was enthusiastic, but exhausted. She slept less than two hours that night.

It rained Tuesday night at A.P.C.I., and I was restless. What would happen in the morning? I was gratified to hear over the radio that Attorney General Jim Smith would not oppose my parole, but I was still concerned. I could still see Georgieff in my mind's eye. What would *he* do tomorrow?

SEPTEMBER 26, 1979

It was a clear, crisp fall day in Tallahasee. Mary had spent the early morning hours wondering if she had left anything undone. She decided finally to leave it alone since what was going to happen would happen. Time had run out.

Dr. John Feegel had informed The Press that he had come prepared with the detailed scientific testimony in the event that Georgieff opposed parole. John said bluntly, "We're loaded."

Fleet had gone over detail after detail with Mary. He wanted his presentation in front of the Commission to be a complete package, leaving no string dangling for Georgieff to pull.

Doctors Fiorese and Webb had answered any last-minute questions raised by Representative Girardeau.

Everybody was ready. It was time.

At approximately 8:30 Parole Commission Chairman Maurice Crockett opened the session. He explained to The Press, television, radio personnel and spectators that the panel would vote on approximately 300 to 400 cases that day and that they would begin with the case of Carl A. Coppolino.

Crockett pointed out that the panel of commissioners would base their decision solely on my behavior in prison, my rehabilitation, rather than on any arguments about my innocence.

Leonard Fleet was the first to address the Commission. He stressed the longevity of my imprisonment (Florida prison records indicated that I had served longer than any other convict imprisoned for second degree murder), the three years I spent in the community on furloughs, and my close family and neighborhood ties. Fleet said, "I ask you to put aside the publicity and treat him just like another human being convicted of murder in the second degree."

Georgieff followed. He did not formally protest the recommendation for parole. Instead he urged the commissioners, "Leave for the courts any legal questions and allow them to make their own judgment about his rehabilitation." It was obvious to the observing press that Georgieff was acting under instructions from Attorney General Jim Smith.

Next to speak was Representative Arnett Girardeau. In a brief but unprecedented speech, Dr. Girardeau begged the Commission, "Please consider favorably this petition for parole."

The vote was taken immediately—six to one in favor of parole. The only negative vote was cast by Ray Howard. Commissioner Roy Russell set my parole date for October 16 and stipulated that I receive a lifetime parole with only one restriction—I could not practice medicine unless I had written permission from the Parole Commission.

Chairman Crockett called for an immediate recess and the newspaper reporters raced for the telephones. Mary went scurrying for a telephone to call Lisa and tell her the news, so that Lisa, in turn, could call me at the prison.

My defense team congregated in the hallway and were peppered by questions from The Press. Dr. Franco Fioresi was emphatic in his position, "I was, and am to this day, medically positive that Carmela Coppolino could not have died from an overdose of succinylcholine."

"The amount (of succinic acid) found in Mrs. Coppolino's brain was less than the amount found in the brains and livers of other people who died of other causes," Dr. Fioresi told reporters, as reported in the *St. Petersburg Times*.

John Van Giesen of the *Miami Herald* spoke to Leonard Fleet right after my favorable vote. Fleet charged that Helpern deliberately withheld evidence of my innocence while the conviction was on appeal. Fleet was referring to Dr. Fioresi's report.

When asked about the report by Van Giesen, Dr. Fioresi said, "When I gave them (Helpern and Umberger) the results, I thought they were going to use them, but they did not."

Dr. John Feegel told Ed George of the *Sarasota-Herald Tribune* that Dr. Fioresi and Helpern's assistants "were intimidated by Helpern's national acclaim and his tremendous reputation." Feegel said apparently Helpern went to the 1967 trial in Naples, testified against me, and then returned to New York City and told his assistants to prove what he had testified to. In fact, Feegel said that the specific tests for succinylcholine had not been made before the trial.

Representative Arnett Girardeau commented to Jim Walker of the *Tampa Tribune* that he was convinced that the State's chief medical witness, the late Dr. Helpern, "perjured himself knowingly and that the conviction was fraudulent."

Meanwhile, Mary found a telephone and called Lisa. "We're going to pick up Daddy on the sixteenth. Call him!" Mary told the throng of supporters and the national media, "I'm ecstatic. The day I had hoped and prayed for and dreamed of has arrived."

When asked what our next step would be, Mary said, "I really don't know what the next move will be. This has been like a brick wall and now we are on top. Our big concern now is getting home, getting our lives back together and playing with our grandchildren. I think Carl has a big adjustment to make living at home with a bunch of women, but I think he's going to love it."

WAITING FOR OCTOBER 16

The daylight hours were filled with interviews by newspapers, television, and radio stations. Letters of congratulations poured into the prison and were totaled in the thousands before I left on the sixteenth. People from all walks of life, from coast to coast, sent me telegrams, mailgrams, and letters, wishing me well. Many of the communications voiced outrage over my lost years in prison. Others admitted they didn't know what they would do to their tormentors if they had been "unjustly convicted" as I was.

My friends—Lamar Baker, James Russ, Troy Browning, Dominic, Jane and Bob Miller, Carmen and Tom Benoit—sent me their love, affection, and good wishes.

I had written Representative Arnett Girardeau several letters telling him how much I owed him. I owed him my total life. He answered back with a five-page letter saying, "It's a good feeling to know that you have helped to bring happiness into another person's life."

As I waited for October 16, 1979, FREEDOM DAY, there were still many unanswered questions—Why didn't F. Lee Bailey put Doctors March, Coumbis, and Calise on the stand in Naples in 1967? The verdict, no doubt, would have been different if he had done so. How much knowledge, if any, did the Florida prosecutors have about the falsification of the evidence by their witnesses, Doctors Umberger and Helpern? Did they know that Umberger and Helpern planned to offer perjured testimony? Dr. Helpern had deliberately suppressed Dr. Fioresi's report—a report which, if made public, would have freed me. Who besides Dr. Helpern knew about the report? Did the Florida prosecutors, for instance, know about its existence? When would the American public wake up to the brutality that exists, not only in Florida's prisons, but in the prisons throughout the country? How many crimes have to be committed against convicts before the consciousness of America will be jarred sufficiently to take steps to improve the nation's correctional system? How many of the reading public, those people who are professionals, blue-collar workers, or housewives, how many of them could have survived and functioned and left prison whole and complete after spending 12 years for a crime that they had not committed . . . in fact, for a crime which never happened?

ABOUT THE AUTHOR

Dr. Carl Coppolino lives in a spacious condominium complex in Tampa, Florida, with his wife, Mary, and daughter, Lisa. After completing *The Crime That Never Was*, he has become involved in securing manuscripts for future release by Justice Press, Inc. In addition, Dr. Coppolino is associated with Raintree Investments, Inc., a successful commodity trading advisory service. Finally, he is President of C.U.F.F.S. (Citizens For a Free Society), a non-profit prison reform organization with branch offices in Florida and New York.